TODAY'S TEACHERS, TOMORROW'S LEADERS

A GUIDE TO IDENTIFYING AND DEVELOPING FUTURE ADMINISTRATORS

PETER MARSHALL

FOREWORD BY TOM HIERCK

Solution Tree | Press

a division of
Solution Tree

I0112748

Copyright © 2025 by Solution Tree Press

Materials appearing here are copyrighted. With one exception, all rights are reserved. Readers may reproduce only those pages marked "Reproducible." Otherwise, no part of this book may be reproduced or transmitted in any form or by any means (electronic, photocopying, recording, or otherwise) without prior written permission of the publisher.

555 North Morton Street
Bloomington, IN 47404
800.733.6786 (toll free) / 812.336.7700
FAX: 812.336.7790

email: info@SolutionTree.com
SolutionTree.com

Visit **go.SolutionTree.com/leadership** to download the free reproducibles in this book.

Printed in the United States of America

FSC
www.fsc.org
MIX
Paper | Supporting
responsible forestry
FSC® C008955

Library of Congress Cataloging-in-Publication Data

Names: Marshall, Peter (Retired school administrator), author.
Title: Today's teachers, tomorrow's leaders : a guide to identifying and
   developing future administrators / Peter Marshall.
Description: Bloomington, IN : Solution Tree Press, [2024] | Includes
   bibliographical references and index.
Identifiers: LCCN 2024018910 (print) | LCCN 2024018911 (ebook) | ISBN
   9781960574725 (paperback) | ISBN 9781960574732 (ebook)
Subjects: LCSH: Teachers--Training of--United States. | Professional
   socialization. | Teachers--Professional ethics. | School administration
   teachers. | Educational leadership--Social aspects.
Classification: LCC LB2165 .M35 2024 (print) | LCC LB2165 (ebook) | DDC
   371.0068/3--dc23/eng/20240812
LC record available at https://lccn.loc.gov/2024018910
LC ebook record available at https://lccn.loc.gov/2024018911

Solution Tree
Jeffrey C. Jones, CEO
Edmund M. Ackerman, President

Solution Tree Press
President and Publisher: Douglas M. Rife
Associate Publishers: Todd Brakke and Kendra Slayton
Editorial Director: Laurel Hecker
Art Director: Rian Anderson
Copy Chief: Jessi Finn
Senior Production Editor: Suzanne Kraszewski
Cover and Text Designer: Fabiana Cochran
Acquisitions Editors: Carol Collins and Hilary Goff
Content Development Specialist: Amy Rubenstein
Associate Editors: Sarah Ludwig and Elijah Oates
Editorial Assistant: Anne Marie Watkins

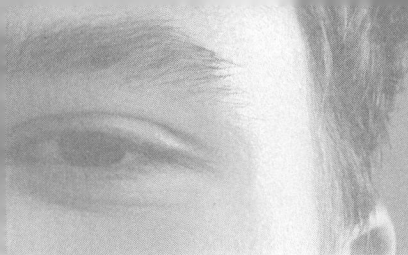

ACKNOWLEDGMENTS

As a retired school administrator, I have always known the power and the benefits that come with working on a team. I would like to thank the wonderful team at Solution Tree for their guidance, knowledge, and patience with supporting a new author. I have felt welcome and included from start to finish.

I'd like to also acknowledge good friend and mentor Tom Hierck. We may cheer for different teams, but he has always been a marvelous coach.

To all those I have worked with in the past and were part of my school teams, I hope the stories and thoughts presented in the book put a smile on your face as you recognize the ideas from our time together. Thank you for being part of very fond memories. I am glad we were able to make a difference together in the lives of students.

To the next generation of administrators who worked with me as teachers and assistant principals and moved into careers as school leaders: Alison, Amanda, Andrea, Brent, Carolyn, Cheryl, Chris, Christopher, Fatimah, Gail, Gary, Gus, Lois, Luke, Melanie, Michelle, Phil, and Scott. I have watched your growth and marveled at your development as a leader. I thought of you often as I was writing, and I am so glad that you have accepted and taken on the most challenging and most rewarding role in education.

Most important, to my home team! Mary, you have been there for every part of my education career and are still right alongside me on this new exciting journey. You really are the best travel companion.

To our great children, Kate and Jon, who grew up in a home with two teachers who became administrators and had to listen to all the stories. You make me proud every day and I cherish the title "Dad" over every one of my other accomplishments.

Solution Tree Press would like to thank the following reviewers:

Ian Landy
District Principal of Technology
School District 47
Powell River, British Columbia, Canada

Louis Lim
Principal
Bur Oak Secondary School
Markham, Ontario, Canada

Laura Quillen
Retired Principal
Fairview Elementary School
Rogers, Arkansas

Jennifer Rasmussen
Literacy Specialist and Instructional Service
Director
CESA 4
West Salem, Wisconsin

Katie Saunders
Principal
Anglophone School District West
New Brunswick, Canada

Kim Timmerman
Principal
ADM Middle School
Adel, Iowa

Visit **go.SolutionTree.com/leadership** to download the free reproducibles in this book.

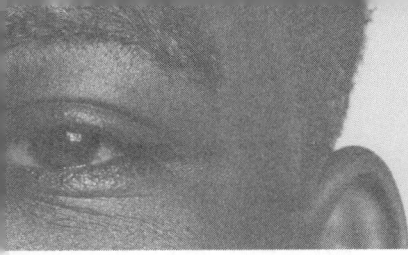

TABLE OF CONTENTS

Reproducibles are in italics.

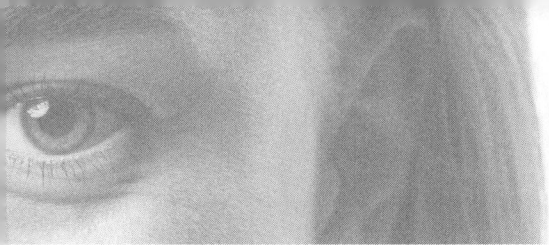

ABOUT THE AUTHOR

Peter Marshall has more than thirty-five years of experience as an educator. He started out as a teacher and then served as a school administrator in four different schools before finishing his career in education as the first principal of Boyne Public School, Milton, Ontario, Canada. During his twenty-two years as a school leader, he also spent time as the principal for leadership and staff development in the central office. Peter retired from the Halton District School Board in 2021 and joined Solution Tree as an Assessment Center associate. In addition to assessment and evaluation, Peter specializes in educational leadership, developing school culture, and effective staff learning.

Peter's vision, leadership, and dedication led to him being recognized as one of Canada's Outstanding Principals (The Learning Partnership) in 2018. As principal of Boyne Public School, Peter led the development of one of Halton's newest schools. He supported the staff, students, and families in growing a school from the middle of an empty field into a community that is recognized for its innovation and its commitment to student achievement and well-being. It also provided a neighborhood hub for what is considered the fastest-growing area in Canada: Milton, Ontario. This success was due to the fostering of an environment that celebrated the cultural diversity of the large student population.

In his system role, Peter worked with both the corporate and academic components of the organization. Peter was responsible for developing and implementing programs for onboarding new staff, mentoring and coaching new administrators and staff, and facilitating training programs for schools and departments across the district.

A graduate of the University of Toronto in physical and health education, Peter received his bachelor's degree at the Ontario Institute for Studies in Education, University of Toronto. He earned his master's degree in curriculum studies/assessment and evaluation from Brock University.

To learn more about Peter Marshall's work, visit petermarshallconsulting.com and follow @petermconsult on X.

To book Peter Marshall for professional development, contact pd@SolutionTree.com.

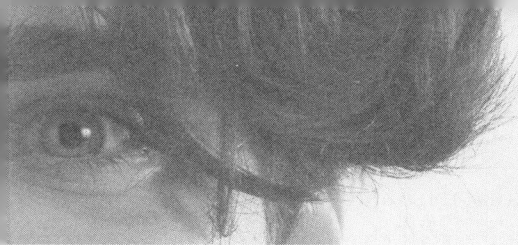

FOREWORD

By Tom Hierck

As I was drafting this foreword, some troubling evidence about the leadership crisis in schools crossed my desk in a National Association of Secondary School Principals (NASSP, 2021) survey.

- Job satisfaction is at an ultimate low, with almost four out of ten principals (38 percent) expecting to leave the profession by 2025.

- Recruiting and retaining school leaders will become even more difficult if more is not done to support educators in our schools.

The National Center for Education Statistics (NCES, 2023) further validates this finding in its National Teacher and Principal Survey that reveals roughly one in ten public school principals (11 percent) left the profession between the 2020–2021 and 2021–2022 school years. Of the report, NCES commissioner Peggy G. Carr notes, "Principal attrition is higher in public schools than it was 5 years ago, and veteran public school leaders with more years of experience leave the profession at higher rates than those with less experience" (NCES, 2023).

She goes on to say that "principals are critical supports for a school's teachers and learners" and that schools need leaders "who are committed to the success of each student." She also states that "these data are a valuable snapshot for those at the district and state levels who must address the issue of principal turnover in their schools" (NCES, 2023).

These data remind me of some thoughts from one of my mentors—the late Wayne Hulley, president of Canadian Effective Schools—who shared a personal message as we were talking about leadership and its impact on school improvement. He said that the improvement process in every school is unique, affected by demographics, existing culture, staff characteristics, and leadership. Hulley's words, along with the concerning data on school leadership and my role as an educational consultant, led me to look for solutions in existing literature to help schools overcome their leadership challenges so the school-improvement process can continue on a smooth trajectory. I uncovered very little but found hope in what my colleague Peter Marshall presents in the pages of this book.

In *Today's Teachers, Tomorrow's Leaders: A Guide to Identifying and Developing Future Administrators*, Marshall provides school leaders with the research, strategies, tools, and motivation needed to become inspirational leaders who both identify and nurture other leaders and thrive in their current role. Marshall does this with ten "ways of being"—competencies of aspiring leaders—that he considers vital for teachers to demonstrate to be successful administrators in the future. Marshall makes the case that successful leadership is very much about individual people using their ways of being in concert with their leadership skills to make an impact for teachers and students in schools. Evaluating potential future leaders through these ten ways of being helps current leaders reflect on the contributions they make while making the most of the contributions of their current teachers.

Marshall doesn't leave school leaders to their own devices when structuring how to approach and implement finding the next wave of school leaders. In addition to presenting and exploring the ten ways of being, he outlines a three-step process for identifying and developing future administrators using three tools—(1) the leadership action matrix, (2) the mentoring planning page, and (3) the mentoring meeting planner—that provide current leaders with a plan to work with staff members. Marshall also exemplifies what the development and coaching process could look like for each of the ten ways of being using sample teachers and school examples drawn from his experience as an administrator. This truly is the complete package of support!

As an educational consultant, I have been fortunate to work with Marshall for more than ten years in schools he has led. I have seen how he has guided and coached great educators to move into leadership roles while also supporting many new assistant principals on their journey to becoming even better leaders of their own sites. There is no substitute for authenticity, and Marshall has lived every step of the journey he so effectively describes in this book.

In reflecting on the importance of Marshall's book to the field of education leadership, I was reminded of a few lines from one of my favorite poems, which is often referenced on Canada's Remembrance Day. Poet John McCrae (1919/2008) wrote "In Flanders Fields" in tribute to his fellow soldiers who lost their lives in battle. Two lines stand out as I reflect on the actions Marshall suggests in this book regarding cultivating the next generation of school leaders:

> To you from failing hands we throw
> the torch; be yours to hold it high.

The compelling mission of this book is clear: as leaders, we must recognize that part of our responsibility and duty is to pass the torch of leadership. Tomorrow's leaders are among us; this masterful book will give school leaders the tools they need to wisely pass that torch to those who have been prepared to hold it high.

REFERENCES

McCrae, J. (1919/2008). *"In Flanders Fields," and other poems.* Accessed at www.gutenberg.org /cache/epub/353/pg353-images.html on October 28, 2024.

National Association of Secondary School Principals. (2021, December 8). *NASSP survey signals a looming mass exodus of principals from schools.* Accessed at www.nassp.org /news/nassp-survey-signals-a-looming-mass-exodus-of-principals-from-schools on October 24, 2024.

National Center for Education Statistics. (2023, July 31). *Roughly one in ten public school principals left profession in 2021–22 school year.* Accessed at https://nces.ed.gov/whatsnew /press_releases/7_31_2023.asp on October 10, 2024.

INTRODUCTION

Take a moment to think of a school leader who inspired you—someone who made a difference in your life and impacted who you are today. What attributes did they possess? What actions did they take? What did they value? How would you describe their "ways of being"—the truly outstanding qualities of leadership that they exhibited. What are the attributes that made them special? Most people have little difficulty recalling a leader who inspired them with their outstanding qualities.

Now imagine a school leader in the future reflecting on a leader who inspired them. Is it you who they picture? Why do you think you inspired them? What qualities do you possess as a school leader that made them want to follow in your footsteps? How did your daily interactions with staff, students, and families in your community illustrate to them that the role of school administrator is important and rewarding and something they wanted to do?

Schools need outstanding administrators. As current school leaders, we are in the unique and important position to identify, prepare, and support teachers to become effective future administrators. This is the central idea of this book. It will guide you to answer the questions, Which teachers have the potential to be future administrators? How do I become their guide, their coach, and their mentor? How do I invest in their success? This book will provide you with the tools, strategies, and motivation to become a leader who inspires others to lead.

At the time of the writing of this book, eleven teachers from Boyne Public School have gone to be assistant principals or principals; another five were assistant principals who are now principals. I was privileged to be a witness to their journeys and to help them along their paths. Why did they stand out? What made them appear destined for leadership? What ways of being made me want to invest in them as future school leaders? What skills did they demonstrate and what behaviors did they show on a daily basis? Some expressed that they were interested in school administration, but many did not articulate a desire to move into a leadership role. My observations along with research and reading on effective leadership and effective teaching led me to develop a process to identify, encourage, and support potential school leaders that begins with the following ten ways of being.

TEN WAYS OF BEING

We know that school leaders are successful because they use a large set of leadership skills; however, it is a smaller handful of personal attributes that create the largest difference in leadership effectiveness (Leithwood, Harris, & Hopkins, 2008). Successful leadership is about using personal attributes in concert with leadership skills to make an impact and using these attributes within the context of the school community. There are many books available about the most important leadership qualities for a school administrator. Many jurisdictions have evaluation processes for school administrators that try to identify the vital aspects of leadership. Selection committees and performance reviews attempt to list the key elements of leadership. Ask any parent or community member and they will share a list of traits that they want to see in their local school leader. School staffs have opinions on what makes the most effective leader. I have identified ten attributes—the ways of being—that I believe and the research identifies as critical for a teacher to demonstrate to be a successful future administrator. My coaching conversations with aspiring leaders and the opportunities I provide for them to develop and improve as future leaders focus on these ten attributes.

To one day be effective as school administrators, teachers must demonstrate that they are the following.

1. **An advocate for all students:** The teacher is relentless in their pursuit to provide equal access and opportunities for all students. They speak up for those that have been marginalized and have no voice. They make sure students and families get what they need.

2. **A creator of a safe and welcoming environment:** The teacher builds and maintains a culture where all students feel safe, included and valued. *All* means *all*.

3. **An effective communicator:** The teacher is able to share on a wide variety of topics, while constantly modeling the expectations of how to communicate effectively and with candor and respect. They use a variety of communication methods and continually demonstrate the most important aspect of communication: being a good listener.

4. **A goal setter who uses data:** The teacher continually seeks out and uses the data that is available to set goals and inspire. They are driven

to improve the learning conditions and outcomes for all the students in the school.

5. **Innovative:** The teacher is creative and on the lookout for necessary and effective change that can lead to new perspectives and learning. They are open to new ideas and consider the most current and effective programs and ideas for the classroom.

6. **Knowledgeable of effective teaching:** The teacher knows what good teaching looks like and sounds like. They are aware of the individual differences within students and strive to modify their teaching to match the students they have in front of them.

7. **Optimistic:** The teacher understands that their mood and disposition have an impact on others. While staying realistic, they are positive about the future and they provide hope for others. They work within their means to achieve the best outcomes for students.

8. **Present:** The teacher is available and can be seen. They are approachable and people want to interact with them. They are effective in their interactions with others and people feel better after being with them.

9. **A problem solver with situational awareness:** The teacher must address situations quickly and effectively while being aware of all stakeholders involved. They must treat all people with dignity while addressing issues and have an awareness of when situations could be prevented with some proactive interventions (situational awareness).

10. **A relationship builder:** The teacher has successful, healthy relationships with many different stakeholders. Particular attention is given to their relationships with their class and with individual students. Relationships with adults are also a key to success.

These are not ranked in importance as all ten are crucial in making a difference for students, staff, and the school community.

School leadership is complex and requires an integrated approach using multiple skills and behaviors on a minute-by-minute basis. This means leaders and aspiring leaders must work on perfecting isolated skills, much like an athlete who must perfect many discrete movements to perform a sport at a high level (Leithwood, 2012). Aspiring and current leaders can work on individual skills to impact their leadership ability as a whole. They might have strengths in some leadership skill areas and may need to consciously target and build proficiency in other aspects to benefit their schools and students (Goldring, Rubin, & Herrmann, 2021).

The shift in role from a teacher in the classroom to a school leader in the administrator's office is a challenge. As a current administrator, you can play a vital role in supporting teachers so they can be successful future administrators. In a study looking at the transition from teaching to administration, Denise E. Armstrong (2014) found that there were three key aspects for a teacher to feel prepared for the new role.

1. Professional learning that is timely and targeted for the individual.
2. Job-embedded opportunities to develop leadership skills.
3. Having a healthy coaching and mentoring relationship with those currently in the role.

By using the ten ways of being, you will be able to incorporate all three of these key aspects for a successful transition for your teachers. You will be equipped to provide targeted, needed, in-time professional learning that is aligned with the work that assistant principals and principals do in schools.

Additionally, teachers must be given opportunities to flex their leadership muscles. By having real-life leadership experiences, future leaders can come to understand what is expected of them and what behaviors successful school leaders exhibit (Mertz, 2006). Having opportunities to take on leadership tasks reinforces the fact that leadership is not exclusive to the person holding the title of school administrator. Instead, leadership must be distributed throughout the school; spreading opportunities to others is an acknowledgment that the principal is no longer seen as the single source of leadership in a school (Goldring et al., 2021). This provides a wider perspective that Jack L. Bagwell (2013) refers to as "leader plus" (p. 53).

Through mentoring and coaching, you will be able to address many of the recommendations made in Katina Pollock's (2017) report *The Changing Nature of Vice Principals' Work*, which focuses on improving the success of assistant principals after they leave the teaching role. For example, you will be able to reduce the feeling of isolation that assistant principals experience. Your coaching and guidance will improve job satisfaction when they are in the role. You will be providing effective professional development that is aligned with their future work. Use your experience and guidance to find those future administrators who should be in the role and help to develop a diverse and successful next generation of leaders. Few programs and school systems have in place mentoring that targets teachers who want to move into administration or beginning assistant principals and focus on the work that is generally assigned to the assistant principal (Pollock, 2017). This book looks to assist principals in mentoring teachers while they are still in a teaching role and within the school, where interactions can occur daily.

WHO THIS BOOK IS FOR

If you are a current experienced school administrator considering which teachers have what it takes to move into administrative roles and you want to provide them the opportunities and guidance to get them there, this book is primarily for you. However, there are many different roles requiring strong leadership in education. All teachers are leaders, and some leave the classroom to take on educational lead positions that do not include becoming assistant principals.

Educators in other leadership positions will also benefit from reading this book. The ten ways of being are certainly transferrable to many educational leadership positions.

If you are a district leader, you can use this book to help guide your decision making when hiring school leaders. In addition, experienced administrators can use this book for personal goal setting and career growth planning. If you are a new administrator, use this book to develop your entire leadership skill set. Finally, if you are a teacher considering a future in administration, you will also find this book helpful as it highlights the skills, knowledge, attitudes, and behaviors that are important for you to have to be effective and fulfilled in a future leadership role. I invite you to seek out a mentor who can help you use this book as a guide for personal and professional development as well as self-reflection.

WHAT IS IN THIS BOOK?

This book is about recognizing the brilliant people you work with and what you can do to support and coach them. This book is grounded in research about leadership but also provides real school examples of practices you can use to foster leadership in others and build a positive school climate and culture.

In my career, I have used the term *vice principal*—the leadership title used in my local district— to describe a teacher moving into a beginning administrator role. In many places in the United States and Canada, the role may be referred to as the assistant principal. Where the research is specific to one role (principal, vice principal, or assistant principal), I highlight this fact. Much of the research does not separate the two roles and will often mention school leaders only. The roles of vice or assistant principal can be very different from the principal role based on school, board, or district context and current policies and procedures that are unique to particular locations. Throughout this book, I use the more common term *assistant principal* when referring to this leadership position.

Chapter 1 presents a tool based on the important work of Paul Hersey and Kenneth Blanchard (1993). Hersey and Blanchard's Situational Leadership Model is a leadership construct focusing on the skill-level abilities of employees as well as their willingness and motivation to perform (Hersey & Blanchard, 1993). This model is intuitively appealing and easy to apply. Research (Meirovich & Gu, 2015) continues to find a significant relationship between the readiness of workers and their performance and satisfaction. As you will read in this chapter, positive outcomes for those seeking leadership positions are strongly related to both willingness and abilities (Meirovich & Gu, 2015). Readiness does matter, and current leaders have a role to play in supporting and mentoring aspiring leaders. I highly recommend you begin with chapter 1 before digging into the ten chapters that follow. Chapter 1 provides foundational information and an explanation of the process that you will follow throughout the book. The remaining chapters present the leadership action matrix as a tool to assist you in determining the most appropriate actions to take to aid in teacher professional development using the ten ways of being.

Starting in chapter 2, each chapter focuses on one of the ten ways of being, first describing the way of being and the related research followed by descriptors and observations for leaders to consider about the attribute. You will be encouraged to think deeply about the aspiring leaders you lead, considering where they show strengths and possible areas for growth. After reading about each way of being, you will chart the people you lead on a leadership action matrix by assessing their current skill level with that attribute as well as their desire and motivation to learn and improve. Where you place the individual on the matrix will help determine your next steps to move them forward in their journey to becoming an administrator.

Chapters include communication starters for conversations about next steps like coaching, providing responsibility, providing guidance, and supporting future leaders in leadership tasks. The next steps also include the teacher creating growth goals and plans for improvement based on sharpening their skills and knowledge in the ways of being. Working with the future leader and involving them in the goal setting will plan a course for success as they enter roles in administration. If you are a teacher, you will be able to plot yourself on the matrix and determine the next steps in your growth.

Each way of being chapter introduces a fictional teacher and administrator. You will see sample templates and planning pages that have been completed by the teacher's administrator and the teacher themselves to assist you through the process of using the ways of being and the materials found within this book. The examples and stories I share are based on my experiences in my thirty years as a teacher, teacher leader, assistant principal, principal, district leader, and instructor of leadership and principal qualification courses.

HOW TO USE THIS BOOK

There are a variety of ways you can use this book.

- Consider a single teacher who you believe has the potential to be a future leader. Work your way through the book by providing feedback, conducting mentoring conversations, goal setting, and planning with this individual to prepare them for the role of school leader.

- Consider a single teacher and select individual chapters that you think would be most beneficial for their growth. Be aware, however, that even though a teacher may appear to have strengths in the overall way of being and you might consider skipping the chapter, there may be specific behaviors within that way of being that require growth and increased understanding. Also, note that each chapter shares practical examples that you can use with highly skilled and motivated teachers to provide leadership experiences where they can use their strengths and gain leadership confidence.

- Consider using this resource with a team of individuals. You may be fortunate to be leading a school with many aspiring leaders. There are aspects of this resource that should be done individually with an administrator, but many activities and discussions could occur with a collaborative leadership team.

- Consider using this resource personally. As a current administrator or a teacher considering moving into an administration role, use this book as a self-reflection tool. The planning pages and templates will fit into any growth plan or goal-setting process and the effective observable behaviors themselves are excellent practices for reflection.

- Consider which leadership ways of being are most needed in your region or district and select those for further study. Also, consider adding additional ways of being that are not included in the ten presented here. Use the resources and templates to create your own list of observable behaviors to align with your school or district context more closely.

- Consider handing this book to a teacher you think would benefit from the content. Use it as a celebration of what you have observed and a springboard for future conversations. It is a wonderful way to recognize their talents and share with them your belief and commitment to their growth.

CONCLUSION

In a summary of high-quality principals, the Wallace Report finds that school climate is improved when talented principals empower teachers (Grissom, Egalite, & Lindsay, 2021). This occurs when administrators focus on and promote teacher leadership (Sebastian, Allensworth, & Huang, 2016). This happens when administrators delegate tasks to teachers and actively mentor them. This happens when administrators assist teachers in finding and selecting professional learning opportunities that are matched with their needs (Brown & Militello, 2016). This book will provide examples of how you can use all these strategies and become a more influential administrator, which is key for the development of your aspiring leaders.

Can you be a leader who prioritizes influencing others? We need great school leaders like you—those who discover, inspire, and model others to lead. This book will help you to continue to motivate and find those who will take on your role someday—today's teachers who will become tomorrow's administrators.

CHAPTER 1

THE LEADERSHIP ACTION MATRIX

My good friend and colleague Tom Hierck (2019) speaks about how the very best teachers learn the DNA (dreams, needs, and abilities) of their students so they can be an important and significant influence in students' lives. The very best principals do the same regarding their staff; they invest in knowing their staff members' expertise, personalities, aspirations, and goals (Grissom et al., 2021).

In their book *Ready to Lead on Day One: Predicting Novice Principal Effectiveness with Information Available at Time of Hire*, authors Jason A. Grissom, David S. Woo, and Brendan Bartanen (2020) share that the standard information on a resume such as education, degrees, and years of experience as a teacher are poor predictors of future leadership effectiveness. Even prior teaching experience at a particular school level in and of itself does not translate to being more effective at that same level as a school leader in the future. What does translate into success? Successful leaders were higher performing as teachers (Grissom et al., 2020).

This finding seems obvious. Success as a school leader does not come from some innate ability to lead; it stems from being an excellent teacher. When given opportunities, high-performing teachers develop the motivation and capacity to lead a school because they accumulate the required knowledge, behaviors, attitudes, and skills (Grissom et al., 2020). Those elements—opportunities, motivation, capacity, leadership, knowledge, behaviors, attitudes, and skills—provide the framework for the leadership action matrix, the tool this chapter explores in the following sections.

If we believe that students are unique individuals and require different approaches to excel in their learning, then we must believe the same is true for teachers. School leaders must be able to tailor their guidance and coaching to what an aspiring leader needs most at a particular moment in time. Research finds that professional learning within leadership development programs has impact when it is personalized to meet the specific need of the aspiring leader (Oleszewski, Shoho, & Barnett, 2012). The leadership action matrix this chapter presents will help you understand individual teachers' levels of skill and motivation so you how to adapt your leadership to assist future leaders the most.

THE TWO AXES OF THE LEADERSHIP ACTION MATRIX

The leadership action matrix consists of two axes, as shown in figure 1.1. The *x*-axis of the matrix is labeled with the words *motivation, desire, passion,* and *interest.* The *y*-axis is labeled with the words *skill, knowledge,* and *understanding.* This matrix supports the premise that professional learning for assistant principals should focus on skill development, as seen on the *y*-axis, and support for a passion and desire for leadership, as seen on the *x*-axis (Oleszewski, Shoho, & Barnett, 2012).

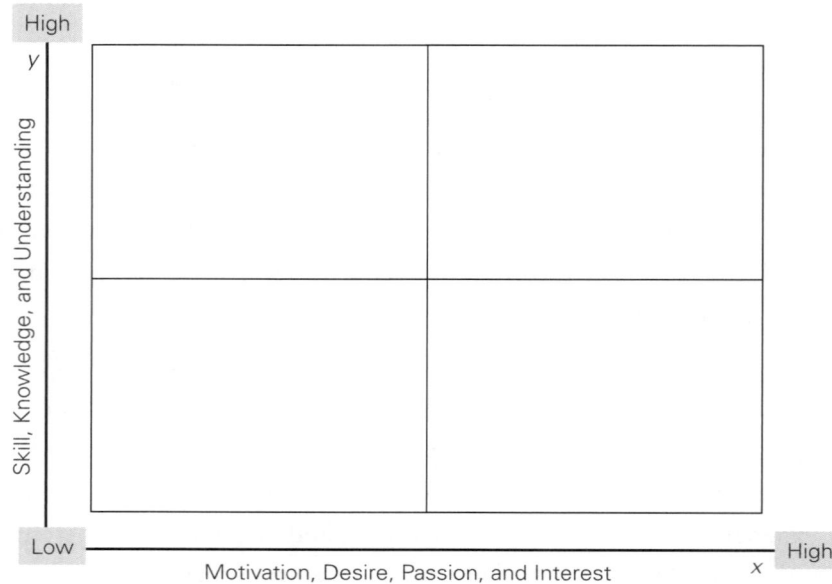

FIGURE 1.1: The leadership action matrix.

THE FOUR QUADRANTS OF THE LEADERSHIP ACTION MATRIX

Kenneth Blanchard and Paul Hersey (1993) developed the Situational Leadership Model, a theory suggesting that the context in which a leader is placed determines the leadership style they should use to have the most impact. Leaders are much more influential if they can adapt to the features in their surroundings and adjust their leadership stance to match what those they lead most need. As the followers develop their abilities and change their attitude toward a task, leaders then adapt their behaviors to move the organization forward. One leadership style does not work in all situations and with all people. Since ability and attitude change over time, leadership must also change. A leader needs to be versatile and demonstrate different ways to lead even though they may have a preferred style.

The foundation of Hersey-Blanchard's model is the idea that leadership actions should match the followers' maturity level. The word *readiness* was then introduced instead of *maturity* to better define the term as meaning followers' abilities and willingness (Meirovich & Gu, 2015). The original model introduced four leadership styles: (1) telling, (2) selling, (3) participating, and (4) delegating (Sridharan, 2022). Ten years after the introduction of the model, Blanchard branched out on his own and changed the terminology slightly, and these terms reflect leadership styles more common in the work we do as school administrators: (1) support, (2) delegate, (3) direct, and (4) guide/coach (Blanchard, 2024; de Bruin, 2020; Kruse, 2019).

The four leadership styles from Blanchard's adaptation of the Situational Leadership Model (SLII, Blanchard, 2024; de Bruin, 2020) make up the four quadrants in the leadership action matrix, as shown in figure 1.2. We will use this leadership action matrix to identify where a potential leader's skills and motivation lie for each observable behavior. The words in each quadrant (support, delegate, direct, and guide/coach) indicate what the administrator will do to assist the teacher moving forward.

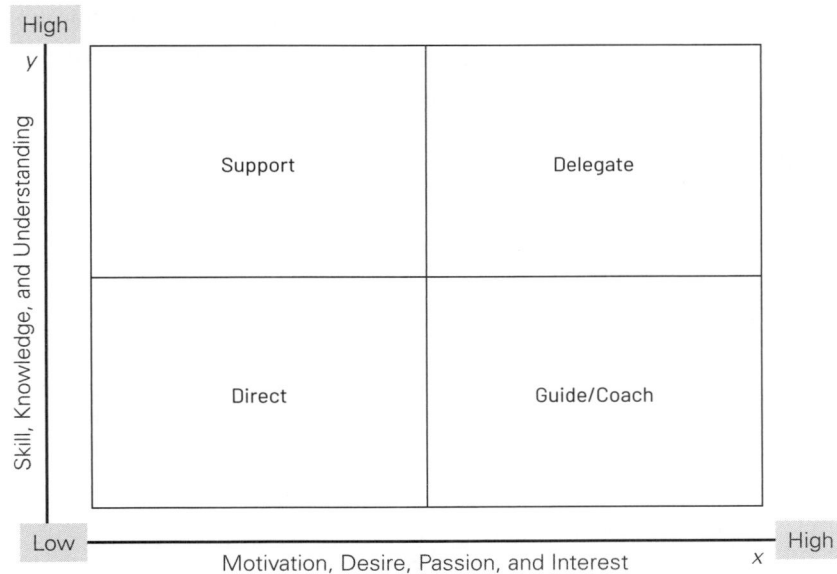

Sources: Blanchard, 2024; Hersey & Blanchard, 1993.

FIGURE 1.2: The leadership action matrix.

In *Give and Take: A Revolutionary Approach to Success*, Adam Grant (2013) writes that the most successful individuals have three things in common: motivation, ability, and opportunity. We will plot two of these on the matrix: motivation and ability. The third also directly connects to you. Find your teachers who have motivation and ability and give them opportunities to lead.

As you read each chapter in this book, you will plot your identified future leaders on the matrix based on the degree to which they exhibit each way of being. Following are descriptions of each quadrant of the matrix: direct, guide/coach, support, and delegate.

The Direct Quadrant: Low Motivation and Low Skill

This quadrant indicates low skill, knowledge, and understanding and low motivation, desire, passion, and interest, as shown in figure 1.3. Teachers who fall into this quadrant are the most challenging for leaders because they lack skills and knowledge and may have little desire or interest to improve. Individuals may be in this quadrant for several ways of being, or sadly, they might be in this quadrant for many aspects of their teaching role. School administrators have a role to play in moving all staff along in their development. A teacher who is lacking both knowledge and willingness to improve is detrimental to student learning, other staff members, and your community. This is not the representation of your school you wish to project. While we should be working with an individual in this quadrant for a particular way of being, we should not be promoting the idea of future administrative roles until they exhibit behaviors that take them out of this quadrant. As Michael Fullan (2014) notes in *The Principal: Three Keys to Maximizing Impact*, talented schools will improve a weak teacher. Equally true is that talented teachers will leave a weak school. So, be the exceptional school that improves a weak teacher. Having a teacher in this quadrant for any of the ways of being is a challenge, but not an insurmountable one. All ways of being are important for leadership success; therefore, leaders must assist teachers out of this quadrant before moving forward with professional development.

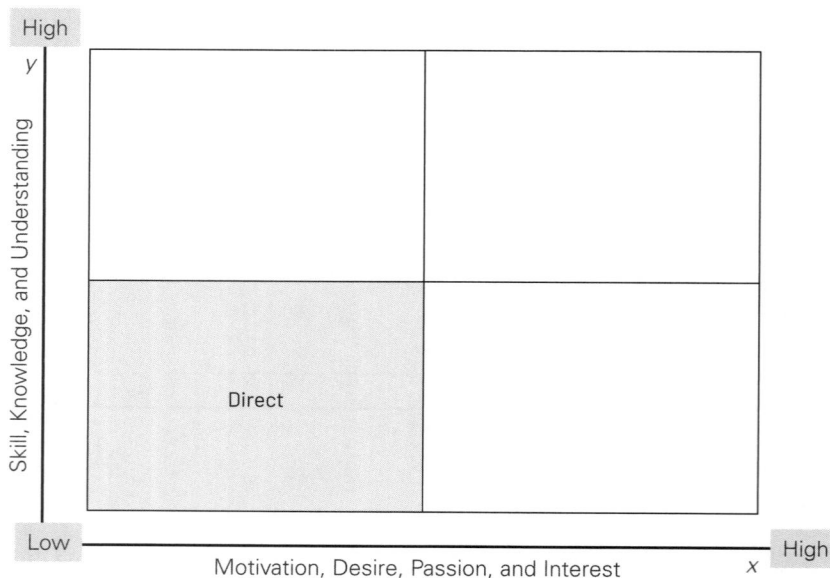

FIGURE 1.3: The direct quadrant: Low skill and low motivation.

Individuals in this quadrant may be unskilled in the specific way of being for various reasons. They may not have considered the importance of the way of being or made it a focus in their development. Others may realize they do not have the ability, but they may be reluctant to reveal that they struggle in the area. It is easy for school leaders to get angry or become disappointed with this behavior from teachers. Leaders might even question their abilities for being unable to turn these people around. Or they might blame previous administrators for not acting on the staff members' deficiencies sooner. Become curious—it will take time to determine why a teacher lacks motivation and passion (Corporate Finance Institute, n.d.; de Bruin, 2020; Freeman, 2016; Oelschlager, 2021; Spira, 2010; Sridharan, 2022).

You can never fully understand someone's past experiences and what challenges they might be dealing with on a daily basis. You can, however, create the conditions in the school and with your leadership that influence the teacher's motivation, learning, and development. Build trust by giving them space to be heard, inviting them into caring conversations, and providing a helpful perspective. The goal is for them to be more comfortable so they will begin to experiment, then fail, and then try again (Evers-Gerdes & Siegle, 2022). Show individuals how to be successful with their way of being or help them build a relationship with someone else who can help (Corporate Finance Institute, n.d.; de Bruin, 2020; Freeman, 2016; Oelschlager, 2021; Spira, 2010; Sridharan, 2022). Being politely relentless in directing individuals about how to make improvements will help them get out of this quadrant.

The work of Simon Sinek (2009) is extremely valuable in inspiring others about why we do the things we do, or why a particular way of being is important or valuable. Why is a particular way of being so vital for effective leadership success? This understanding might start to motivate a teacher to help move them into the guide/coach quadrant. In that quadrant, they still have low skills and abilities, but they will become more willing to accept resources, coaching, and support once they have improved their level of motivation. They need to see how the way of being is key to student success, and important for well-being, equity, or overall school success.

For many educators, it comes naturally to work with students using Dweck's (2008) theory of mindsets as growth or fixed. As leaders, we need to work with staff members in this same way. If a staff member is stuck, consider what you would say to a student who is stuck. Have the mindset each day that the individual is going to get to where they need to be. As a leader, do all you can to help improve their skills to move them out of this quadrant. Provide clear, brief directions about what the teacher needs to do. Be direct about what you would like to see, set up small wins to build confidence, and provide frequent feedback to help the teacher be successful. Have frequent check-ins and provide timelines if necessary; helping teachers move out of this quadrant can be a lot of work as they may have short-term success and then stall (Corporate Finance Institute, n.d.; de Bruin, 2020; Freeman, 2016; Oelschlager, 2021; Spira, 2010; Sridharan, 2022).

As educators, we can all picture a struggling student who lacks motivation and desire to improve, and then something clicks—something motivates or inspires improvement for the individual, and positive results start to build momentum. Be that motivator or inspiration for the teachers in your school. I have met many teachers who could be difficult to work with; however, my mindset was that I was always going to be politely relentless in my pursuit of benefiting students.

The Guide/Coach Quadrant: High Motivation and Low Skill

This quadrant indicates low skill, knowledge, and understanding; however, the individual exhibits high motivation, desire, passion, and interest, as shown in figure 1.4. A teacher who has many observable behaviors for ways of being that fall into this quadrant has shown you that they are highly motivated to learn more, do more, and develop, but currently do not have the skill and knowledge they need to succeed. For example, this teacher might be brand-new to your school and ready to climb mountains, but they do not yet possess the experience or understanding to deal with some of the complexities of teaching. Or this could be an experienced teacher who, when introduced to a new idea or process, sees the value and wants to get on board but doesn't know where to start or where to turn to get the necessary information. These are individuals who may express that they are not skilled or confident in their abilities in a way of being, but you see the potential. They are curious, want to improve, and want to do professional learning (Corporate Finance Institute, n.d.; de Bruin, 2020; Freeman, 2016; Oelschlager, 2021; Spira, 2010; Sridharan, 2022).

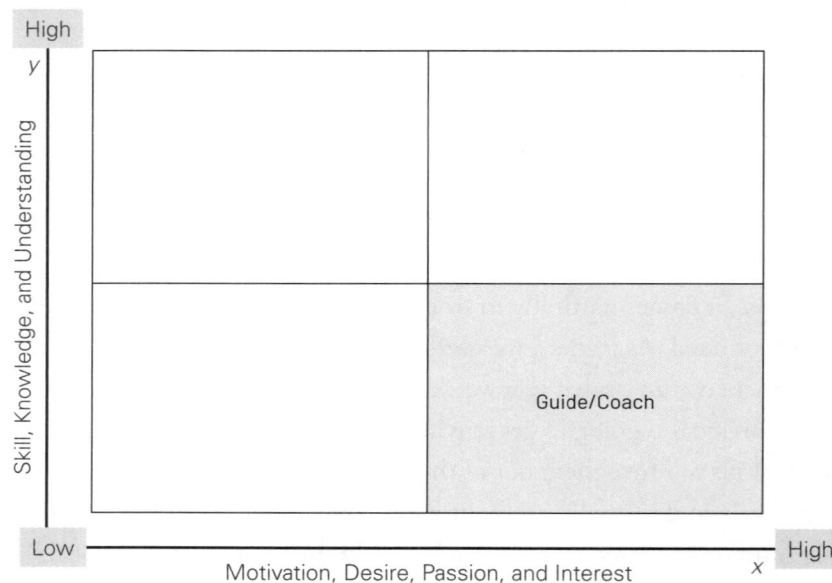

FIGURE 1.4: The guide/coach quadrant: High motivation and low skill.

Individuals in this quadrant need you to be their guide and their coach to provide them with the tools and training they need. They may have shared that they want to move into administration and will do all they can to learn the skills and knowledge to achieve this goal. Organizational psychologist Adam Grant (2023) explains that:

> When considering a new role, the most important question isn't "can I do it?" It's "do I want it?" It's up to the employer to decide whether you're qualified. Only you can gauge whether you're motivated. Values should align with the job. Skills can be learned on the job.

They do not need convincing from you to develop a particular way of being. They have the motivation (Corporate Finance Institute, n.d.; de Bruin, 2020; Freeman, 2016; Oelschlager, 2021; Spira, 2010; Sridharan, 2022)—you just have to provide the opportunity.

An important resource that you control and can provide is time—both your time and personal time to learn. Individuals in this quadrant will have a lot of questions since they are highly motivated. Give them the parameters and boundaries for what could be possible and involve them in finding what is needed (Corporate Finance Institute, n.d.; de Bruin, 2020; Freeman, 2016; Oelschlager, 2021; Spira, 2010; Sridharan, 2022). For example, when possible, include them in making decisions about resources, learning materials, conferences, workshops, and so on, to develop their skills. This could mean providing your budget and parameters, such as the number of days allowed away from the classroom, and then working with the teacher to identify professional development opportunities. Reduce the obstacles and constraints as much as possible. You have a highly motivated individual who wants to learn; that is worth investing in!

For professional development, consider others on staff who shine in a particular way of being. Workshopping and staff learning sessions can be a key way to help staff members improve their skills. Modeling is important because staff who fall into this quadrant are enthusiastic, willing to learn, and ready to adopt best practices. It is prudent for leaders to ensure teachers in this quadrant are learning from the right sources. These individuals might learn from formal and informal mentors things that you as an administrator never want to see in your school. It is important for the individuals in this quadrant that you set up learning opportunities connecting the right content with the right people.

This quadrant also provides an opportunity for leaders to learn alongside staff members. As the teachers learn and develop, provide coaching and feedback. Have discussions about the learning and ask them to share with others; their enthusiasm will be contagious.

The Support Quadrant: Low Motivation and High Skill

This quadrant indicates high skill, knowledge, and understanding, but low motivation, desire, passion, and interest (figure 1.5, page 16). A teacher in this quadrant knows quite a bit about the way of being and can show they have talents in that area, but they currently have little desire to examine their practice, learn more, or share with others (Corporate Finance Institute, n.d.; de Bruin, 2020; Freeman, 2016; Oelschlager, 2021; Spira, 2010; Sridharan, 2022). An example of someone in this category is an experienced teacher who is highly skilled but has become unmotivated, has decreased their engagement with a way of being, or has displayed less-than-ideal attitudes and behaviors. They may seem to be in a rut. They are not putting in the effort and commitment you might have seen in the past. These individuals are lacking in team involvement, and the staff are suffering because these teachers are not sharing their talents.

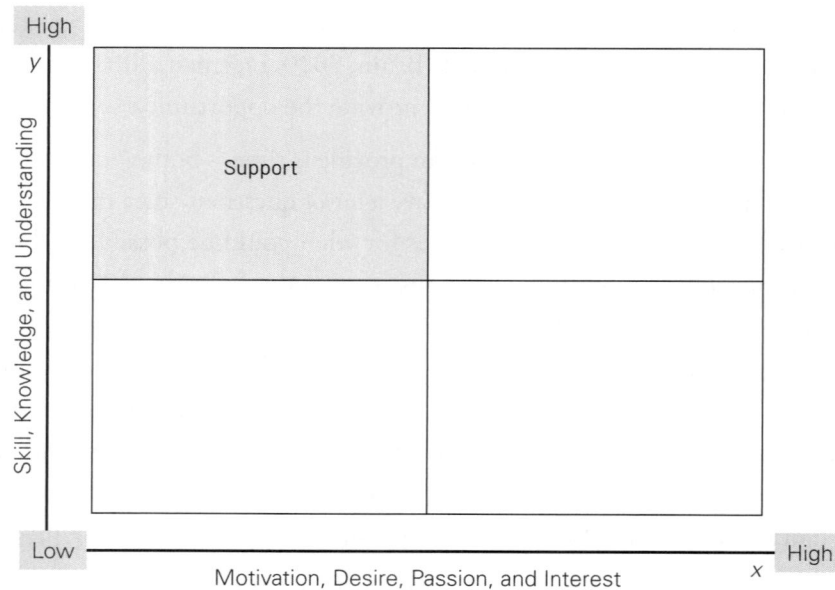

FIGURE 1.5: The support quadrant: Low motivation and high skill.

Education is not a solo effort. Being a school administrator requires working with teams and interacting with others constantly. As Richard DuFour and colleagues (2024) have written, "No one person will have the energy, expertise, and influence to lead a complex change process until it becomes anchored in the organization's culture without first gaining the support of key staff members" (p. 35). If a highly skilled and knowledgeable teacher is to embark on a leadership journey, they must focus on their passion and motivation for each of the ten ways of being in relation to working with others. This quadrant requires leaders to support teachers so that they will see the benefit of sharing their knowledge and expertise with others.

This quadrant requires a bit of problem solving for leaders. Is the teacher's lack of motivation in this particular moment, semester, term, or school year, or has the individual exhibited this behavior for a long time, maybe even before your arrival at the school? Utilize your strong communication abilities and consider having a caring and candid conversation with the individual to share your perceptions. Why are they not sharing their talents?

In this quadrant, leaders help individual teachers see why a way of being is valuable and that they, too, can embody the way of being to their students, colleagues, and the school community. You might have to be heavy on the compliments to reestablish in their mind that they have the skill and ability, you just want to see it more. Fill their bucket—give them back their confidence. You need to be genuine and honest with them; they have the skill set, and you want them to share it with others.

Once you have identified the leadership behaviors you want to see more of, monitor for the behaviors and recognize when they occur to reinforce the positive (Corporate Finance Institute, n.d.; de Bruin, 2020; Freeman, 2016; Oelschlager, 2021; Spira, 2010; Sridharan, 2022). Keep in mind it might take time to see the future leader's passion reemerge. You might have to share how this individual impacts their colleagues and what your expectations are about behavior they must exhibit as part of a team.

Individuals in this quadrant need to become mentors to other teachers or take on leadership roles with staff. When they do, be sure to be available and check in, but do not micromanage them and take away the positive momentum they have created (Corporate Finance Institute, n.d.; de Bruin, 2020; Freeman, 2016; Oelschlager, 2021; Spira, 2010; Sridharan, 2022); however, monitoring is necessary. A low-motivation teacher mentoring someone with high motivation could result in both teachers having low motivation. To avoid this, agree on what the skill sharing will involve, provide the necessary resources, and then get out of the way. Celebrate and thank the teacher and ensure that they see the positive outcomes of their involvement and impact. They have to hear about the success of others, and how their knowledge and skills assisted others. This will stoke their motivation.

The Delegate Quadrant: High Motivation and High Skill

The individuals in this quadrant are those whom leaders wish they could replicate and staff an entire school with—the teachers who have excellent skills combined with high motivation and a positive attitude toward students and learning. As shown in figure 1.6, this quadrant indicates high skill, knowledge, and understanding and high motivation, desire, passion, and interest. These teachers are confident in their abilities. Their high motivation makes them curious and they never stop learning (Corporate Finance Institute, n.d.; de Bruin, 2020; Freeman, 2016; Oelschlager, 2021; Spira, 2010; Sridharan, 2022). These individuals are looking for opportunities to grow and learn; they are by far the easiest for current school leaders to work with. Some of these future leaders will already exhibit all the ways of being, but plotting each attribute is still important because aspiring leaders can always improve. Your goal is to move every individual you are coaching and mentoring into this quadrant for all ten ways of being.

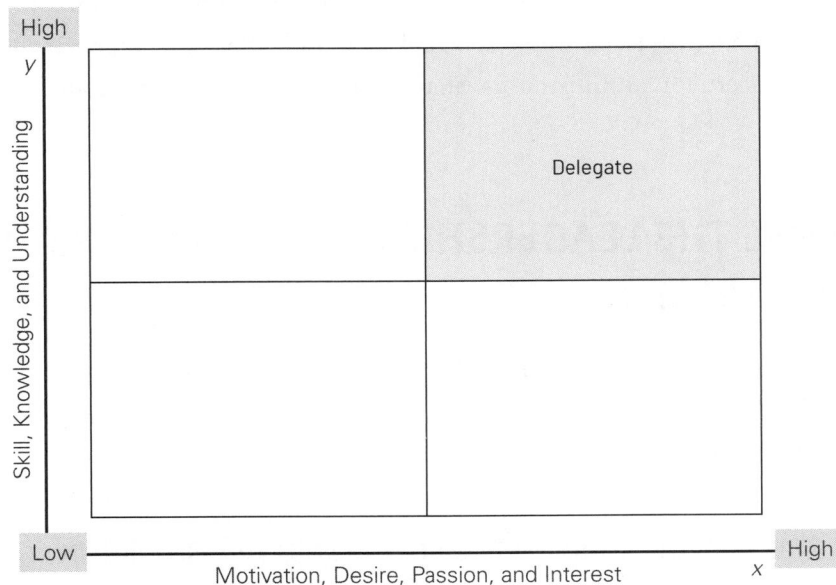

FIGURE 1.6: The delegate quadrant: High motivation and high skill.

Individuals in this quadrant are often the ones who jump right in. They notice what needs to be done and start activities and initiatives without you even knowing. Working with individuals in this quadrant involves deep discussion and reflection. Do they understand the importance of the way of being you are discussing? Can they picture the way of being not just at a school level but at the system level as well? One of the most important discussions to have with individuals in this quadrant is what they can do to bring others along to help develop their skills (Corporate Finance Institute, n.d.; Freeman, 2016; Oelschlager, 2021; Spira, 2010; Sridharan, 2022).

It is important to give these individuals autonomy. They have shown you in the past that they are competent and can be trusted. Give them a license to be creative. They do require acknowledgment of a job well done, so stay close enough to the project or activity so you can give thoughtful feedback. Look for opportunities to stretch them, giving them broader responsibilities within what is permissible (Corporate Finance Institute, n.d.; de Bruin, 2020; Freeman, 2016; Oelschlager, 2021; Spira, 2010; Sridharan, 2022). Remember, however, that they cannot and should not be doing your job; there are aspects of the school administrator role that can only be done by the assistant principal or principal. Look to provide your teachers with opportunities such as organizing events, running meetings and professional development, problem solving issues, and being visible throughout the school. Your district might have a process to have teachers support administrators when they are absent—a "teacher in charge" program. Every experience that you can orchestrate for them will provide exposure to the role and assist them in preparing for their leadership journey.

You should not feel a loss of influence or power when you share your leadership with individuals in this quadrant. Best practices multiply in schools where influence and sharing are the norm (Leithwood et al., 2008). So, give up some of your leadership to people in this quadrant in the areas in which they show excellence. Distributed leadership is a good thing! Just make sure not to overload teachers with leadership responsibilities. Talk about the importance of work–life balance, a major concern for administrators. Share how you balance the roles and responsibilities in your life.

HOW TO USE THE LEADERSHIP ACTION MATRIX AND OTHER MATERIALS

Once you have identified a teacher who could potentially move into a leadership position in the future, or a teacher has expressed interest in moving into such a position, choose the first way of being you would like to focus on and take the following steps.

Step 1: Plot the Way of Being on the Leadership Action Matrix

Read the list of observable behaviors for the way of being you are focusing on (found in chapters 2–11 of this book). For each observable behavior, determine the teacher's current status and plot the number of that behavior on the leadership action matrix tool.

For example, let's plot four observable behaviors from the first way of being—an advocate for all students—found in chapter 2 (page 28) and place one in each of the four quadrants. If the teacher demonstrates low skills and low interest for observable behavior five per the following description, put a five in the direct quadrant.

Behavior 5: *The teacher recognizes, respects, and employs student strengths, diversity, and culture as assets for teaching and learning. They use asset-based language, focusing on what students do have and how they can use these strengths to build success, rather than language that focuses on what students cannot do.*

If the teacher demonstrates strong knowledge but low interest for observable behavior six per the following description, put a six in the support quadrant.

Behavior 6: *The teacher is committed to addressing misconduct in a positive, fair, and unbiased manner. They work well with larger school teams to develop behavior plans, school guidelines and policies; and accommodation and modification techniques that treat all students respectfully.*

If they demonstrate low skills but high interest for observable behavior one per the following description, put a one in the guide/coach quadrant.

Behavior 1: *The teacher understands the need for continual learning and self-reflection in the areas of diversity, equity, and inclusion. The teacher engages in professional learning around serving the needs of all students. Professional learning includes topics of social justice and ways of teaching diverse students.*

If they demonstrate that they have strong skills and a strong interest for observable behavior four per the following description, put a four in the delegate quadrant.

Behavior 4: *The teacher makes efforts to connect with students in ways that respect cultural and personal differences. They learn greetings in the languages of their students and make classroom signs using students' languages. They use students' preferred names and pronounce them correctly. They ensure substitute teachers have guidance so that respectful interactions occur in their absence.*

Figure 1.7 (page 20) shows an example of a filled-in template. A blank reproducible template appears at the end of this chapter (page 24).

You might choose to plot each behavior precisely within each quadrant to rank it compared to others to target which behavior requires immediate attention. Or you can view all the behaviors for a particular quadrant equally. When you have plotted the teacher on all observable behaviors for a way of being, you will likely have some numbers in each of the quadrants.

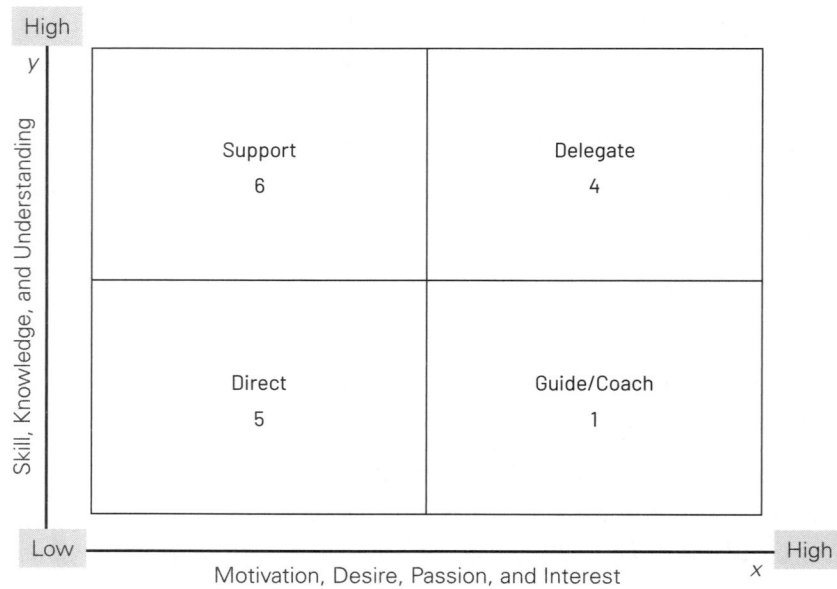

FIGURE 1.7: Leadership action matrix example—Student advocate qualities.

Step 2: Complete the Mentoring Planning Page

The mentoring planning page (figure 1.8) is a tool to use to organize your notes that correspond to the observable behaviors in each way of being. Record the numbers you placed in each quadrant of the leadership action matrix tool from step 1 in the number section of each quadrant on the mentoring planning page. Figure 1.8 is a sample that continues the example from figure 1.7. A blank reproducible template appears at the end of this chapter (page 25).

After recording the behavior number, write any observation notes, comments, or evidence of the observable behavior in the column beside it. Your comments indicate why you placed the observable behavior in that particular quadrant and will provide potential discussion topics to address with the teacher. Provide good information for growth and development but take care not to overwhelm the teacher with a long list of suggested next steps. Use your judgment based on your relationship with the aspiring leader to determine the appropriate number of statements and the level of concern you want to share. While you may feel that growth is required in many areas, a systematic and carefully developed plan of professional learning will be key to sustaining improvement. Bold or circle the notes that require further discussion during mentoring conversations. These notes will go in the mentoring meeting planner (explained in the following section) to plan your meeting time with a future leader.

Way of Being: An Advocate for All Students

Teacher: K. M.

Administrator: Principal Marshall

Directions: Record the numbers for observable behaviors from the leadership action matrix in the appropriate quadrants along with your notes for each. Bold or circle the statements you want to address with the teacher (to include in the meeting planning tool).

Support		Delegate	
Behavior Number	**Notes**	**Behavior Number**	**Notes**
6	Has rules and expectations, but needs to develop them with students, work with others in the school, and contribute more in teams	4	Builds strong relationships with students that respect cultural and personal differences

Direct		Guide/Coach	
Behavior Number	**Notes**	**Behavior Number**	**Notes**
5	Sometimes uses deficit-based language in staff meetings when speaking about students; should use asset-based language when discussing students	1	Wants to improve understanding of our diverse student population, equity, and inclusion; should provide professional development to support

FIGURE 1.8: Mentoring planning page example.

Step 3: Use the Mentoring Meeting Planner

Use the mentoring meeting planner (figure 1.9) before, during, and after meetings with your aspiring leader. Highlight comments using bold or circled notes from the mentoring planning planner to frame your meeting conversations. There are also sections teachers can use to be involved in planning and goal setting; together, you chart a course for growth and development. A blank reproducible template appears at the end of this chapter (page 26).

Date: October 6

Administrator: Principal Marshall

Teacher: K. M.

Focus

Which way or ways of being will we discuss?

An Advocate for all Students

Agenda for Sharing and Discussion

What specific points about the way or ways of being will we discuss?

- Review many of the positives about K. M.'s classroom environment and relationships with students.
- Discuss the need for K. M. to be well-rounded in many aspects of leadership.
- Discuss her perspective on her strengths and needs in this way of being.
- Review behavior 5 in the direct quadrant and direct on how to use asset language.
- Review behavior 1 in the guide/coach quadrant and provide resources for support.
- Review behavior 4 in the delegate quadrant and how K. M. can share with the rest of the staff.

Key Points

For each of the following sections, list the bold or circled items from the mentoring planning page.

- **Direct**
  - » Sometimes uses deficit-based language in staff meetings when speaking about students; should use asset-based language when discussing students.
- **Support**
  - » Has rules and expectations, but needs to develop them with students, work with others in the school, and contribute more in teams.
- **Guide/Coach**
  - » Wants to improve understanding of our diverse student population, equity, and inclusion; provide professional development to support.
- **Delegate**
  - » Builds strong relationships with students that respect cultural and personal differences.

Teacher Plans, Comments, and Ideas

What plans, comments, and ideas did the teacher have during the meeting?

Goal Setting

What is the teacher's goal?

Potential Resources
What are some potential resources to recommend to the teacher that address their areas of needed growth from the direct and guide/coach quadrants?
Suggest the following books: • *Beyond Conversations About Race: A Guide for Discussions With Students, Teachers, and Communities* by Washington Collado, Sharroky Hollie, Rosa Isiah, Yvette Jackson, Anthony Muhammad, Douglas Reeves, and Kenneth C. Williams

Final Thoughts
What are your final thoughts about next steps and when to check back in?
• K. M. is engaged in this process and thankful for the assistance.   • She is interested in moving into school administration and would like to continue meeting on a regular basis.   • She would like to review the other ways of being to see how she can improve.

FIGURE 1.9: Mentoring meeting planner example.

CONCLUSION

With an understanding of Hersey and Blanchard's Situational Leadership Model (1993) in place, it is now time to utilize the leadership action matrix with members of your school staff. Each of the remaining chapters focuses on one of the ways of being that is vital for success as a school administrator. While reading about each way of being, consider in which quadrant the future leader falls within the leadership action matrix: direct, guide/coach, support, or delegate. Each way of being includes a list of observable behaviors that current leaders would hope to see in effective future school leaders. The chapters provide blank templates and completed examples to assist with the next steps so future leaders can move "up and to the right" on the matrix for the leadership ways of being.

REPRODUCIBLE

Leadership Action Matrix

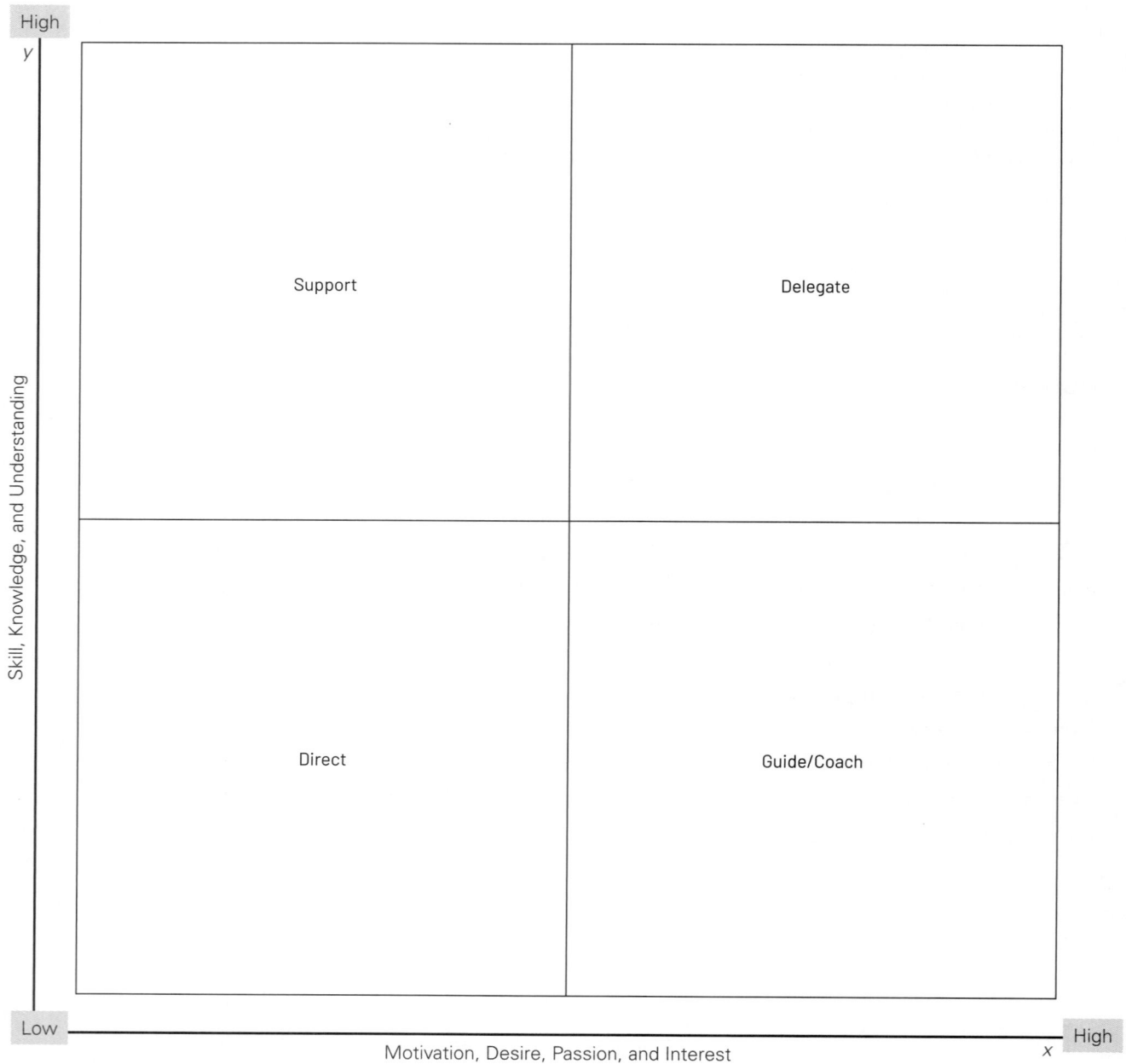

High
y

Skill, Knowledge, and Understanding

Support	Delegate
Direct	Guide/Coach

Low

High

Motivation, Desire, Passion, and Interest

x

Mentoring Meeting Planning Tool

Way of Being:

Teacher:

Administrator:

Directions: Record the numbers for observable behaviors from the "Leadership Action Matrix" (page 24) in the appropriate quadrants along with your notes for each. Bold or circle the statements you want to address with the teacher (to include in the meeting planning tool).

Support		Delegate	
Behavior Number	**Notes**	**Behavior Number**	**Notes**

Direct		Guide/Coach	
Behavior Number	**Notes**	**Behavior Number**	**Notes**

Mentoring Meeting Planner

Date:

Administrator:

Teacher:

Focus

Which way or ways of being will we discuss?

Agenda for Sharing and Discussion

What specific points about the way or ways of being will we discuss?

Key Points

For each of the following sections, list the bolded or circled items from the mentoring planning page.

- **Direct**

- **Support**

- **Guide/Coach**

- **Delegate**

Today's Teachers, Tomorrow's Leaders © 2025 Solution Tree Press • SolutionTree.com
Visit **go.SolutionTree.com/leadership** to download this free reproducible.

Teacher Plans, Comments, and Ideas

What plans, comments, and ideas did the teacher have during the meeting?

Goal Setting

What is the teacher's goal?

Potential Resources

What are some potential resources to recommend to the teacher that address their areas of needed growth from the direct and guide/coach quadrants?

Final Thoughts

What are your final thoughts about next steps and when to check back in?

Today's Teachers, Tomorrow's Leaders © 2025 Solution Tree Press • SolutionTree.com
Visit **go.SolutionTree.com/leadership** to download this free reproducible.

CHAPTER 2

AN ADVOCATE FOR ALL STUDENTS

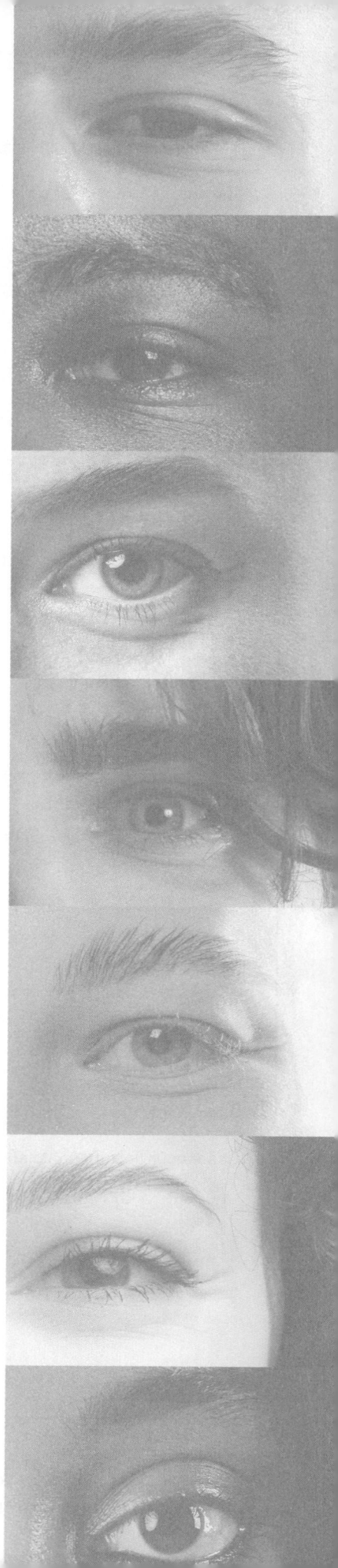

When school systems work in your favor, it can be difficult to see how the system could be unfair to others. Today's school leaders must make a concerted effort to examine their mindset to not only understand one's own privilege but also to make a commitment to disrupt the systems that perpetuate inequality to improve the conditions for all. Therefore, teachers who move into administration must develop an equity lens and become advocates for all students. They must be able to build a school climate where all students feel welcome, safe, and valued. To do this, a school should embrace the diversity that is in their community and ensure that school leaders are advocates for the diverse needs of all students.

The Canadian Association of Principals and the Alberta Teachers' Association (2014) study defines diversity as:

> [The] endless variations in student needs, including medical conditions, learning disabilities, language learning needs, mental health issues, cultural differences and—in too many cases—basic needs. . . . There is no such thing as a "typical" student in the classroom when so many sources of diversity must be taken into consideration. (p. 10)

Schools are becoming more diverse, and proper leadership can make schools more inclusive and guide teachers to be more culturally responsive (Grissom et al., 2021). However, the United States Government Accountability Office (2022) published a report stating that even though public school K–12 student populations are growing more diverse, the country's schools remain divided along economic, racial, and ethnic lines. While school administrators are becoming more ethnically diverse in overall numbers, the increase is not keeping pace with the student and community population, and the representation gap with students is growing (Grissom et al., 2021). The research is clear: when schools are populated with staff who reflect the social identities of their students, there are immediate and long-lasting positive effects (Blazar & Lagos, 2021). Administrators must explore all opportunities to hire educators who reflect the communities they serve (Ontario Ministry of Education, 2020). However, research also shows that a principal's identity or ethnicity is not a final marker of success. Every administrator who leads using an antiracist lens—looking closely at the structures and opportunities provided for all their students—can create positive and successful school experiences for all students. To do this, administrators must examine how their actions remove barriers and create opportunities for historically underserved student groups. They must promote access to support and important resources for the success of all students and confront systemic factors that inhibit the realization of the full potential of those who have been marginalized (Grissom et al., 2021).

While school leaders see diversity as an asset, they often describe their staff as playing the role of first responders who struggle to do the work they want to do and need to do with the resources available. While there are challenges, great school leaders express positive feelings about the changing social and cultural diversity in their communities (Grissom, Egalite, & Lindsay, 2021; Pollock, Wang & Hauseman, 2014).

Culturally responsive and relevant pedagogy recognizes that students do best when learning is connected to their background, their language, and their social and cultural identity. An inclusive school is one where students see themselves in the curriculum and within their physical surroundings. The policies, practices, and programs within a school must be tailored to meet the diverse needs of a school population. Effective administrators lead staff in conversations that address equity issues, inquire about the unique needs of individuals, and examine the current practices that exist within their school. Such a framework strives to build positive school cultures, encourage family-school relationships, and build stronger community connections with the ultimate outcome of improving student success (Ontario Ministry of Education, n.d.).

The role of the assistant principal is uniquely positioned to promote equitable outcomes for all students. When teachers become assistant principals, they work closely with students, staff, families, and their community. They can play a direct role in improving outcomes by engaging in effective and equity-oriented practices (Goldring et al., 2021). Provide teachers with the opportunity to experience and lead equity work prior to getting into the administration role. Public school principals are beginning their leadership careers with less teaching experience, especially in high-needs schools, and this is an equity concern as students from marginalized groups benefit from having experienced administration (Grissom, Egalite, & Lindsay, 2021).

According to the Wallace Report's synthesis of two decades of research on how principals affect students and schools, "the fair, just, and non-discriminatory treatment of all students, the removal of barriers, the provision of resources and supports, and the creation of opportunities with the goal of promoting equitable outcomes requires specific skills, orientations, and behaviors" (Grissom et al., 2021, p. 3). The observable behaviors this chapter provides showcase the specific skills, orientations, and behaviors that are necessary for teachers to demonstrate if they are to become effective future administrators.

Your leadership work with teachers to advocate for all students is extremely important for changing the future for all students. A conscious effort to find leaders whose voices are not typically heard will lead to better educational experiences for diverse and marginalized students, so leaders must understand the need to advocate for all students. The behaviors in this way of being are too important to wait until a teacher is a school leader to develop. As Michael

Fullan (2019) writes, school leaders must be "courageously and relentlessly committed to changing the system for the betterment of humanity" (p. 12). Those teachers who move into administration must not just "do school," they must use their position and leadership to create better outcomes for all students.

KEY OBSERVABLE BEHAVIORS

Following are behaviors that aspiring leaders who advocate for all students should exhibit. When rating a teacher in this way of being, think about the knowledge and skills involved with each behavior as well as the passion and motivation it requires. Consider providing the list of observable behaviors for this way of being to future leaders for self-evaluation and reflection prior to the mentoring planning meeting. (Visit **go.SolutionTree.com/leadership** for a free reproducible of this list.)

1. The teacher understands the need for continual learning and self-reflection in the areas of diversity, equity, and inclusion. The teacher engages in professional learning around serving the needs of all students. Professional learning includes topics of social justice and ways of teaching diverse students.

2. The teacher rises to the challenge of teaching all students; they do not believe any student is a burden in the classroom. They welcome students with diverse needs and look for integration opportunities for them.

3. The teacher designs equitable classroom practices based on cooperation, not competition. They focus on closing the opportunity gap rather than just closing the achievement gap.

4. The teacher makes efforts to connect with students in ways that respect cultural and personal differences. They learn greetings in the languages of their students and make classroom signs using students' languages. They use students' preferred names and pronounce them correctly. They ensure substitute teachers have guidance so that respectful interactions occur in their absence.

5. The teacher recognizes, respects, and employs student strengths, diversity, and culture as assets for teaching and learning. They use asset-based language, focusing on what students do have and how they can use these strengths to build success, rather than language that focuses on what students cannot do.

6. The teacher is committed to addressing misconduct in a positive, fair, and unbiased manner. They work well with larger school teams to develop behavior plans, school guidelines and policies; and accommodation and modification techniques that treat all students respectfully.

7. The teacher views the focus on equity, diversity, and inclusion as necessary work—not as an add-on. The work is not a single lesson or unit of study, but an inclusive curriculum that is woven into all learning practices and allows for connections to be made.

8. The teacher ensures that students see themselves and their classmates' lived experiences in the classroom, curriculum, and teaching materials throughout the year, not just during awareness months. They use a critical lens to evaluate and make decisions about which books, posters, texts, resources, and materials to use.

9. The teacher seeks out resources that have well-rounded and multidimensional characters and stories. Their students see positive, whole, and empowering examples of themselves that go against any one-dimensional, stereotypical representation of their culture and themselves. Overall, the resources they select for students are relevant, current, accessible, inclusive, and monitored for bias.

10. The teacher identifies and removes barriers. They continually search for alternative instructional approaches to meet the needs of all students. They provide students with multiple opportunities to demonstrate success by providing numerous ways to engage with classroom materials, resources, and assessments.

11. The teacher considers whose voices are being marginalized and makes a concerted effort to amplify and give space to those voices.

12. The teacher utilizes a calendar and identifies days of cultural and faith-based significance when making decisions about special events, activities, and the timing of tests and major assignments to ensure all students are included and do not have their special days impacted by schoolwork. They also use days of significance as a vehicle to raise awareness and knowledge of diverse cultures, faiths, and practices, and when planning activities, field trips, and special events, to ensure students can participate.

13. The teacher demonstrates an understanding that teaching and learning is a two-way relationship in their classroom—that they are learning from their students as well. Students are empowered to "teach" and celebrate who they are. They are learners in the areas where they lack knowledge and expertise.

14. The teacher promotes learning in the classroom that includes opportunities for students to participate in a justice-driven curriculum to recognize, analyze, and discuss barriers and injustices.

15. The teacher works with others to make sure that school and classroom practices and materials reflect and respond to the diversity of students in

the classroom and society as a whole. Their classroom does not need to be diverse for the practices and materials to reflect diversity.

16. The teacher provides materials that families can use in the home to support and contribute to student success at school, and their communication is clear, respectful, and accessible for all families. For example, the teacher uses translation software or translators when needed.

17. The teacher displays cultural competence as they seek out opportunities to interact, engage, and communicate with people across cultures. They welcome and interact with others from backgrounds different from their own. They demonstrate comfort, respect, and curiosity.

18. The teacher indicates they are moving toward a culturally sustaining pedagogy (McCray, 2022) where cultures are sustained instead of eradicated. Step one is when the teacher critically self-reflects and asks what they are trying to sustain in their teaching, materials, and resources use this in their work to be better.

19. The teacher initiates or facilitates contact with other professionals and community agencies to assist students and their families where appropriate.

20. The teacher communicates to their peers the high expectations for achievement of students who have traditionally struggled to be successful at school. They are a champion for students and address the causes and issues that create inequities.

SAMPLE TEACHER

This section presents an example using a fictional teacher and an administrator. It shows the results when the administrator plots the future leader's observable behaviors from the way of being, analyzes the data, plans the next steps, and conducts a meeting with the teacher.

Paula is a sixth-grade teacher who has a classroom of twenty-eight students from a variety of cultural backgrounds. Paula is strong at building positive relationships with her students, and they love being in her class. She is a popular teacher with staff and is very involved in the school. She is knowledgeable about the curriculum and works hard to create engaging lessons for her students. She has been teaching for ten years and is interested in administration. Her administrator, Principal Martin, has been supporting her journey as a future leader and has a good relationship with her. One area where the administrator feels Paula needs to improve to be an effective future leader is as an advocate for all students.

Step 1: Plot the Way of Being on the Leadership Action Matrix

Principal Martin plots Paula's observable behaviors for the first way of being—an advocate for all students—using the leadership action matrix. The results appear in figure 2.1.

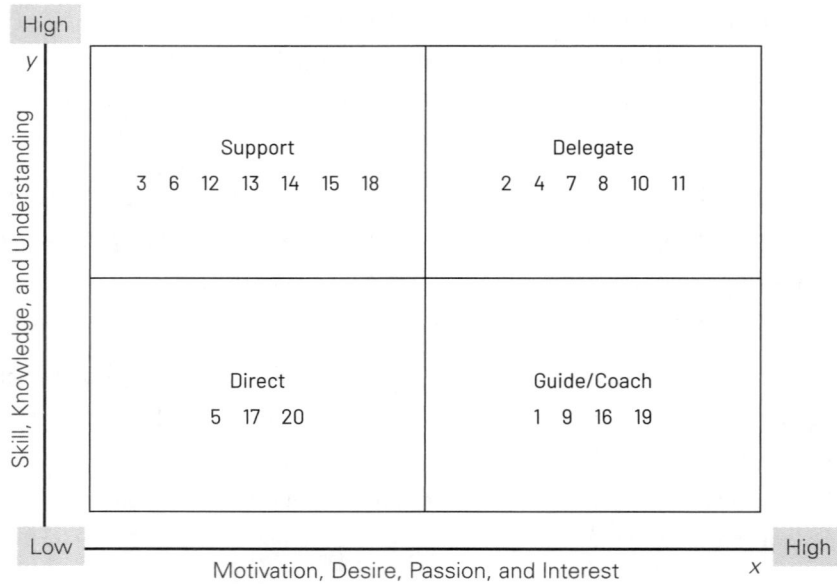

FIGURE 2.1: Paula's leadership action matrix for an advocate for all students.

Step 2: Complete the Mentoring Planning Page

After plotting the observable behaviors for Paula on the leadership action matrix, Principal Martin transfers the numbers to the mentoring planning page (see figure 2.2), adding comments about the behaviors she observed and her thoughts about the next steps. Then, she bolds the items she wants to discuss further when she meets with Paula. Paula could use this tool for self-evaluation before the mentoring meeting as well.

Way of Being: An Advocate for all Students

Teacher: Paula Sample

Administrator: Principal Martin

Support		Delegate	
Behavior Number	**Notes**	**Behavior Number**	**Notes**
3	Uses data as a magnifying glass, not a hammer, by giving students opportunity to learn and grow, not just using data to sift and sort into ability groups; uses data not only for evaluation, but to determine next learning for each student	2	Always accepts and teaches all students

6	**Has rules and expectations, but needs to develop them with students, work with others in the school, and contribute more to teams**	4	Builds strong relationships with students that respect cultural and personal differences
12	Recognizes days of significance, but must use them for planning and scheduling	7	Sets up classroom as welcoming and inclusive to all students
13	Looks for opportunities for students to share about themselves—lots of presenting; should consider using small groups	8	Uses inclusive materials and resources
14	Examines curriculum for real-life connections, and is justice driven	10	Uses lots of diverse instructional practices to meet all student needs and is assessment literate
15	**Shows diversity in her classroom; should work more with others to share strengths from her classroom to implement schoolwide**	11	Seeks involvement of all students to incorporate strong student voice in the classroom
18	Has many curriculum experiences and resources; should review resources to determine what is being sustained		**Recommendations for delegation:** • **Recommend for ambassador program**

Direct		Guide/Coach	
Behavior Number	**Notes**	**Behavior Number**	**Notes**
5	**Sometimes uses deficit-based language in staff meetings when speaking about students; should use asset-based language when discussing students**	1	**Wants to improve understanding of our diverse student population, equity, and inclusion; should provide professional development to support**
17	Has involvement during school events but needs to seek out and speak with students' families during these events	9	Has culturally appropriate resources, but should use what she learns from professional development in this way of being to update curriculum and resources
20	**Champions students in the classroom, but should also be public in support of all students**	16	**Has outstanding communication with families, but should be sure to be more inclusive to reach all families**
		19	**Has concerns about some students' families not being in contact with support agencies, and should look into that to extend reach past classroom**

FIGURE 2.2: Sample mentoring planning page for Paula as an advocate for all students.

The following are explanations of some of Principal Martin's ratings for Paula and the rationale for them.

Behavior 5: *The teacher recognizes, respects, and employs student strengths, diversity, and culture as assets for teaching and learning. They use asset-based language, focusing on what students do have and how they can use these strengths to build success, rather than language that focuses on what students cannot do.*

Principal Martin placed a five in the direct quadrant because based on her observations of the language Paula uses when describing students, she believes Paula is low in both skill and passion in this area. Principal Martin is concerned that there are times when Paula can become frustrated or negative about student performance and too often during team meetings she shares how the student struggles and very little about the student's positive aspects. At times, she speaks negatively about students in the presence of her colleagues. Principal Martin is hopeful that directly identifying this with Paula will assist her as she moves into the role of administration.

Behavior 15: *The teacher works with others to make sure that school and classroom practices and materials reflect and respond to the diversity of students in the classroom and society as a whole. Their classroom does not need to be diverse for the practices and materials to reflect diversity.*

While Paula's motivation seems a bit low in this area, her knowledge and skill are strong, so Principal Martin placed behavior fifteen in the support quadrant (high knowledge and skill, low motivation). Principal Martin observed that Paula is doing excellent work in her classroom related to equity and inclusion. The administrator would like to support Paula in sharing her work on equity and inclusion with others in the school.

Behavior 1: *The teacher understands the need for continual learning and self-reflection in the areas of diversity, equity, and inclusion. The teacher engages in professional development around serving the needs of all students. Professional learning includes topics of social justice and ways of teaching diverse students.*

Principal Martin placed behavior one in the Guide/Coach quadrant because Paula is high in motivation but lower in knowledge. Paula is an excellent candidate for guiding and coaching because she has expressed interest in learning more and improving her skills in the areas of professional development, communicating with families, and assisting families with community-support agencies. Her interest in learning is strong, and Principal Martin is going to guide and coach Paula to provide the information the teacher desires.

Behavior 7: *The teacher views the focus on equity, diversity, and inclusion as necessary work—not as an add-on. The work is not a single lesson or unit of study, but an inclusive curriculum that is woven into all learning practices and allows for connections to be made.*

Principal Martin placed behavior seven in the delegate quadrant because Paula is both high in knowledge and high in passion and interest. Paula has a strong commitment to equity, diversity, and inclusion, and her classroom reflects what should be happening in every classroom. Principal

Martin wants other staff members to observe Paula in her classroom to experience her success in this behavior and how she has created a learning space for all her students. The delegate quadrant allows Principal Martin to share all the extremely positive qualities that Paula possesses and celebrate her abilities. Principal Martin has also written, "ambassador program," which is a program she would like to see started at the school. She believes Paula would be an excellent leader to begin this program. Delegating this responsibility to Paula will provide her with some practical experience working with staff, students, and the community before beginning an administrative role. The ambassador program is described in detail later in this chapter (page 40).

Step 3: Use the Mentoring Meeting Planner

Principal Martin fills in most of the information on the mentoring meeting planner tool in preparation for her meeting with Paula. Figure 2.3 shows the completed mentoring meeting planner including notes from the meeting.

Date: February 12

Administrator: Principal Martin

Teacher: Paula Sample

Focus

Which way or ways of being will we discuss?

An Advocate for All Students. Discuss what it means to be an advocate for all students and why it is important as a school administrator that you advocate for all students. Ask Paula for input.

Agenda for Sharing and Discussion

What specific points about the way or ways of being will we discuss?

- Review many of the positives about Paula's classroom environment and relationships with students.
- Discuss the need for Paula to be well-rounded in many aspects of leadership.
- Discuss Paula's perspective on her strengths and needs in this way of being.
- Review notes from the twenty observable behaviors.
- Review notes from the mentoring planning page.

Key Points

For each of the following sections, list the bolded or circled items from the mentoring planning page.
- **Direct**
  - » Use asset language when discussing students.
  - » Be public in your support of all students.
- **Support**
  - » Develop classroom rules and expectations with students, work with others in the school to develop plans, and contribute more to teams.
  - » Work more with others to share advocacy perspective and show strengths from the classroom schoolwide.

FIGURE 2.3: Sample mentoring meeting planner for Paula as an advocate for all students.

continued ▶

- **Guide/Coach**
  - » Provide professional development around our changing population of students.
  - » Communication with families is outstanding; need to be more inclusive to reach all families. How can we work together to communicate with hard-to-reach families or families that require different communication methods?
  - » Contact agencies for support for families that may need help.
- **Delegate**
  - » Ambassador program

Teacher Plans, Comments, and Ideas

What plans, comments, and ideas did the teacher have during the meeting?

- Paula is going to wait on the ambassador program idea for now.
- Paula was unaware of her choice of words when describing students and will focus on using asset-based language. She wants immediate feedback on this when it occurs.
- Paula wants to turn attention to her own professional development in this area by focusing on what is available in the community to help her families, and on available communication resources such as interpreters and getting materials translated in multiple languages.
- She is willing to do some coaching of other staff at staff learning opportunities and wants to allow staff to come into her classroom to see her resources and how she interacts with her students.

Goal Setting

What is the teacher's goal?

- Paula will reach out to the district and local agencies to find out what supports are available in the community for families. She will also find where materials can be translated and will report back before the end of the month.
- Paula will frame her discussions about students using asset-based language and has asked some critical friends to identify when she uses deficit-based language so she can correct it in the moment. She wants an update the next time we meet.
- Paula will run a session at the next staff learning day in her classroom to share her ideas and suggestions.

Potential Resources

What are some potential resources to recommend to the teacher that address their areas of needed growth from the direct and guide/coach quadrants?

- Connect Paula with district leadership responsible for equity, diversity, and inclusion.
- Suggest the following books:
  - » *Evident Equity: A Guide for Creating Systemwide Change in Schools* by Lauryn Mascareñaz
  - » *Not Yet . . . and That's Ok: How Productive Struggle Fosters Student Learning* by Peg Grafwallner
  - » *Beyond Conversations About Race: A Guide for Discussions With Students, Teachers, and Communities* by Washington Collado, Sharroky Hollie, Rosa Isiah, Yvette Jackson, Anthony Muhammad, Douglas Reeves, and Kenneth C. Williams

Final Thoughts

What are your final thoughts about next steps and when to check back in?

- Paula is engaged in this process and thankful for the assistance. She is interested in moving into school administration and would like to continue meeting on a regular basis. She would like to review the other ways of being to see how she can improve.

AN ADVOCATE FOR ALL STUDENTS IN ACTION: SCHOOL EXAMPLES

The following—story time and the ambassador program—are two examples of what advocating for all students could look like in your school. These examples show staff and the larger community that the school advocates for all students and understands the importance of the behaviors in this way of being. Programs such as these also provide leadership opportunities for staff identified for this way of being and plotted in the leadership action matrix who require experiences for further development in advocating for all students.

Story Time

As principal of leadership and staff development, I had the pleasure of meeting Karen L. Mapp, a senior lecturer on education at the Harvard Graduate School of Education and the faculty director of the Education Policy and Management master's program. Karen is one of the authors of *Beyond the Bake Sale* (Henderson, Mapp, Johnson, & Davies, 2007), which speaks to the importance of including families in school initiatives in meaningful ways. When I left that central office position and transitioned to a position in a newly opened school, I knew the important concepts from Karen and her coauthors would support our major goal of a commitment to advocating for every student. In this diverse school, 75 percent of the student population was designated as English learners. In our first year, we had thirty-nine different primary languages used in the homes of our students. For many students, English was their second, third, or even fourth language learned. For many students, the first time they had any education or instruction in English was when they came to us for kindergarten. Making sure our communication was available in multiple languages would be key to valuing and welcoming families into the school.

One of the strategies we used to advocate for all students was to create a regular story time activity during which parent and community volunteers read to students in the library during student break times. This might not sound like a revolutionary idea; however, it was a key activity for advocating for all students in our diverse school. We started with four different story time days in our school: Arabic, Punjabi, Turkish, and Urdu. Students were invited to come to the library on designated days to hear a library book read in the language of the day—their home language.

With students speaking about the opportunity at home and the school sharing the initiative with our community, we had more volunteers than we had spots or times available to read. We used our school resources from the dual-language section of the school library. This highlighted to our students and the community that we valued the importance of having multilanguage resources available for students. Books featured during story time were popular choices for students to sign out and take home.

Supporting all students with resources that families can access shows that your school is accepting and inclusive. Investing in resources in multiple languages reflects a diverse school community. Including break-time activities that allow students a choice that caters to their needs and interests. Such activities engage with students and families in a way that goes beyond bake sales. This idea is a perfect activity to delegate to teachers looking for leadership opportunities. It requires working with staff within the school to create schedules, working with students, and communicating and interacting with the community before and during the initiative.

School Ambassador Program

In the first years after opening our doors, we had a constant flow of new students we wanted to feel welcome and included right away. Many families came from outside Ontario or were new to Canada. We wanted our new families and students to receive an amazing first impression. This is what led to the development of the school ambassador program in our school. School ambassadors—who are students—have many roles, with one of the most visible being as school tour guides.

Students filled out a short application expressing their interest in the program. Because new students entered the school at every grade level, we attempted to have ambassadors from all age groups. Being an ambassador was a sought-after position of responsibility. Students were eager to show their school pride.

In the first year, the team of students and staff developed a tour script to use when new families were visiting the school, which included descriptions of the classrooms and learning spaces. Students auditioned and practiced by taking staff members and administrators on mock tours. Ambassadors shared up-to-date registration numbers, languages spoken in the school, number of classes, and unique behind-the-scenes information about the school building and maintenance.

Selected ambassadors were able to speak the language of the family. Having many multilingual students in the school was an asset we harnessed when providing diverse and accommodating experiences for students and their families. This program built school spirit and pride, one conversation at a time, as tours were conducted before, during, and after school.

Staff were usually informed about when tours would be coming through the school, and they were welcoming. Families did not enter classrooms unless invited, but they were able to see the real goings on in the school, as this was not a performance or show. If administrators were available, the tour would end outside the office to answer any questions students could not answer.

Ambassadors also did more than school tours. They came to kindergarten orientation sessions for students and families and other special community events like movie nights, guest speaking events, curriculum nights, and graduation. Students wore ambassador t-shirts and badges with their names and the languages they could speak. Early on, families were able to see their relationship with the school and the importance of the students, their talents, the pride they have in the school, and the inclusiveness of the environment.

Once we implemented the ambassadors program, we noticed that attendance increased at school events. Having the team of students available increased the likelihood that families would engage with our school and our special events.

The ambassadors program is another example of an initiative that a teacher can set up, organize, and run. The program will make them keenly aware of the diversity in the school that may be hidden from them and has them examining demographic data about students and their families, as well as experiencing the coordination necessary for schoolwide activities that might include ambassadors.

CONCLUSION

School administrators work in complex, challenging, and ever-changing environments. Two strong indicators of those most suited to be future administrators are having the skill and motivation to advocate for all students and a firm belief that all students can be successful. Advocating for all students can generate numerous success stories like those in this chapter; however, it is also an area in education that is politically charged. Tomorrow's leaders need to educate themselves on policies and issues that promote an inclusive environment as well as be aware of those that do not. They must address systemic practices, recognize and interrupt patterns, and provide alternatives to the practices that have denied equitable outcomes for all students (Ontario Principals' Council, 2023). Effective administrators face the immediate needs of today while always looking at what is coming tomorrow and into the future. We must all aspire for a better future for every student.

CHAPTER 3

A CREATOR OF A SAFE AND WELCOMING ENVIRONMENT

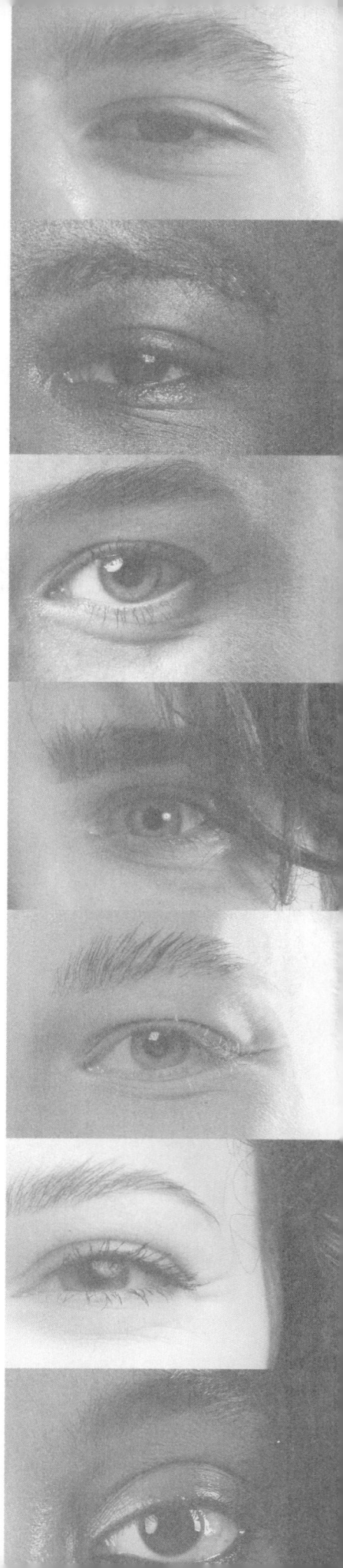

There are two parts of a school environment—what is visible and what is felt. While a school's physical building must be hazard-free, organized, and clean as a safe and welcoming environment, most of us in education picture the aspects that cannot be seen: a mentally healthy, orderly, and accepting environment necessary for students to be successful. No student can be expected to reach their potential if they are feeling intimidated, insecure, or unsafe.

The Wallace report *How Principals Affect Students and Schools: A Systematic Synthesis of Two Decades of Research* gathered numerous quantitative and qualitative studies and found that there are four principal practices that are directly linked to positive and effective outcomes for students (Grissom, Egalite, & Lindsay, 2021). The first of these is the building of a productive culture and climate, which is the focus of this chapter.

Research indicates that a safe and welcoming environment is a major contributor to a school's climate. Benjamin Kutsyuruba, Don A. Klinger, and Alicia Hussain (2015) define school climate as "the quality and character of school life based on patterns of people's experience . . . that reflect norms, goals, values, interpersonal relationships, teaching and learning practices, and organizational structures" (p. 136). They note that "students flourish emotionally, socially, and academically based on the quality of relationships among students, parents, school personnel, and the community" (Kutsyuruba et al., 2015, p. 136). They conclude that it is vital for administrators to develop ways to improve school climate to fully satisfy students' academic, social, and emotional needs.

The Ontario Ministry of Education's (2022b) approach to creating safe and accepting schools focuses on promoting positive student behavior, providing early and ongoing intervention, preventing inappropriate behavior, and addressing inappropriate behavior with appropriate consequences. The Centers for Disease Control and Prevention (n.d.) stresses the importance of student connection to a network of caring peers and adults. A safe and welcoming classroom allows students to feel better about themselves; they report stronger mental health, have better relationships, attend school more regularly, and have more confidence in their ability, which leads to performing better academically (Diamanti, Duffey, & Fisher, 2018). In addition, safe and welcoming schools increase well-being, provide a sense of connection, reduce high-risk substance abuse, and help keep students from committing and being victims of violence (U.S. Department of Health and Human Services Centers for Disease Control and Prevention, 2020).

A literature review on safe schools by Benjamin Kutsyuruba and colleagues (2015) shows that school environments that are unsafe disproportionally affect certain groups of students based on gender, race, ethnicity, sexual orientation, social status, and ability. Students identified with exceptionalities are bullied and victimized more than their peers. Students who identify as part of the 2SLGBTQI+ communities often feel unsafe, unwelcome, and are more frequently bullied. Gender differences and unequal social relations in schools can also result in incidents of violence, harassment, and bullying (Kutsyuruba et al., 2015). The response to bullying and harassment is not felt to the same degree by all students, and unfortunately, those students who have been traditionally underserved continue to be impacted at a higher rate when it comes to unsafe school environments.

So, what must we do to create a safe and welcoming environment? The school administrator contributes largely to the physical, social, and academic aspects of school climate, and therefore they have an exceptionally important role in building a schoolwide focus on school climate and collaborative school cultures by first establishing and then maintaining, sustaining, and developing trust relationships in schools. In each classroom, educators have to provide a support network for students and help them develop the knowledge and skills needed to develop their humanity within their safe school environment (Kutsyuruba et al., 2015). Taking strong skills and understanding from the classroom level and combining them with a passion and desire to create positive change for an entire school is what future leaders will be called to do.

KEY OBSERVABLE BEHAVIORS

Following are the behaviors that aspiring leaders who are creators of a safe and welcoming environment should exhibit. When rating a teacher in this way of being, think about the knowledge and skills involved with each behavior as well as the passion and motivation it requires. Consider providing the list of observable behaviors for this way of being to future leaders for self-evaluation and reflection prior to the mentoring planning meeting. (Visit **go.SolutionTree.com/leadership** for a free reproducible of this list.)

1. The teacher makes themselves available for students by being present and visible. They have positive relationships with students, making it a priority to check in with students to find out how they are feeling and doing. They take a personal interest and show they care about more than just student academic performance. They show they care about students' mental health. They have a professional, respectful, and appropriate relationship with the students.

2. The teacher optimizes the physical classroom space to be safe, positive, welcoming, functional, and organized. Students can find materials quickly

and easily. The teacher cares about the appearance of their classroom and the school in general.

3. The teacher utilizes positive classroom management. They emphasize with students the desired behaviors rather than focusing on what students should not do. They provide an abundance of one-to-one feedback with students and avoid public reprimands. They are discreet and maintain confidentiality about student difficulties. They manage classroom behaviors effectively and demonstrate appropriate boundaries and expectations for how everyone should be treated in the shared learning space.

4. The teacher has worked with students to create clear expectations (common commitments) rather than rules to obey. They speak about being a community and being there for each other. They build a sense of inclusion as students have a stake in establishing a culture of respect and responsibility. The classroom commitments align with schoolwide expectations; they are simple and understandable, posted and understood by students using wording appropriate for the age group. The teacher enforces common commitments fairly, reviewing and discussing them regularly—not just at the start of the year or when issues arise.

5. The teacher is a role model within a respectful classroom environment. They do not participate in disrespectful behavior, gossiping, or other inappropriate behavior toward students, staff, or community members. The teacher "walks the talk" and promotes positive behavior and respect in all daily interactions with students and staff.

6. The teacher utilizes school and district discipline policies. They align with other staff members about classroom expectations. Although they develop common commitments with their students, they do not allow behaviors or actions that run counter to the agreed-upon expectations of their teaching colleagues, school, or district.

7. The teacher listens and engages in conversations with students about their lives and interests. They listen to student concerns and demonstrate empathy and an understanding of student needs without jumping in to fix a problem before taking time to truly understand. They demonstrate in their listening behaviors that the speaker is important to them.

8. The teacher never embarrasses students, uses sarcasm in hurtful ways, or tears down a student. They provide affirmations and build students up.

9. The teacher responds when they are aware of name-calling and bullying. They do not downplay what a student says or how they are feeling. They take student issues seriously and do not pass them off as "kids being kids"

or "just a joke." They step up, intervene, and use their position as teachers to identify concerns and offer solutions and guidance. When moving through the hallways or outside the school, they identify problematic situations and problem solve. Their assistance to students is effective and appropriate for the age and individual.

10. The teacher is aware of their own beliefs, biases, and stereotypes. They do not expect individuals to behave in a particular way based on their gender, race, ability, sexual orientation, or other personal attributes. They challenge their own beliefs and respond when they hear others using outdated and questionable assumptions.

11. The teacher remains positive. They model positive thinking and show elevated levels of engagement. They are aware of students' individual strengths and talents and identify and interact with students in a friendly, professional manner.

12. The teacher creates and maintains a safe environment in the classroom by having class meetings and addressing issues that arise. They seek guidance from others for feedback and advice before meeting with students and involve others when situations are serious and require more intervention. They work with students to create topics of conversation and model effective discussion processes.

13. The teacher is aware of students' abilities and provides the necessary accommodations and modifications in the classroom so that every student can experience success.

14. The teacher helps students learn how to be effective allies and provide support for others. They provide time for and demonstrate how students can be a friend and help a friend. They discuss safety concerns and when it is appropriate and necessary to directly intervene, when to go for help, and when to use alternative strategies during a conflict. They take time to work with students to learn and practice positive, respectful behaviors targeting the age and maturity of students with their relationships and interactions but do not single out individual students. By emphasizing the difference between inappropriate dialogue, name-calling, rude behavior, and respectful debate, they demonstrate and teach about civil discourse.

15. The teacher uses student names and gets to know students by name. They ask students for the correct pronunciation of their names and use it during conversations. They never tease or make fun of names or change the name to make it easier for them. They help students learn each other's names. They correct students when any student ridicules another student's name.

16. The teacher has fun with students. You hear laughter in their classroom. The teacher uses humor appropriately to build positive connections. They model for students humor that is appropriate in a school setting.

17. The teacher makes a positive, safe, and welcoming classroom the norm. They talk about bullying regularly and how the classroom is going to function as a safe space for everyone. They know the appropriate school codes of conduct, local policies and procedures, and they share with students the impact of inappropriate behavior from the perpetrator, victim, and others. They focus on why the classroom needs to be a safe and welcoming space and the benefits of coming to a school that operates in this manner instead of only sharing the consequences of bullying and inappropriate behavior.

18. The teacher is comfortable being themselves with students. They share appropriate personal information to create a welcoming learning environment so a teacher can bond with students. The teacher shows they are a real person who values their community enough to be open.

19. The teacher creates an environment where families are welcome and encouraged to participate in the teaching of their children. Families are respected and valued as partners.

20. The teacher uses inclusive language when referring to others. They model in their word choices that they are respectful of all students, staff, and those outside the school.

SAMPLE TEACHER

This section presents an example using a fictional teacher and administrator. It shows the results when the administrator plots the future leader's observable behaviors from the way of being presented in this chapter; analyzes the data; plans the next steps; and conducts a meeting with the teacher.

RJ is a fourth-grade teacher, although he spent most of his career teaching secondary. He wants to move into administration, so he asked to be moved to grade four to experience teaching at the junior level before applying to be an assistant principal. His classroom is a warm, welcoming, and fun place to be. He has worked hard preparing for this new grade assignment and the curriculum pieces of his role have come easily for him. Students love being in his class, and he is popular with families. He steps up when there are conflicts or difficulties with students. He does not allow any bullying behavior.

Step 1: Plot the Way of Being on the Leadership Action Matrix

Principal Rodriguez plots RJ's observable behaviors for the second way of being—a creator of a safe and welcoming environment—using the leadership action matrix. The results appear in figure 3.1.

Way of Being: A Creator of a Safe and Welcoming Environment

Administrator Name: Principal Rodriguez

Teacher Name: RJ Sample

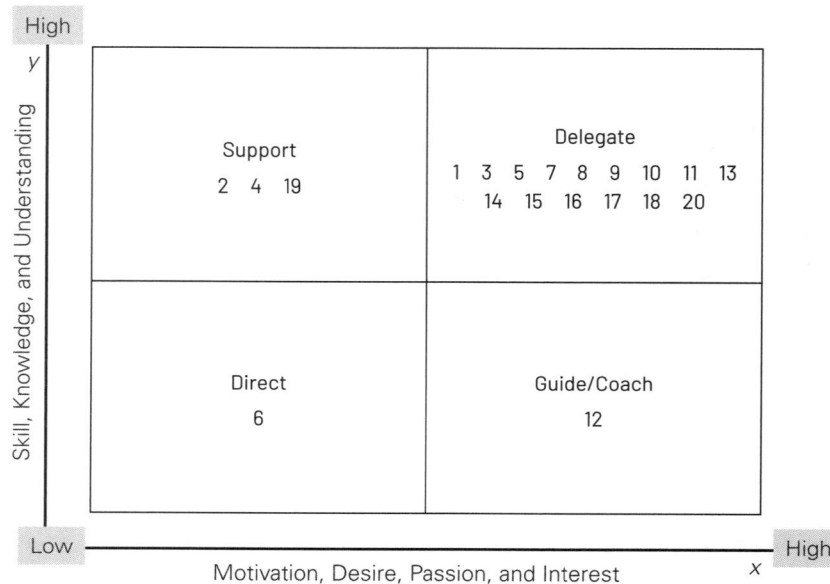

FIGURE 3.1: RJ's leadership action matrix for a creator of a safe and welcoming environment.

Step 2: Complete the Mentoring Planning Page

After plotting the observable behaviors for RJ on the leadership action matrix, Principal Rodriguez transfers the scores to the mentoring planning page (see figure 3.2), adding comments about the behaviors he observed and his thoughts about the next steps. Principal Rodriguez bolds the items he wants to discuss further when he meets with RJ. RJ could use this tool for self-evaluation before the mentoring meeting as well.

Way of Being: Creator of a Safe and Welcoming Environment

Teacher: RJ Sample

Administrator: Principal Rodriguez

Support		Delegate	
Behavior Number	**Notes**	**Behavior Number**	**Notes**
2	Has a classroom that is safe, positive, welcoming, and functional, but he does not have to do all the work himself; solicits student involvement and voices	1	**Makes himself available for students in the hallways and at the classroom door, and takes a personal interest in students and their mental health**
4	**Uses teacher-created expectations that are the same each year—should not recycle! Aligning with schoolwide expectations and creating with student input critical**	3	Uses positive and excellent class management
19	Has some student involvement, but not enough; should have more	5	Shows professionalism in conduct and appearance
		7	Has many interactions with students that involve listening to them
		8	Acts respectfully toward students and builds them up
		9	Responds quickly and seriously to concerning student behavior, such as bullying
		10	Has awareness of biases and stereotypes and does not use generalizations about students
		11	Has a positive, "can-do" attitude
		13	Uses evidence from tests and assignments to assess student abilities and supports student needs with modifications and accommodations
		14	Has classes, lessons, and discussions on being a friend and ally; discusses any issues between students modeling positive and respectful dialogue
		15	Has learned names of all students—even in other classes

FIGURE 3.2: Sample mentoring planning page for RJ for a creator of a safe and welcoming environment.

continued ▶

Support		Delegate	
Behavior Number	**Notes**	**Behavior Number**	**Notes**
		16	Includes laughter and fun activities—students love the class
		17	Has conversations with students about the classroom as a safe space
		18	Shares appropriate information about himself, family, pets, and interests
		20	Has awareness of inclusive language, always learning and teaching other staff
			Recommendations for delegation: • **Has excellent skills in greeting students each morning and developing positive relationships; should take a leadership role to teach others about this behavior.**
Direct		**Guide/Coach**	
Behavior Number	**Notes**	**Behavior Number**	**Notes**
6	**Allows students to exhibit behavior in class that is not consistent with other classrooms, which causes confusion for students and potential conflicts with staff; should focus on being part of the team**	12	**Needs to incorporate student voices in maintaining safe and welcoming environment—for example, could hold class meetings; should look for resources online that school could provide for him**

Following are explanations of some of Principal Rodriguez's ratings for RJ and the rationale for them.

Behavior 6: *The teacher utilizes the discipline policies that are in place in the school or the district. They are in alignment with other staff members about what the expectations are within the class. Although they develop common commitments with their students, they do not allow behaviors or actions that run counter to the agreed-upon expectations of their teaching colleagues, school, or district.*

Principal Rodriguez placed behavior six in the direct quadrant (low understanding/low motivation) because this is the one behavior he believes RJ's understanding and motivation are both low, and this will need to improve as he considers the pathway to administration. RJ allows certain behaviors from students that are not consistent with what other fourth-grade teachers allow. When students move to other classrooms for subjects that RJ does not teach, those teachers have different expectations. He is no longer teaching high school students, and he is part of a larger collective team. Principal Rodriguez has a good relationship with RJ, which will help him be direct in their discussions about consistency being key. Principal Rodriguez has some concerns that RJ wants to be a popular and fun teacher and the message he sends to his colleagues when he does things on his own. Principal Rodriguez will also discuss the importance of a school-wide or system approach to school culture and remind RJ about the importance of being part of a larger team.

Behavior 4: *The teacher has worked with students to create clear expectations (common commitments) rather than rules to obey. They speak about being a community and being there for each other. They build a sense of inclusion as students have a stake in establishing a culture of respect and responsibility. The classroom commitments align with schoolwide expectations; they are simple and understandable, posted and understood by students using wording appropriate for the age group. The teacher enforces common commitments fairly, reviewing and discussing them regularly—not just at the start of the year or when issues arise.*

Principal Rodriguez observed RJ is doing excellent work; however, he had not included student voices in building the classroom community together. While his desire to include students seems a bit low in this area, his knowledge and skill in classroom management are strong, so Principal Rodriguez puts behavior four in the support quadrant (high knowledge and skill, low motivation). Principal Rodriguez noticed that RJ displayed a set of classroom rules that he presented to the students at the start of the year. They are the same rules he used in the past with older students and not developed for the students he was currently teaching. RJ had yet to make the adjustment. He did not involve students in the creation of their common classroom commitments, and he only refers to the expectations when students have not obeyed "his rules." Principal Rodriguez wants to support RJ in understanding the importance of including students, changing the terminology from rules to classroom commitments, and how all of this contributes to building and sustaining a safe and welcoming environment.

Behavior 12: *The teacher creates and maintains a safe environment in the classroom by having class meetings and addressing issues that arise. They seek guidance from others for feedback and advice prior to meeting with students and involve others when situations are serious and require more intervention. They work with students to create topics of conversation and model effective discussion processes.*

Principal Rodriguez put behavior twelve in the guide/coach quadrant because RJ is high in motivation but low in knowledge. RJ has heard about class meetings and is an excellent candidate for guiding and coaching because he has expressed interest in learning more and improving his skills such as having positive classroom discussions with students. He has a strong relationship with students so class meetings will work well when he learns the structure and processes. He wants to learn how to have students politely, positively, and civilly discuss issues.

Behavior 1: *The teacher makes themselves available for students by being present and visible. They have positive relationships with students, making it a priority to check in with students to find out how they are feeling and doing. They take a personal interest and show they care about more than just student academic performance. They show they care about student mental health. They have a professional, respectful, and appropriate relationship with the students.*

Principal Rodriguez placed behavior one in the delegate quadrant because RJ is high in knowledge and high in passion and interest. RJ positions himself in the hallway and at his classroom doorway to greet students every morning and as they return to the classroom throughout the day. He carries on conversations with students about their interests. You can often find him discussing topics other than school with students while they are outside, eating their lunch, or walking in the hallways. He has a strong commitment to getting to know each student in his class and the names of students throughout the school. Principal Rodriguez wants to have other staff greet students this way, so he will ask RJ to share his strategies. Delegating this leadership opportunity to RJ will provide him with some practical experience working with staff. (Strategies for greeting students each morning are described later in this chapter on page 54).

Step 3: Use the Mentoring Meeting Planner

Principal Rodriguez fills in most of the information on the mentoring meeting planner tool in preparation for his meeting with RJ. Figure 3.3 shows the completed mentoring meeting planner including notes from the meeting.

Date: December 4

Administrator: Principal Rodriguez

Teacher: RJ Sample

Focus

Which way or ways of being will we discuss?

A Creator of a Safe and Welcoming Environment. Discuss why it is important as a school administrator to consider what it means to be safe. What does it mean to be welcoming? Why is it important to have schoolwide common language and expectations? Ask RJ for input.

Agenda for Sharing and Discussion

What specific points about the way or ways of being will we discuss?

* RJ exhibits a lot of positives concerning relationships with students, dealing with issues, and classroom atmosphere.
* There is a need to be well-rounded in many aspects of leadership.
* Find out RJ's perspectives on his strengths and needs in this way of being.
* Review notes from the twenty observable behaviors.
* Refer to notes from the mentoring planning page.

Key Points

For each of the following sections, list the bolded or circled items from the mentoring planning page.

* **Direct**
    » Provide direction on providing consistency for students across classrooms, avoiding potential conflict with team members and other staff, and being part of a team.
* **Support**
    » Provide support in working with students on collective commitments to replace rules and explain why the process is important and expectations need to be schoolwide.
    » Provide support to create student involvement and involve student voices.
* **Guide/Coach**
    » Guide his interest in running class meetings. Provide resources (online and books).

- **Delegate**
    - » Ask him to share his strategies for interacting with students in hallways, at the door, and so on.
    - » Ask him to share his strategies for greetings each morning.

Teacher Plans, Comments, and Ideas

What plans, comments, and ideas did the teacher have during the meeting?

- RJ will definitely talk at the next staff meeting about greeting students each day, what it means, and how it makes a difference. He is going to work with his grade-level team to create a morning plan where one teacher will be at the entrance door, one will be just inside, another teacher will be at the bottom of the staircase, another at the top, and the final teacher will be outside of the classrooms allowing students to enter. Each teacher will have a location when the day begins so students are greeted.
- RJ justified his classroom rules by stating he has always worked with high school students and is still getting used to the younger age. He did not really consider how his classroom impacted the other classrooms in the junior level.
- RJ was not aware that other staff were upset about his class rules. He was thankful to be made aware of the issue.
- RJ is thankful to be on a large team of teachers and is learning a lot about working with others; he is used to having only one teaching partner in the past. He is very interested in learning more about teams, structures, and processes as he mentioned he will need to know this in the future.
- RJ wants to start class meetings with his students and asked if he could share with others once he has them up and running.
- RJ will use his first class meeting to generate classroom commitments. He has a process that he will follow and is comfortable starting this soon.

Goal Setting

What is the teacher's goal related to this way of being?

- RJ will check out online resources while waiting for a book on class meetings to arrive.
- RJ will use a class meeting structure to develop a set of classroom commitments and then share them with Principal Rodriguez and teaching partners.
- RJ will present at the next staff meeting about the importance of greeting students each morning and what he has noticed as a teacher since adopting this strategy.
- RJ will establish a morning routine with the fourth-grade team. The plan will position each individual in different locations in the morning to welcome students. He will bring a copy of the plan to the office to share.
- RJ will focus on what it means to be a collaborative team member with the junior teachers. He also wants to have regular discussions with the administration about working with a team, guiding a team, and the structures of teams.

Potential Resources

What are some potential resources to recommend to the teacher that address their areas of needed growth from the direct and guide/coach quadrants?

- RJ is going online to find resources available about class meetings.
- Suggest the following book (purchase for him):
    - » *Morning Meetings and Closing Circles: Classroom-Ready Activities That Increase Student Engagement and Create a Positive Learning Community* by Monica Dunbar

Final Thoughts

What are your final thoughts about next steps and when to check back in?

- RJ wants a lot of feedback prior to beginning the process to become an assistant principal. He is interested in the dynamics of working with a large group. He is working toward a better understanding of whole school and systems thinking in regard to creating a safe and welcoming school.

FIGURE 3.3: Sample mentoring meeting planner for RJ for a creator of a safe and welcoming environment.

A CREATOR OF A SAFE AND WELCOMING ENVIRONMENT IN ACTION: SCHOOL EXAMPLES

The following—morning greeting and five key words for mental health—are two examples of what creating a safe and welcoming environment could look like in your school. These examples show staff and the larger community that the school understands the importance of creating a safe and welcoming environment. I also share them here to provide examples of leadership opportunities for staff who require experiences for further development.

Morning Greeting

Mornings can be difficult. Even the smallest interruptions to the routine can reroute us from our preferred path. Now imagine coming from a home where the morning routine is impacted by serious difficulty or trauma. Add to that the knowledge that the school could not be a safe or welcoming environment and often involves teasing or harassment. Students should feel welcome at school and that they have entered a safe space.

It does not matter the age of your students—feeling welcome never stops being good for us. Greeting students at the door, welcoming them with a smile and positive words, and ensuring these types of encounters continue throughout the day help create a safe and welcoming environment.

Schools often have designated entrances for students in different grades. For example, in our school, kindergarten students had their own entrance and area of the school. The primary students were met by their teachers and brought in a main door. Students in grades 7 and 8 had a different start to their day—a morning greeting that involved various strategies for welcoming students.

Staff from grades 7 and 8 met students at the entrance, on the stairway, and at the top of the stairs so students would pass and be greeted by their teachers as they entered the school. In addition, every Friday, the intermediate team of teachers "played in" the students by singing and clapping to music in the hallway as students walked past—an incredibly welcoming and positive start to the day and celebration of the week students completed. Such a strategy would work at the start of the week as well to welcome students and celebrate the week to come. Some students walked through while others paused to do a little dance; even those who moved quickly had smiles on their faces.

Think about the students in your school. What do they experience when they first come into the school? Is there a safe place to gather before the day begins? Do they have a place to go if they want to start the day calmly and quietly? Are adults a comforting presence? Are there any activities in the morning to join? Do the adults in the school want to be there? Are happy students there too?

RJ, the teacher in this chapter, was asked by his administrator to work with his grade team to create a plan for student entry into the school. Each individual on the team assigned themself to a location in the school to greet and welcome students as they entered. The team also decided that each teacher would have a good morning sign in their doorway that asked students how they would like to start the day using five options that changed often: (1) with a hello, (2) with a wave, (3) with a greeting in their first language, (4) with a high five, or (5) with a fist bump. This process allowed teachers to quickly evaluate each student's well-being as they entered. Teachers even welcomed students back to their classrooms using the same process. This welcoming routine ensured students had at least several positive interactions with their teacher every day.

Five Key Words for Mental Health

The Canadian Mental Health Association (n.d.) shares that "approximately 1 in 5 children and youth in Ontario has a mental health challenge. . . . That is why early identification and intervention is so critical and can lead to improved achievement in school and better health outcomes in life." Mental Health America (2024) reports "1 in 5 youth had at least one major depressive episode in the past year. Over half of them—nearly 3 million youth—did not receive treatment." The report goes on to say that "60.5 percent of youth in the U.S. are flourishing, which is associated with school engagement and other positive outcomes for youth." The Aligned and Integrated Model (AIM) from School Mental Health Ontario (2023) is useful when thinking of student mental health. It provides a continuum of support for students in schools in the shape of a pyramid divided into three sections. The first tier at the base of the pyramid is the majority of the students with no mental health issues but are occasionally upset. The second tier of students, a lower percentage, have some mental health distress. At the top of the pyramid are students with mental health disorders requiring medical intervention (School Mental Health Ontario, 2023).

In our school, we focused our work where we had the greatest impact to help with prevention and identification: the base of the pyramid. Our work in tier one focused on five key words (School Mental Health Ontario, 2023) related to a safe and welcoming environment.

1. Welcome
2. Include
3. Understand
4. Promote
5. Partner

Our leadership team created a graphic with students in the center. Moving out from the center are rings of stakeholders with relationships to students: staff, families, neighboring schools, the community, and the district office. Have your teacher leaders create such a diagram identifying all the individuals and groups you must communicate with, interact with, and factor into decisions when operating a school. This exercise provides a sense of the large number of stakeholders one must consider as a school administrator. We developed key questions using the following key words—welcome, include, understand, promote, and partner—to self-evaluate our work as a safe and welcoming school.

- How do we *welcome* new students? *Welcome* new staff? *Welcome* new families?

- How do we *include* student voices in our teaching?

- How do we *include* our families in important school decisions?

- What do we need to *understand* about our student demographics that will help us with our teaching?

- What do we need to *understand* about the diversity in our community to be better?

- What do our front hallway and reception area *promote* to our community?

- In our assemblies and school gatherings, what do we *promote* as a major feature of our school?

- What does our mission statement *promote* for our stakeholders?

- Who do we need to *partner* with in our community to support our students?

- Who do we need to *partner* with at our central office in order to move forward with our professional development plan?

Thinking deeply about these key words promotes conversations and provides a starting point for future and beginning administrators by concentrating on what it means to welcome, include, understand, promote, and partner with for success to create a safe and welcoming environment. Use this strategy with aspiring leaders to help them learn to consider multiple stakeholders. It also helps identify areas of focus and initiatives to help improve the school's ability to welcome, include, understand, promote, and partner.

CONCLUSION

Schools should be safe and welcoming places for students. No student can be expected to learn if they are not physically, psychologically, and socially safe within an environment that is welcoming and attractive to attend, accepting of who they are, and responsive to what they need to learn and grow. Students spend a great deal of their waking hours in school and must feel it is somewhere that they can come each day and receive respect, care, and support. Community members and families must feel it is a place they can attend and have their voices heard. Staff need to have their health and safety considered and protected in order to do good work. A major part of a school administrator's responsibilities centers on making sure the school is a safe place for everyone. No one is in a better position to influence the climate and culture of a school than the school administrator. Teachers who are considering moving into the school leadership role must understand the importance of creating and maintaining a safe and welcoming environment.

CHAPTER 4

AN EFFECTIVE COMMUNICATOR

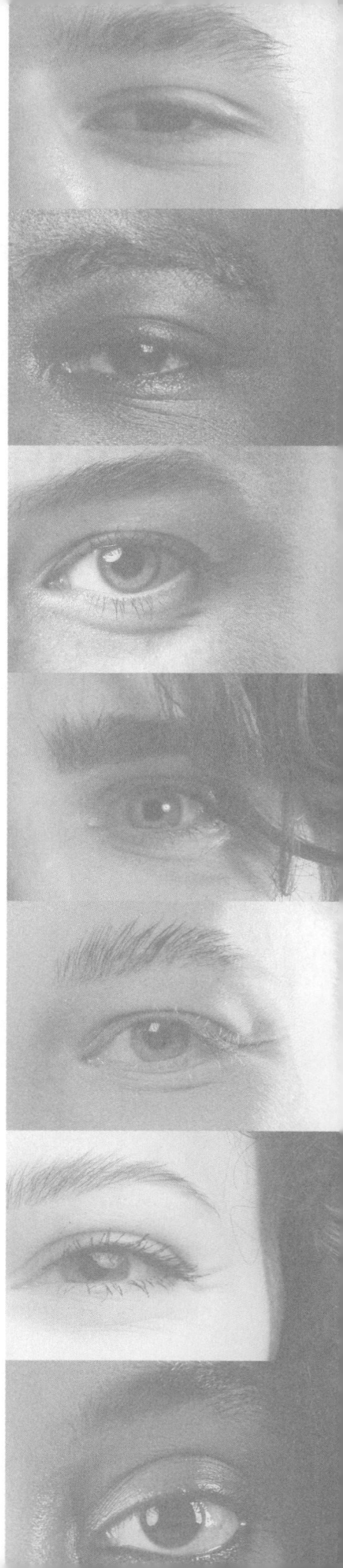

Research in the field of education has shown that communication is the number one most important element of highly effective administrators (Tyler, 2016). A key contributor to the emotional, social, and academic success of students is effective communication within the educational setting between and among all stakeholders (Natale & Lubniewski, 2018). Communication is a central part of daily life and an important aspect of effective leadership. Every day, school leaders are involved in an extensive amount of communication. It is key to building relationships and gaining and holding trust. Administrators can establish strong connections with students, staff, families, and the community, and they can do this quickly if they have strong communication skills. Communication, however, is more than simply transmitting information and coordinating activities. Incorporating strong communication skills is how an administrator creates understanding and acceptance of the school's mission, vision, values, and goals.

At its core, communication is an indication of the quality of the relationships in a school. If the relationships are poor, many will point to a lack of communication or little trust in the person providing the messaging (Salamondra, 2021). Effective communication will build a solid school culture, while poor communication can lead to dissatisfaction; communication is all about trust and transparency (Salamondra, 2021). How leaders choose to communicate indicates how they want others to perceive them. School leaders must consciously consider both their methods of communication as well as the frequency of communication.

School leaders must be able to communicate effectively with students, staff, families, and the community about a wide variety of topics, including expectations and requirements, while constantly modeling and demonstrating appropriate behavior. They must also stay connected with the district's main office, feeder schools, and the school board. School leaders must be able to communicate effectively orally, in writing, and when using social media and other forms of technology. They must also demonstrate what is arguably the most important part of communication: being a good listener.

Communication is vital to creating, nurturing, and growing a collaborative school culture and continually striving for school improvement. Administrators are called on to have important and sometimes difficult conversations. They challenge current practices and foster change and innovation through communication. They must listen and act on feedback as well as provide feedback to support improvements in student outcomes (Ontario Ministry of Education, 2013). *The Ontario Leadership Framework* (Leithwood, 2012) includes engaging in courageous conversations—conversations that are difficult and uncomfortable—as one of five core leadership capacities. How a school leader manages these challenging conversations can make or break their reputation; handling them with effective communication builds trust, collaboration, and a sense that students and staff are in a safe and respectful place (Ontario Principals' Council, 2011).

There was a time when the words of teachers and administrators were taken as incontestable truth; schools and classrooms have changed for the better, and schooling is now more focused on inquiry-based, experiential learning utilizing critical thinking skills (Di Lucia, 2014). School leaders of today have come to understand that their comments, ideas, and plans will no longer be accepted at face value; rather, they must use strong communication skills to support their ideas and opinions (Di Lucia, 2014). Mentors working with aspiring leaders are more effective when they model appropriate responses, showing how to use communication effectively, whether in person or digitally when responding to opposing opinions (Di Lucia, 2014).

Administrators are called on to have important and sometimes difficult conversations and not shy away from discussions that must occur for the benefit of students and their families. Difficult conversations can be emotional and unpredictable. Interacting with upset or aggressive people is one aspect of leadership that teachers moving into administration feel most concerned about (Ontario Principals' Council, 2011). Some leaders avoid challenging conversations because they do not want to jeopardize relationships, they do not realize the significance of an issue or concern, or they lack confidence in their communication skills (Ontario Principals' Council, 2011). The desire to always be kind can hinder a leader's ability to have hard conversations or give honest feedback. Talented communicators find a way of being both honest and respectful.

Roberta Salmirs Barber (2020) highlights four key components that an administrator must consider when communicating. These components are:

1. How to share the day-to-day operations and events of running a school. All stakeholders need to know about the use of calendars as well as important reminders of procedures, policies, and so on

2. The crisis communication plan, including all emergency information and rehearsal and practice plans

3. Feedback, and not just the feedback from administration to staff, but also from teachers to students and families, like expectations for formal documents like report cards as well as the daily updates and formative assessment data that lead to student improvement

4. The communication process administration uses to recognize individuals, motivate staff, and share the accomplishments of the school with everyone

All four of these components are important for the success of aspiring leaders when communicating with all stakeholders—staff, students, parents, families, the community, and the district office.

The COVID-19 pandemic magnified the need for school leaders to seriously consider their personal communication skills and how their school interacts and engages with the school community (Orta & Gutiérrez, 2022). Communicating in one single way (via handouts, for example) would no longer be effective in meeting the variety of needs within a school community. The increased use of technology is a benefit for getting information out; however, it only works when all families have access to the internet, have the devices necessary for learning and communication, and have the support to use the technology (Orta & Gutiérrez, 2022).

For families to feel connected to school, administrators must now play a key role in creating communication pathways. An important leadership responsibility made clear during the COVID-19 pandemic was the need for school leaders to coordinate professional development for communication along with a clear set of norms and expectations for it. In the time since 2020, administrators have come to see the value in having very clear expectations of their staff about engaging and communicating with families (Smith et al., 2021).

Those of us who worked in schools throughout the pandemic experienced the importance of solid communication when school leaders used their entire staff to help make connections with families and students—for wellness checks, to address technology issues, to answer questions about remote learning, among many others. This shift in the typical ways schools communicated with families required everyone to become gifted in communication skills (Orta & Gutiérrez, 2022).

Some specific communication behaviors of administrators have been found to be motivational. Frequent face-to-face and personal communication between the school leader and their teachers (Turkle, 2015) has been shown to motivate teachers; however, while there is significant value with face-to-face communication, technology has eliminated the barriers of time and space (Yumurtaci, 2017). Stakeholders can now communicate with the school quickly with the use of email, text messaging, online portals, and discussion boards. School administrators have come to understand that the ability to quickly communicate has now created an expectation of promptness.Staff and the school community are expecting to have their questions and comments read and responded to in a timely manner (Yurmurtaci, 2017).

Face-to-face communication still matters, however. Phone calls still matter. Technology has made it convenient to communicate, but as Sherry Turkle in *Reclaiming Conversation: The Power of Talk in a Digital Age* (2015) writes, "Human relationships are rich, messy, and demanding. When we clean them up with technology, we move from conversation to the efficiency of mere connection" (p. 21), and in most cases in education, simple connection is not good enough. Turkle's (2015) ideas are not anti-technology; they are pro-conversation.

Having school leaders and staff well versed in communication is good for students, and effective communication with parents and families is vital to ensuring participation and support for students, school activities, programs, and events. Effective communication between schools and families has been shown to be a foundational aspect of a student's social and academic success (Natale & Lubniewski, 2018). Schools should do all they can to communicate well with parents and family members. When families and educators collaborate on communication strategies it has an overall positive effect on student outcomes (Can, 2016). When schools consult and work with families to find communication strategies that are effective, parent involvement increases. This increased parent involvement has been linked to academic and emotional development in students (Barajas-López & Ishimaru, 2020; Kyzar & Jimerson, 2018). Parental involvement leads to better student outcomes; thus, parent participation should be deeper than just bake sales (Henderson et al., 2007). The National PTA cites the following advantages for having parents involved in schools (ParentSquare, 2022).

- Students achieve more, regardless of the socioeconomic and ethnic or racial background of the parent.

- Students show more positive attitudes toward school and better behavior.

- When parents and teachers work together to understand the culture of the home, students from diverse backgrounds do better (Barajas-López & Ishimaru, 2020; Ishimaru, 2019).

- When positive communication exists and a reciprocal relationship is formed, families are treated with more dignity and respect and begin to share in more decision making (Barajas-López & Ishimaru, 2020; Ishimaru, 2019).

- Teacher morale is higher and ratings of teachers by parents increase.

If educators want parents and families to be more involved, then they must take the lead in communicating to form a more powerful partnership (Weber, 2020), using a variety of strategies to attract, inform, and engage with parents and families to make them feel welcomed and heard. Parents want to be more involved than ever; remote learning has brought parents into the daily life of their child's classroom. The best schools value this increased engagement and want to continue to deepen it. Having effective communication processes in place between the school and home benefits this engagement and supports improved outcomes (Orta & Gutiérrez, 2022).

School leaders must also know how to filter communication from the outside. This includes information from the state, provincial, and district levels, as well as from the school board and community organizations and businesses to understand what information is important, not important right now, or not important at all.

Effective communication also involves effective listening. Tracey Salamondra (2021) has identified two different kinds of listening behaviors for effective communication in schools.

1. Deep listening where the expectation of the speaker is to be heard and understood by the other person

2. Strategic listening that involves responding to the speaker with guiding questions, prompts, and suggestions

In addition, effective communication involves active listening that includes behaviors such as validating, encouraging, summarizing, clarifying, reflecting, and restating (Ontario Principals' Council, 2011). Administrators must avoid poor listening behaviors such as interrupting, passing judgment internally to themselves, giving unwarranted advice, and not maintaining confidentiality (Salamondra, 2021).

Tyler (2016) finds that principal certification programs have little impact on future leaders' communication abilities. What does improve a teacher's ability to communicate as they move into administration is mentoring and school- and district-level training in communication (Tyler, 2016).

KEY OBSERVABLE BEHAVIORS

Following are the behaviors that aspiring leaders who are effective communicators should exhibit. When rating a teacher in this way of being, think about the knowledge and skills involved with each behavior as well as the passion and motivation it requires. Consider providing the list of observable behaviors for this way of being to future leaders for self-evaluation and reflection prior to the mentoring planning meeting. (Visit **go.SolutionTree.com/leadership** for a free reproducible of this list.)

1. The teacher provides ongoing communication about learning and their classroom. The information is consistent, timely, and enough to allow students, other impacted educators, and parents and families to have a vision of what occurs in the classroom and show they support student outcomes.

2. The teacher shares information in a way that illustrates to parents, families, and community members that the teacher welcomes and respects them as valued partners in student learning. They engage in regular and open two-way communication with families and the community about the school, students, needs, accomplishments, and problems. They do not communicate only when there is a problem. They make phone calls, schedule meetings, and strive to have personal, face-to-face conversations when needed.

3. The teacher uses multiple methods of communication and finds out the preferred method for individual families. They initiate teacher-parent communication with phone calls, notes, emails, newsletters, a classroom

website, student agendas, or using communication technology approved in the school, such as apps like Schoology. They maintain records of parent communication like phone logs and an email filing system to keep notes of important family information. All of this is done within the school's rules governing access to information and confidentiality. At a minimum, they retain the time, date, and general topic of conversation to indicate an ongoing communication record for each student and family.

4. The teacher shares learning opportunities, resources, and supports to assist parents and families who want materials for home to partner in student learning and have productive ongoing parent-teacher-student conversations. They are supportive and respectful of families with differing home environments that may not allow for much work to be done at home. They understand and support as needed.

5. The teacher contributes productively to meetings and staff learning sessions, encouraging others to do so as well. They demonstrate positive, polite communication skills to promote a positive working environment and do not dominate the conversation.

6. The teacher makes effective use of email to staff and families if email is a preferred form of communication in the school. When dealing with a challenging situation, a situation that could lead to misunderstanding, or there are more than just a few lines of text to communicate, the teacher uses face-to-face or phone communication.

7. The teacher demonstrates respect by showing positive and productive listening skills. They truly listen to others, they are open to other ideas, and they genuinely consider the value of what others share.

8. The teacher probes appropriately while listening to make others comfortable enough to share information. They skillfully dig deeper when necessary. They make use of the AWE question—"And what else?"—when speaking with students and parents. They effectively work through problems to reach amicable solutions by encouraging others to share their feelings and thoughts first.

9. The teacher makes sure that students leave a conversation feeling heard. Their conversations with students are appropriate for the staff-student relationship. Conversations with students are not focused on building a friendship. Feedback and corrections to students are caring, respectful, honest, and helpful.

10. The teacher is clear in outlining the context and outcomes of lessons. They communicate directions and procedures to students in a way that ensures understanding of students' ages and stages. Classroom procedures and commitments communicate achievable expectations for students. The teacher assists students by posting important messages, dates, assignment due dates, and so on, to help students organize their time and responsibilities.

11. The teacher employs an appropriate balance of teacher- and student-directed discussion and learning during teaching. The teacher does not do all the talking and instructing; they encourage and welcome student voices.

12. The teacher uses questioning techniques in class that encourage higher-level thinking skills. They vary the format of questions and prompts and provide students with adequate response time. Their instructions and questioning empower and engage students to explore content.

13. The teacher uses appropriate language (avoiding the use of slang; using appropriate humor; avoiding conversational placeholders; using appropriate pace, volume, pitch; and so on) when working with students, when interacting with other staff, and when engaging with families.

14. The teacher actively participates in conversations that focus on students and student learning. They make students the focus of their conversations with other staff, speaking positively and with hope.

15. The teacher conducts effective teacher-student conferences with students and families. They represent the school positively when discussing student progress. They balance their talk time with families and work to provide collaborative next steps and a positive outlook moving forward.

16. The teacher has experience with the formal structure of high-stakes meetings, such as on a school board or school committee, and understands timed agendas, meeting outcomes, and so on.

17. The teacher recognizes the power of providing feedback to students. They provide high-quality feedback that is supportive, timely, useful, respectful, and authentic, and feedback is a significant part of their teaching.

18. The teacher references the school's vision and mission frequently, demonstrating to others that they are supportive and have a positive outlook on the school's direction. They make explicit reference to school

goals when providing direction or feedback about schoolwide issues. They reference the school mantra or motto.

19. The teacher uses strong communication skills to problem solve with staff and students. They follow a process and communicate well when identifying and resolving conflicts. If responsible for doing so, they effectively communicate any outcomes of problem-solving situations to those who require explanation. They understand that problem solving involves resolution and reconciliation.

20. The teacher is mindful of student nonverbal communication. They recognize when students are under stress and provide comfort. When their own words create misunderstanding, discomfort, or fear in students, they make adjustments, correct any misunderstandings or concerns, and make sure the student is comfortable and feels safe. The message is still important; however, they understand the need to focus on the student over the message.

SAMPLE TEACHER

This section presents an example using a fictional teacher and administrator. It shows the results when the administrator plots the future leader's observable behaviors from the way of being presented in this chapter; analyzes the data; plans the next steps; and conducts a meeting with the teacher.

Selina is an experienced kindergarten teacher of more than twenty years. She has started to ask more questions about the role of administration and has shared that she would like to leave the classroom and finish her career as a school leader. Selina has a wealth of knowledge about the kindergarten program, and her classroom is often used to demonstrate best practices to new teachers. Selina has strong communication skills with her students and within the school. She is traditional in her communication with families, relying heavily on a monthly email newsletter. She welcomes students and their families each morning in the kindergarten entry area and is present at dismissal times as well. Using the list of observable behaviors, her administrator, Principal Nguyen, has noticed some aspects of Selina's communication that she would like to highlight to assist Selena as she considers an administrative role.

Step 1: Plot the Way of Being on the Leadership Action Matrix

Principal Nguyen plots Selina's observable behaviors for the third way of being—an effective communicator—using the leadership action matrix. The results appear in figure 4.1.

Way of Being: An Effective Communicator

Administrator Name: Principal Nguyen

Teacher Name: Selina Sample

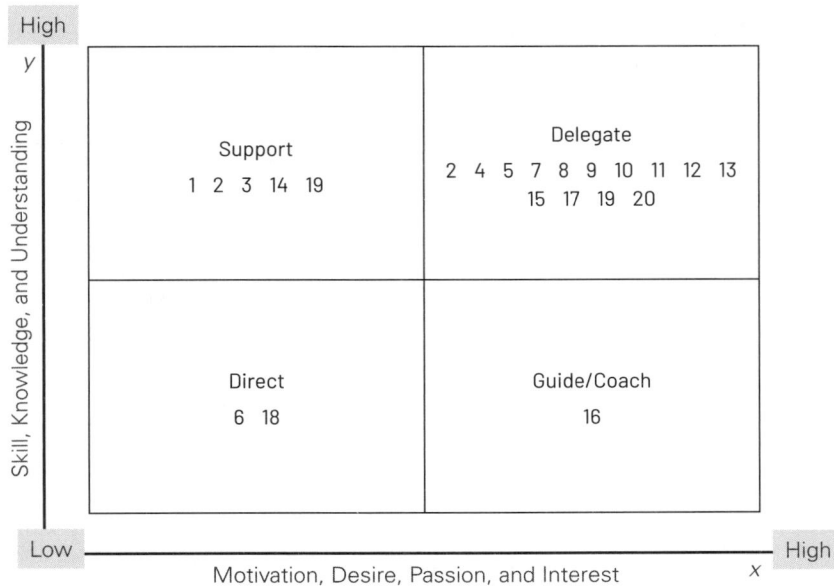

FIGURE 4.1: Selina's leadership action matrix for an effective communicator.

Step 2: Complete the Mentoring Planning Page

After plotting the observable behaviors for Selina's leadership action matrix, Principal Nguyen transfers the numbers to the mentoring planning page (see figure 4.2), adding comments about the behaviors she observed and her thoughts about the next steps. She bolds the items she wants to discuss further when she meets with Selina. Selina could use this tool for self-evaluation prior to the mentoring meeting as well.

Way of Being: An Effective Communicator

Teacher: Selina Sample

Administrator: Principal Nguyen

Support		Delegate	
Behavior Number	**Notes**	**Behavior Number**	**Notes**
1	Uses a newsletter consistently to communicate, however using it requires more precise timing and frequency	2	Engages in regular communication and is available for families at drop off and pick up
2	Communicates often, but should consider the form of communication for the type of message	4	Sends home a lot of program information by email

FIGURE 4.2: Sample mentoring planning page for Selina for an effective communicator.

continued ▶

Support		Delegate	
Behavior Number	**Notes**	**Behavior Number**	**Notes**
3	Relies too heavily on face-to-face meetings at school since some families cannot come for drop off or pick up; sends emails, but they provide content and not connection	5	Always participates in staff meetings by listening and providing input
14	Shows some frustration with staff when speaking about the level of student skill; should speak with optimism	7	Observed in meetings as active listener who seeks to understand
19	**Needs to communicate about problem solving when necessary; some parental concerns about lack of communication**	8	**Probes students in class to create many invitations for learning**
		9	Communicates with students to build strong relationships
		10	Has a visually appealing and organized classroom with directions and procedures for students; uses multiple languages
		11	Listens intently and probes to ensure student voices are heard in classroom
		12	Uses questioning with students to encourage them to speak, share, and explain; has an invitational style
		13	Uses appropriate language and is a role model
		15	Has received many positive parent comments about experiences during classroom visits
		17	Provides constant feedback during learning
		19	**Should use effective communication skill with students and staff to reach out to families by implementing Friday phone calls**
		20	Understands student nonverbal communication and expression of feelings; very patient

Direct		Guide/Coach	
Behavior Number	Notes	Behavior Number	Notes
6	Has an overreliance on email	16	**Needs experience on a school board or district committee**
18	**Communicates little about what is happening outside of kindergarten to parents; should also communicate about schoolwide issues**		

Following are explanations of some of the administrator's ratings for Selina and the rationale for them.

Behavior 18: *The teacher references the school's vision and mission frequently, demonstrating to others that they are supportive and have a positive outlook on the school's direction. They make explicit reference to school goals when providing direction or feedback about schoolwide issues. They reference the school mantra or motto.*

Principal Nguyen put behavior eighteen in the direct quadrant because Selina is dedicated to her kindergarten program and is a cheerleader for the students and the work done in that area of the school. However, kindergarten is still part of the larger school. Her communication with families shares little about what is happening in the school outside of kindergarten. Principal Nguyen would like to see Selina's communication align with the mission and vision of the larger school and include a reference to the school mantra to connect kindergarten students and families to the rest of the school and promote that relationship.

Behavior 19: *The teacher uses strong communication skills to problem solve with staff and students. They follow a process and communicate well when identifying and resolving conflicts. If responsible for doing so, they effectively communicate any outcomes of problem-solving situations to those who require explanation. They understand that problem solving involves resolution and reconciliation.*

Principal Nguyen observed that Selina is doing excellent work in her classroom related to communication with students. With staff and students, she demonstrates strong communication skills one on one. However, some parents have expressed concerns about her communication, so Principal Nguyen indicated support for behavior nineteen. Selina is having difficulty understanding the importance of and need for deeper conversations with families. Her motivation is to get information out quickly and easily and make a connection, instead of a desire for better understanding and a conversation. Her communication skills are high, but in this particular aspect, her interest in putting in time and effort when required is low. For example, if a student has had an upsetting experience with another student at school, it is difficult for parents to get the full and accurate story. Instead of communicating in a timely manner, Selina often waits until the next day to communicate when a parent is at drop off or pick up. Alternatively, she sends an email that then goes back and forth as the parent attempts to better clarify exactly what went on in class. Principal Nguyen is trying to stress the importance of choosing the appropriate method of communication and the need to be proactive with communication to build community and two-way communication.

Behavior 16: *The teacher has experience with the formal structure of high-stakes meetings, such as on a school board or school committee, and understands timed agendas, meeting outcomes, and so on.*

Principal Nguyen placed behavior sixteen in the guide/coach quadrant because Selina is high in motivation but lower in knowledge. She is an excellent kindergarten teacher with little experience at a school board or district level. To give her experiences of working on a committee that would be highly structured and demonstrate to her the kind of formality and detail she will face in the future as a school leader, Principal Nguyen will assist Selina in gaining membership on a larger kindergarten team. The district sends new teachers to observe Selina's classroom. Selina is an excellent candidate for guiding and coaching because she has expressed interest in learning more before becoming an administrator.

Behavior 8: *The teacher probes appropriately while listening to make others comfortable enough to share information. They skillfully dig deeper when necessary. They make use of the AWE question—"And what else?"—when speaking with students and parents. They effectively work through problems to reach amicable solutions by encouraging others to share their feelings and thoughts first.*

The delegate quadrant allows the administrator to share all the extremely positive qualities that Selina possesses and celebrate her communication abilities. Principal Nguyen put behavior eight in this quadrant because Selina is both high in knowledge and high in passion and interest. Selina works with kindergarten students well and invites them into learning by asking good questions and following up with responses that keep students thinking and speaking. Principal Nguyen wants Selina to extend those excellent communication skills with her parent community, so the principal has also written "Friday phone calls" on the planning page. She would like to see Selina add this strategy to her weekly routine to become accustomed to contacting parents and sharing positive news about students on a regular basis. Principal Nguyen hopes this routine will increase Selina's comfort in speaking with students' parents. Every Friday, Principal Nguyen will read a story to Selina's class to give Selina time to make two phone calls each week to talk to students' parents. (See page 74 for a more in-depth discussion of the Friday phone calls strategy.)

Step 3: Use the Mentoring Meeting Planner

Principal Nguyen fills in most of the information on the mentoring meeting planner tool in preparation for her meeting with Selina. Figure 4.3 shows the completed mentoring meeting planner, including notes from the meeting.

Date: April 2

Administrator: Principal Nguyen

Teacher: Selina Sample

Focus

Which way or ways of being will we discuss?

An Effective Communicator. Why it is important as a school administrator that you communicate well? Who are your stakeholders? What are the best ways to communicate and when, where, and how? Why should communication happen? Ask Selina for input.

Agenda for Sharing and Discussion

What specific points about the way or ways of being will we discuss?

- Selina has excellent classroom communication and relationships with students; however, communication must go beyond the classroom.
- There is a need to be well-rounded in many aspects of leadership.
- What is Selina's perspective on her strengths and needs in this way of being?
- Review notes from the twenty observable behaviors.
- Refer to notes from the mentoring planning page.

Key Points

For each of the following sections, list the bolded or circled items from the mentoring planning page.

- **Direct**
  - » Provide direction about Selina's overreliance on email.
  - » Provide direction for communicating about the larger school beyond kindergarten.
- **Support**
  - » Provide support about communicating concerning problem solving when necessary, since some parents have concerns about lack of communication.
  - » Provide guidance on types of communication since Selina relies too heavily on face-to-face communication at school when some families are not at drop off or pick up. Discuss how email provides content but not connection.
- **Guide/Coach**
  - » Guide Selena to join a board or district committee for experience.
- **Delegate**
  - » Have Selina use the Friday phone calls strategy to apply the communication skills she uses with staff and students to parents.

Teacher Plans, Comments, and Ideas

What plans, comments, and ideas did the teacher have during the meeting?

- Selina loves the idea of Friday phone calls. Principal Nguyen will give release time to read with the class so Selina can take fifteen to twenty minutes to make two or three calls per week.
- Selina is going to consider what should be communicated via email and what should be a face-to-face or phone conversation. She will keep a log in the next month of examples of each.
- Selina wants to use her extensive knowledge of kindergarten teaching to join a district committee on kindergarten to experience formal committee work.

FIGURE 4.3: Sample mentoring meeting planner for Selina for an effective communicator.

continued ▶

Goal Setting

What is the teacher's goal related to this way of being?

- Selina will begin making Friday phone calls to parents this week with release time administration provides. She will take notes after each phone conversation and share her thoughts and feelings with administration at a regularly scheduled leader meeting next month.

- Selina will begin a chart of communications with her families that includes date, time, and topic. She will indicate whether she communicated via email, face to face, or over the phone. She will share the chart to discuss at next month's meeting.

- Selina will wait for an invitation to join the district kindergarten planning team being arranged by administration. Selina would like to set up discussions with administration about the structure and organization of the meetings.

Potential Resources

What are some potential resources to recommend to the teacher that address their areas of needed growth from the direct and guide/coach quadrants?

- Connect Selina with the district leaders responsible for the kindergarten planning committee.

- Suggest the following books:

- *Crucial Conversations: Tools for Talking When Stakes Are High* by Joseph Grenny, Kerry Patterson, Ron McMillan, Al Switzler, and Emily Gregory

- *Reclaiming Conversation: The Power of Talk in a Digital Age* by Sherry Turkle

Final Thoughts

What are your final thoughts about next steps and when to check back in?

Selina will need to experience success with Friday phone calls to see the benefit of making connections with parents. She is still hesitant and wants to use email for the vast majority of her communication with parents. It will be interesting to see what her thoughts are after experiencing a lot more communication with parents.

AN EFFECTIVE COMMUNICATOR IN ACTION: SCHOOL EXAMPLES

The following—prioritized and personalized parent meetings and Friday phone calls—are two examples of what effective communication could look like in your school. These examples also show staff and the larger community that the school understands the importance of this way of being. Strategies such as these also provide leadership opportunities for staff you have identified for this way of being. Once plotted in the leadership action matrix, they will require experiences for further development in being an effective communicator.

Prioritized and Personalized Parent Meetings

Regardless of the meeting format, school leaders must be effective communicators to have successful and productive meetings with parents and families. Relationships with families are built one conversation at a time.

Not all parents are comfortable coming into the school. Some may have had negative experiences when they were students. Others may be particularly impacted by worry or anger when having a meeting about their child. Making schools warm and welcoming but still maintaining a formal setting can support parents who are, at times, uncomfortable attending. Leaders must work hard to make the meeting experience as positive as possible. Effective communication is a critical piece.

As a leader, I often discussed with staff what we could do during meetings to make sure parents were comfortable, and felt heard, safe, and supported, and that conversations were productive. One of the key points we focused on was who was doing the talking in meetings. Are leaders and teachers the ones doing all the talking, or are parents engaged in the conversation? Ensuring equal dialogue with parents, not a monologue performed by the school, allows schools to get the full perspective from families.

As an administrator, I would ask aspiring leaders to monitor the conversation to ensure we were sharing the airtime with families. I asked them to focus on the invitational questions I asked parents to encourage them to speak. After the meetings, we discussed what they noticed about my use of paraphrasing or asking for more details. If the conversation became heated, I wanted them to note what calming strategies I implemented. It is extremely important for leaders to model the phrases, body language, and steps we take when involved in collaborative conversations with parents.

I have often shared the following analogy about communication with staff (Grenny, Patterson, McMillan, Switzler, & Gregory, 2022): Think of hot and cold taps that flow into a basin or sink to combine into a shared pool of water. The water represents a shared pool of meaning to which everyone must contribute. This requires everyone in the meeting to have their taps on. In a parent meeting, when a family member is silent, it is up to school staff to make them feel comfortable and safe so they will turn on their taps and contribute to the conversation. Or, if someone has their tap on full blast, staff must have the skills to help them turn down the flow to encourage more equitable conversation. Sometimes, parents need this opportunity to vent their frustration; however, skilled staff members ensure a return to proper dialogue (Grenny et al., 2022). At the end of a meeting, parents should have spoken an equal amount or more than staff.

Some other strategies help make parents feel comfortable. Make introductions at the beginning of the meeting, and state everyone's role in connection to the student. If possible, place name plates and roles in front of staff members. After introductions, state the purpose of the meeting, and ask parents to explain their understanding of how the meeting time will be used. Asking this clarifying question ensures everyone has the same purpose in mind, and if families have broader concerns, leaders can adjust the meeting content or plan to address the added content at another time.

During the meeting, show respect for parents by making eye contact and listening. Designate one meeting participant to take notes to share later with the group. Others in the meeting can then focus their attention on the speaker. Nothing feels more uncomfortable than speaking to a group of individuals who all have their faces buried in their laptops.

Another important aspect of parent meetings is to personalize the amount of time spent. If parents come to a meeting with a long agenda, increase the amount of time for the meeting. If a meeting ends early, that is great, but do not cut meetings short or rush parents out the door. This shows that supporting their child is your top priority. Also, remember that the meeting might be the only opportunity to engage with the parent or family.

When there are multiple meetings in a day with a tight schedule, it is still possible to have a full conversation and respect the family's time. In our school, we displayed an agenda with "Student A," "Student B," and so on (no actual names) listed with times. Seeing the schedule at the start highlights for parents the length of time to be together and an understanding of respect for other families' appointment times as well. If unable to complete the necessary discussions in the time allotted, share how you may continue the conversation at a follow-up meeting. Schedule a follow-up meeting right then to show families continuing support. As you approach the end time, summarize who would do what, by when, and what the follow-up meeting would look like.

Friday Phone Calls

Friday phone calls are a strategy I adopted early in my career as an administrator after learning about them from educational consultant Todd Whitaker at The Summit on PLC at Work conference in Phoenix, Arizona, in 2008. Every Friday afternoon, I made phone calls to the families of three students to share great news about their children. That is three phone calls a week, for forty school weeks, so 120 phone calls a school year bragging about students to their parents. Each call took only a few minutes, but the impact was immense.

Calls can be about a student's academic performance, if they are working well in class, a situation where they were a good friend to others, if they handled a challenge particularly well, or helped another student, to name a few. Our school mantra was, "Work Hard, Be Nice, and Make a Difference"; I often framed my conversation by how the student embodies the mantra. I started each parent conversation sharing how I came to know the great news about their child—I overheard their child's teacher boasting about the student, or that the teacher approached me and shared the good news. I had parents tear up, parents call their partners to the phone and ask me to repeat the news, and I even had parents ask if I had the wrong number.

Principal Nguyen suggested this strategy for Selina because it provides valuable experience for effectively communicating with parents and families in a way that is positive for the teacher and the parents. Opening the lines of communication in this way makes it less difficult for teachers to reach out when there is a problem. And parents shouldn't receive communication from the school only when there are difficulties. Invite aspiring leaders into your office to hear one of the phone calls, especially if it is about a student from their class. Encourage them to begin the practice as a teacher; they will quickly learn how it impacts families in a positive way.

CONCLUSION

Being an effective communicator is critical for administrators because school leaders represent the school in their words and actions, and the information they share is vital for staff, students, families, and other stakeholders. Effective communication requires an appropriate tone and accurate and timely information, so families trust the school and understand what is happening in their child's school life. Teachers who have knowledge and skills in communication as well as a desire to make sure their students, colleagues, and families are well-informed and feel connected will be good candidates for moving into administration in the future.

CHAPTER 5

A GOAL SETTER WHO USES DATA

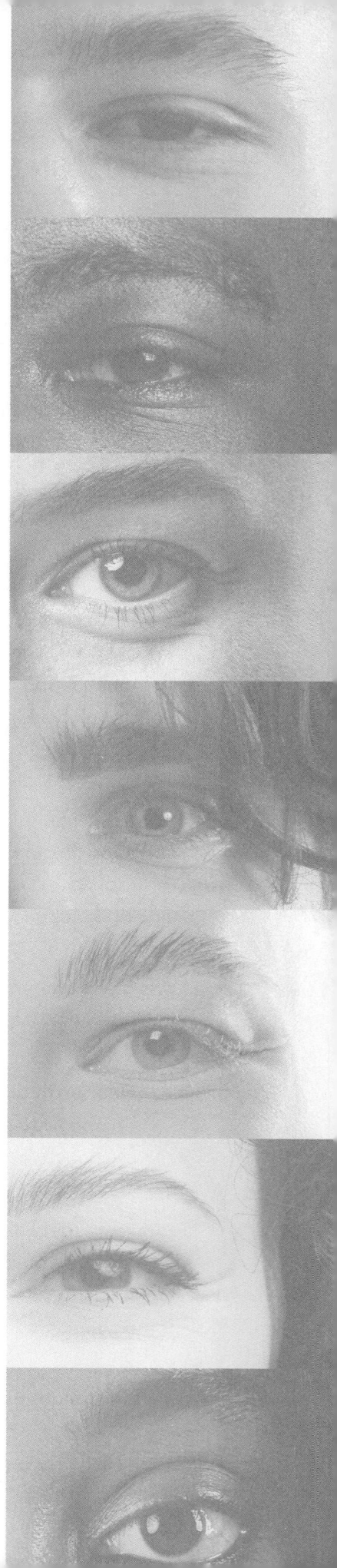

As Michael Fullan (2014) astutely observes, we cannot expect to improve something within our schools if we do not measure it. A teacher who understands the assessment and evaluation cycle and utilizes data along the way to make the necessary changes and adaptations to best support students is well-equipped to continue to use feedback and information to make changes that are necessary for schoolwide improvement. Just like a classroom teacher, a school leader must use data to understand the current landscape, determine what they are trying to achieve, and decide on the best course of action to get there.

The Wallace Report (Grissom et al., 2021) synthesis of research on how principals affect students and schools shows that the most effective administrators use data not just to make good decisions and address school needs, but to also inspire actions in others. They use data for both accountability measures and to improve the climate and culture in the school. The effective use of data creates teacher investment in the initiatives, programs, and ideas necessary for schoolwide improvement. This cycle of using data to create actions that lead to improvement and the generation of more data showing the benefits in student outcomes has a profoundly positive impact on teachers' perspectives about the school's mission, vision, and school climate (Grissom et al., 2021).

The use of data is so important in the role of the administrator that *The Ontario Leadership Framework* has listed using data as one of the five core leadership capacities (Leithwood, 2012). School leaders must be able to gather and analyze a wide range of data. They must engage their teams in looking for trends, strengths, and gaps in school and individual classroom data, and then using the data to focus conversations and next steps on teaching and learning (Leithwood, 2012).

The Ontario Leadership Framework (Leithwood, 2012) makes clear that the primary purpose of using effective leadership practices, and having schools run by those that are effective in these leadership ways, is to "ensure that organizational members and other stakeholders are working towards the same set of purposes and that these purposes are a legitimate expression of both provincial policy and local community aspirations" (p. 13). A key role for the administrator involves making sure all individuals connected to the school understand the purpose. Setting goals provides a unifying sense of direction connected to the school's mission. This requires that everyone involved is well acquainted with where they are going, how they are going to get there, and the role that each person plays in moving forward. Using data and setting goals along this journey keeps the process aligned and moving forward.

Student achievement improves when school administrators align professional learning opportunities for teachers with school goals (Grissom, Egalite, & Lindsay, 2021). An administrator must possess the ability and the desire to set goals using data. Administrators collect a large volume and wide variety of information, data, and feedback in the day-to-day operation of the school. Effective administrators have a sense of what is working well and what they need to examine more closely; however, administrators should systematically collect evidence to justify their thoughts and inform their decision making. An administrator cannot go by feel alone.

Teachers who are already skilled at using data in their classroom, motivated to find out about their hunches by collecting data, and comfortable in understanding what it might reveal are those teachers we want moving into administration. Being comfortable with data, inquisitive, and action oriented is necessary for teachers who want to be future leaders.

KEY OBSERVABLE BEHAVIORS

Following are the behaviors that aspiring leaders who are goal setters who use data should exhibit. When rating a teacher in this way of being, think about the knowledge and skills involved with each behavior as well as the passion and motivation it requires. Consider providing the list of observable behaviors for this way of being to future leaders for self-evaluation and reflection prior to the mentoring planning meeting. (Visit **go.SolutionTree.com/leadership** for a free reproducible of this list.)

1. The teacher has a purpose for their assessment practices and how they will use results. They use formative assessment to improve learning and summative assessment to prove learning (Erkens, Schimmer, & Dimich-Vagle, 2017).

2. The teacher participates effectively in groups to contribute to productive collaboration. When working on goal setting or looking at data with others, they monitor their contributions and invite others to participate. They support their colleagues and add to a positive school climate and culture.

3. The teacher assists in the development of shared group processes and norms of participation, and with determining the goals the team plans to achieve. They work with others to follow a protocol or script to move them through a process together.

4. The teacher is curious and optimistic when working with data. They are comfortable even when data discussions are uncomfortable. They speak positively when discussing data and do not shame or blame students or other staff members.

5. The teacher determines students who are successful with specific standards and those who are not. They participate in conversations about results across classrooms to discover how to improve their instruction and how to use the talents of team members to benefit students.

6. The teacher participates regularly with a team to analyze student work to determine which students and which standards need attention and to calibrate with teaching partners about how they will measure proficiency with consistency. They utilize the information from these meetings to create collaborative formative assessments with their team.

7. The teacher wants to be involved in the school's long-range planning, examinations of school effectiveness, and analysis of school and district data to create goals, as well as discussions of opportunities for staff professional development and growth.

8. The teacher is part of a team, and, as part of that team, focuses on being consistent and works in unison with their teaching partners. The teacher understands that individual effort is not enough, and all students benefit if teams of teachers work collectively. When working in a team, the teacher maintains program, subject or grade, and division consistency.

9. The teacher is aware of and can articulate and use the school's mission, vision, and values statements. They are knowledgeable of the school goals and are working toward achieving them. They discuss the mission and vision of the school with students and families. They align the work they do with teams and partners back to the mission, vision, and goals of the school.

10. The teacher uses quick check-ins with students to collect data to move the learning forward. They share learning goals for the lesson and receive immediate feedback from students about their understanding. They use entry passes or exit passes where students quickly answer questions so the teacher can gauge the students' current proficiency.

11. The teacher effectively motivates students to improve their learning. They have high and realistic expectations for all students. They share data with students in a way that elicits a positive response. They communicate proficiency in a way that motivates students for continual learning. The teacher uses both grades and feedback, realizing the power of feedback and the limits of providing grades only for student investment in learning.

12. The teacher uses a wide variety of assessment strategies and tools. They do not solely depend on pencil-and-paper tasks with a low level of difficulty. They provide students with multiple ways to demonstrate their learning. They also use multiple sources of evidence to diagnose progress and determine next steps. They use multiple sources of data to determine final summative grades.

13. The teacher records accurate data on student performance, by student and by expectation or outcome. They keep comprehensive records to track student learning. The assessment task is aligned to the standard

students are learning. They focus more on what is being learned instead of what is being taught when they consider the essential standards in a course. Their data informs them when they need to change course, make adjustments, and reengage students in the content.

14. The teacher uses data and evidence rather than personal opinion to make decisions about student placement in programs, including benchmark data, test results, classroom observation data, and any additional information to assist them in moving all students forward.

15. The teacher starts with the end in mind, unit planning for the semester and then implementing daily plans to achieve student outcomes. Their individual daily and weekly plans follow a sequential order that includes small learning targets with well-positioned formative assessments to inform instructional decisions; however, there is flexibility based on student needs indicated by data.

16. The teacher is instructionally agile (Erkens et al., 2017). They use evidence from what they see and hear emerging in front of them during class instruction to make just-in-time changes. They adapt and are flexible with what comes next to ensure students meet planned expectations.

17. The teacher encourages students to set goals, work toward them, and gather data about their learning by self-evaluation and reflection using criteria.

18. The teacher uses technology where appropriate to improve the efficiency and effectiveness of data. They use technology for planning, analysis, instructional delivery, reporting, note taking, and decision making.

19. The teacher helps students, staff, and other stakeholders understand the relationship between the school's goals and the board and district initiatives and priorities—that the school is part of a system working toward goals, and that the teacher supports schoolwide and districtwide work.

20. The teacher examines trends in student data over time and is curious to identify potential areas of support for students, particularly those students from marginalized groups.

SAMPLE TEACHER

This section presents an example using a fictional teacher and administrator. It shows the results when the administrator plots the future leader's observable behaviors from the way of being presented in this chapter; analyzes the data; plans next steps; and conducts a meeting with the teacher.

Kelly is the head of the English department in a high school. They have been the department head for many years and have a large team of younger, eager English teachers whom they mentor and coach. Kelly is well respected and supports the teachers in the department with advice for both work and life. The department team meets regularly to share lesson plans and new ideas and resources; however, there is little conversation about students. Kelly has expressed an interest in restructuring the English meetings to focus more on student work samples and student results across different classrooms. The teachers have learned excellent assessment and evaluation practices from Kelly. Individual teachers use student data for their own students and within their classrooms, but there is little sharing of data across grades or teachers. Kelly is focused on the English department, and it is one of the best in the district. Kelly meets monthly with other department heads, but the discussions always move to conversations about budgets, schedules, and schoolwide events. Principal Hanson is supportive of Kelly's desire to move into administration and wants to do all he can to support them. One area he feels Kelly needs to improve to be an effective future leader is as a goal setter who uses data.

Step 1: Plot the Way of Being on the Leadership Action Matrix

Kelly's administrator, Principal Hanson, plots her observable behaviors for the fifth way of being—a goal setter who uses data—using the leadership action matrix. The results appear in figure 5.1.

Way of Being: A Goal Setter Who Uses Data

Administrator Name: Principal Hanson

Teacher Name: Kelly Sample

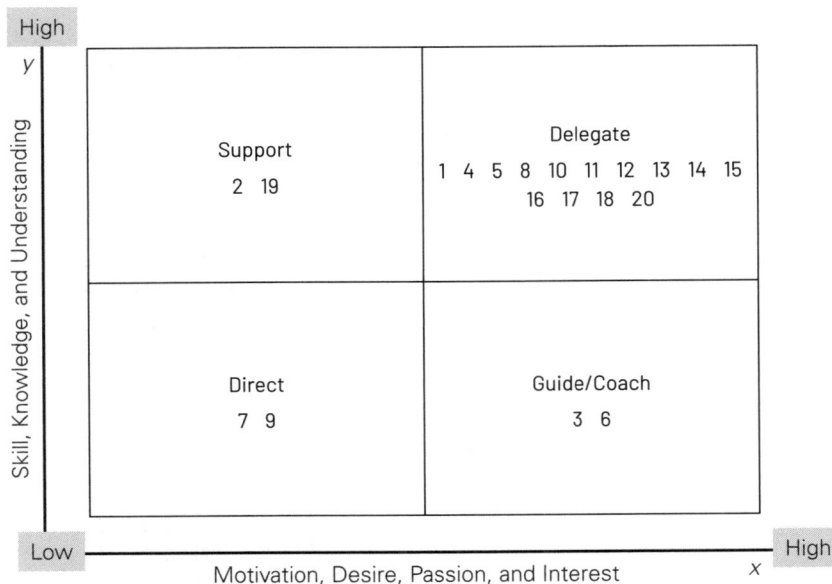

FIGURE 5.1: Kelly's leadership action matrix for a goal setter who uses data.

Step 2: Complete the Mentoring Planning Page

After plotting the observable behaviors for Kelly on the leadership action matrix, Principal Hanson transfers the numbers to the mentoring planning page (see figure 5.2), adding comments about the behaviors he observed and his thoughts about the next steps. He bolds the items he wants to discuss further when he meets with Kelly. Kelly could use this tool for self-evaluation before the mentoring meeting as well.

Way of Being: A Goal Setter Focused on Data

Teacher: Kelly Sample

Administrator: Principal Hanson

Support		Delegate	
Behavior Number	**Notes**	**Behavior Number**	**Notes**
2	**Participates effectively as department head but should share the work; you do not have to run every meeting**	1	Works with department to develop extensive assessment plan
19	Connects work to district and province in subject area; should also consider goals and vision outside of the discipline (equity, well-being, climate, culture, other subjects) and look outside own department	4	Develops comfortable team atmosphere for data discussion
		5	Looks at classroom data and plans reengagement days with staff on essential outcomes
		8	Works as a team with focus on all students across classrooms
		10	Collects a lot of data gathering in classroom about student learning
		11	Uses feedback on student work effectively and provides many opportunities to improve
		12	**Shows extremely high assessment literacy**
		13	Keeps a lot of data on students in all grades in department by expectations and tracks entire program
		14	Always uses data in student discussions, credit recovery, and pass/fail conversations
		15	Develops organized units of study with department based on essential outcomes

		16	Shows instructional agility when working with students
		17	Involves students in their own goal setting and reflection
		18	Applies strong technology skills to data use
		20	Uses data collected over many years for examining trends
			Should share protocols with other department heads
Direct		**Guide/Coach**	
Behavior Number	**Notes**	**Behavior Number**	**Notes**
7	**Immerses herself in data work at department level; should join schoolwide discussions**	3	Wants to learn protocols for data analysis and student evidence of learning; share book resources
9	Needs to branch out to develop schoolwide focus on mission, vision work	6	**Is currently looking at student samples; wants protocols for meetings and to teach department about power of sharing data**

FIGURE 5.2: Sample mentoring planning page for Kelly for a goal setter who uses data.

Following are explanations of some of Principal Hanson's ratings for Kelly and the rationale for them.

Behavior 7: *The teacher wants to be involved in the school's long-range planning, examinations of school effectiveness, and analysis of school and district data to create goals, as well as discussions of opportunities for staff professional development and growth.*

Principal Hanson placed behavior seven in the direct quadrant because if Kelly is interested in administration, they must begin to adopt a big-picture view of the school and the visioning and goal setting leaders do. Kelly has some knowledge and skill using data because they head the English department where teachers use data in their classrooms and track data across classrooms; however, Kelly has little understanding of other forms of data used in schools and should have some experience with this before moving into administration. Kelly has little motivation at this time to look at initiatives, feedback, and results from other departments or the school as a whole. Principal Hanson will strongly recommend that Kelly attend schoolwide meetings to gain that experience.

Behavior 2: *The teacher participates effectively in groups to contribute to productive collaboration. When working on goal setting or looking at data with others, they monitor their contributions* *and invite others to participate. They support their colleagues and add to a positive school climate and culture.*

Principal Hanson placed behavior two in the support quadrant (high knowledge/low interest) because Kelly has knowledge and skills with running and organizing meetings as a department head, but he is concerned that Kelly takes on too much of the responsibility and dominates the conversation during these meetings. Kelly must increase her ability to have others run parts of the meeting and share the responsibility. During meetings, Kelly's department staff have a good relationship with each other; however, they are not collaborative when it comes to contributions and participation. Kelly sometimes uses meeting time to teach the teachers, spending too much time on management and school planning that can be discussed in emails or memos. Kelly's knowledge and skill in meetings are appropriate in some areas, but in others, Principal Hanson wants to support Kelly in her desire to make meetings more productive and collaborative.

Behavior 6: *The teacher participates regularly with a team to analyze student work to determine which students and which standards need attention and calibrate with teaching partners how they will measure proficiency with consistency. They utilize the information from these meetings to create collaborative formative assessments with their team.*

Principal Hanson placed behavior six in the guide/coach quadrant because Kelly is high in motivation but low in knowledge and needs some assistance. Kelly is an excellent candidate for guiding and coaching because they have expressed interest in learning more about collaborative marking and looking closely at student work samples and assessments with colleagues. Kelly knows the English department would improve even more if the teachers analyzed student work together. Kelly knows doing this will improve instruction, providing more consistency of assessment results across classrooms when teachers view proficiency in the same way so team members can create better assessment materials when they work together. Principal Hanson will assist with this by providing some protocols Kelly can use with their team. The hope is that the English department will align their work and then share the protocols and process with the entire school.

Behavior 12: *The teacher uses a wide variety of assessment strategies and tools. They do not solely depend on pencil-and-paper tasks with a low level of difficulty. They allow students multiple ways to demonstrate their learning. Students are encouraged to show, discuss, and perform their learning in a wide variety of ways. They also use multiple sources of evidence to diagnose progress and determine next steps. They use multiple sources of data to determine final summative grades.*

Principal Hanson wrote behavior twelve in the delegate quadrant because Kelly is both high in knowledge and high in passion and interest. They do amazing work with students in all aspects of assessment and evaluation. There is not a teacher on staff who understands the purpose, methods, process, and products of assessment and evaluation as well as Kelly. They are a true leader who has shared assessment knowledge with the entire English department. Principal Hanson wants Kelly to share protocols with other department heads because he recently introduced some protocols for staff to examine student work samples and assessments. Once Kelly is comfortable with the protocols, Principal Hanson hopes Kelly will share them with other departments because they are well respected for their work on assessments and evaluations. Delegating this responsibility to Kelly will provide them with some practical experience working with other staff in an area of great passion prior to beginning her administrative role.

Step 3: Use the Mentoring Meeting Planner

Principal Hanson fills in most of the information on the mentoring meeting planner tool in preparation for his meeting with Kelly. Figure 5.3 shows the completed mentoring meeting planner including notes from the meeting.

Date: March 22

Administrator: Principal Hanson

Teacher: Kelly Sample

Focus

Which way or ways of being will we discuss?

A Goal Setter Who Uses Data. Discuss what it means to be a goal setter focused on data. What sources of data are available to schools? What is the importance of people skills when looking at data? Why is it important as a school administrator that you champion the use of data when discussing students? Ask Kelly for input.

Agenda for Sharing and Discussion

What specific points about the way or ways of being will we discuss?

- Kelly has many positives in assessment and evaluation and the use of data at the classroom level.
- There is a need to be well-rounded in many aspects of leadership.
- Find out Kelly's perspective on her strengths and needs in this way of being.
- Review notes from the twenty observable behaviors.
- Review notes from the mentoring planning page.

Key Points

- **Direct**
  » Encourage Kelly to join schoolwide discussions about data.
  » Direct Kelly about how to develop a schoolwide focus on mission and vision work.
- **Support**
  » Support Kelly in sharing the work in meetings—they do not have to run or direct every meeting.
  » Help her connect her work to the district and province in subject area, consider goals and vision outside of the discipline (equity, well-being, climate, culture, other subjects), to look beyond her own department.
- **Guide/Coach**
  » Share protocols for data analysis and student evidence of learning with Kelly.
  » Share protocols for meetings with Kelly as she is currently looking at student samples and could teach department members about the power of sharing data.
- **Delegate**
  » Kelly is extremely assessment literate and respected in this area.
  » Once Kelly learns protocols, they can share them with other department heads for schoolwide use.

FIGURE 5.3: Sample meeting planner for Kelly for a goal setter who uses data.

continued ▶

Teacher Plans, Comments, and Ideas

What plans, comments, and ideas did the teacher have during the meeting?

- Kelly is interested in sharing the protocols they learn with other departments once they are comfortable with them and will begin using them with their team.

- Kelly is extremely interested in working with Protocols for Examining Evidence and Artifacts found in *The Handbook for Collaborative Common Assessments: Tools for Design, Delivery, and Data Analysis* because the protocols show how to calibrate scoring between classrooms, how to analyze different student errors, and how to improve assessment measuring tools.

- Kelly can see how they have been dominating the meeting and is going to begin having data moments, where staff come with an assessment or student in mind and share.

- Kelly would like to get involved on schoolwide committees such as the School Effectiveness Team, School Data Team, and is interested in seeing other kinds of data other than just student assessments from the English classes.

- Kelly is appreciative of the support and wants to continue to discuss her leadership journey.

Goal Setting

What is the teacher's goal related to this way of being?

- Kelly will begin to use the protocols found in the two books immediately with the English department, using them during team meetings to turn meetings into data meetings.

- Kelly will restructure team meetings, so everyone is involved and focused on student work, instead of managerial issues.

- Kelly will share with the administrator how meetings are going and when they are ready to share the protocols with other school departments.

- Kelly will attend the next School Data Team meeting and other meetings that are schoolwide to gain perspectives outside the English department.

Potential Resources

What are some potential resources to recommend to the teacher that address their areas of needed growth from the direct and guide/coach quadrants?

- Share with Kelly district data and schoolwide data that may be interesting to her to broaden their perspective.

- Suggest the following books:

  » *The Handbook for Collaborative Common Assessments: Tools for Design, Delivery, and Data Analysis* by Cassandra Erkens

  » *The Big Book of Tools for Collaborative Teams in a PLC at Work* (2nd edition) by William M. Ferriter

Final Thoughts

What are your final thoughts about next steps and when to check back in?

Kelly is going to knock this out of the park. They are strong in assessment and evaluation in the classroom and now developing more of a schoolwide focus and looking to structure the department meetings to examine student work and data. A definite win/win that will help the school greatly and give Kelly valuable experience in leading a large initiative.

A GOAL SETTER WHO USES DATA IN ACTION: SCHOOL EXAMPLES

The following—annual learning plans, and significant 72 and community circles—are two examples of what it could look like to set goals and use data in your school. These examples show staff and the larger community that the school sees the importance of using data and setting goals. I share them here to provide leadership opportunities for staff you have identified and plotted in the leadership action matrix who require experiences for further development in setting goals and using data.

Annual Learning Plans

In Ontario, teachers are required to complete an annual learning plan (ALP), a goal-setting document that is part of the teacher performance appraisal in the province. Many schools and districts require staff to do some form of goal setting—or set goals for them—for professional development. These goals can have a profound impact on motivation, especially if staff set goals for themselves.

An ALP is a document teachers use to drive their decisions about learning goals for the year. In Ontario, a collective agreement with the teachers' union indicates goals cannot be given to teachers. A school administrator cannot mandate what the teacher should set as a goal because this aspect of the performance appraisal highlights the need for the teacher to create a goal based on personal wishes and aspirations. However, that does not mean there cannot be a supportive conversation with administration about the goals teachers have identified. Working with aspiring leaders was a golden opportunity each year to talk about their leadership journey and potential next steps.

In our school, the ALP process was transparent. I created a master document of the goals for every teacher. I highlighted common themes in goals, such as training in collaborative problem solving, mathematics instruction, inquiry, equity, technology, communication with families, documentation, and so on. I displayed the master document of goals prominently on the bulletin board in my office so that I could look for partnership and book study opportunities, and determine professional activity day content, staff meeting learning opportunities, and so on. When resources came into the school, I checked the list to match content with noted interests. For example, when the school board asked for a representative to attend a train-the-trainer session and then share resources and practices with others, I knew who to ask. When I was fortunate to receive a new resource through a conference or workshop, after I finished it, I knew who to give it to. After reading a professional journal or article, I knew who to share the information with. The teaching practices and goals that are a focus of the plans should be made public, however, so that teachers with a common focus can support each other, and those that are accomplished at the practice can offer assistance to those at are looking to develop (Fullan, 2014).

By using data from the ALP, staff meetings can become learning sessions where you can group staff with shared learning goals. This is also an opportunity for teachers who are future leaders to assist their peers and learn more in their area or areas of desired professional growth along the way.

Significant 72 and Community Circles

My mentor and colleague Tom Hierck introduced me to the significant 72 strategy. *Significant 72* refers to 72 hours, 72 minutes, and 72 seconds (Wolcott, 2019). In my school, we utilized the concept of significant 72 by focusing 72 minutes each month on real-time data from students on issues that were important to them and us to set goals and work toward the vision of the school we wanted to create.

When our school was formed, we established in our goal-setting and schoolwide plans three key indicators from the *School Effectiveness Framework* (Ontario Ministry of Education, 2013) to focus on. We were going to invest in relationships first.

1. **Indicator 2.5:** Staff, students, parents, and school community promote and sustain student well-being and positive student behavior in a safe, accepting, inclusive, and healthy learning environment (Ontario Ministry of Education, 2013).

2. **Indicator 3.3:** Students are partners in dialogue and discussions to inform programs and activities in the classroom and school that represent the diversity, needs, and interests of the student population (Ontario Ministry of Education, 2013).

3. **Indicator 6.2:** Students, parents, and community members are engaged and welcomed, as respected and valued partners in student learning (Ontario Ministry of Education, 2013).

Using these indicators to inform our Safe School Plan and our School Effectiveness Plan, we created yearly goals focusing on literacy, numeracy, and health and well-being.

The data we used for well-being goals came from staff, students, and community surveys. Our school and every school in the district conducted two schoolwide surveys each year. Typically, such surveys are conducted during a scheduled time in the year and data is then generated for staff use. These provide valuable information; however, we wanted faster and focused data from easier-to-administer tools. So, we connected this need for data to the significant 72 process.

Our staff were trained in how to effectively lead a community circle within their classroom. Each month, we asked teachers to hold a community circle meeting with their students during a large block of instructional time, which in our case could easily be 72 minutes, but in most cases was closer to an hour. Staff could hold more meetings in the month if they wished or when something happened in class that required restorative work or collaborative problem solving. As a leadership team, we wanted a defined community circle once a month to get valuable information from students and we called it significant 72 to align it with the 72 hours and minutes aspect of significant 72. Using this format for collecting student data provided us with the opportunity to make changes as needed rather than waiting until receiving data from formal surveys. Also, including students in this way helped students understand that their voices and opinions mattered.

Experts on staff instructed others on how to operate a community circle, how to set expectations for student input, and how to listen so that the strategy would run smoothly and effectively. Trained individuals took staff through the steps and volunteered to model how to run an effective class circle within a real classroom. These were the opportunities I would look for because they were authentic leadership practice for teachers thinking of moving into leadership roles and it was centered on an initiative that was valuable for students and staff as a whole.

Each community circle focused on a question of the month shared with teachers during staff development meetings. Staff then conducted a community circle meeting during the following week around the question and recorded student responses. Staff development meetings also included reviewing responses from the previous month, reviewing the data, and making changes to practice as needed. Some community circle questions include the following:

- How do your families hear about what you are doing or learning in school?

- How do we welcome new students into our classroom? What will we teach them and show them so they feel included, welcome, and safe?

- Are there places or spaces in our school or on school property where you do not feel safe?

- What do you see or notice the adults at our school doing to make the school a welcoming, safe place where you want to be?

- What opportunities would you like to see available in the school this year?

- What is your "recipe for recess"? If we are inside during breaks, what activities should you be allowed to do, and which materials should you be allowed to use?

Teachers had the freedom to adjust the question slightly to match the ages and stages of the students in their classroom. In addition to providing valuable data to make important changes or confirm what we were doing was working, this strategy also provided the opportunity for teachers to think outside their classroom and their particular roles. Teachers moving into administration will need to think of the school broadly and consider all grades and students of all ages. Having aspiring leaders involved in this initiative provides real insight into their leadership potential.

CONCLUSION

Using data to set goals and measure progress requires both skill and a passion for wanting to dig deeper to find answers to questions. Classroom teachers who are comfortable with collecting data, sharing it with others, and then using the data to make a positive difference in teaching and learning are well on their way to being an administrator who will do the same. Teachers who understand the human aspects of data—that there are real people connected to the scores and results they are analyzing—can make better decisions that do not involve using data as a weapon for shame and blame. When collected and analyzed properly, data brings important information to light.

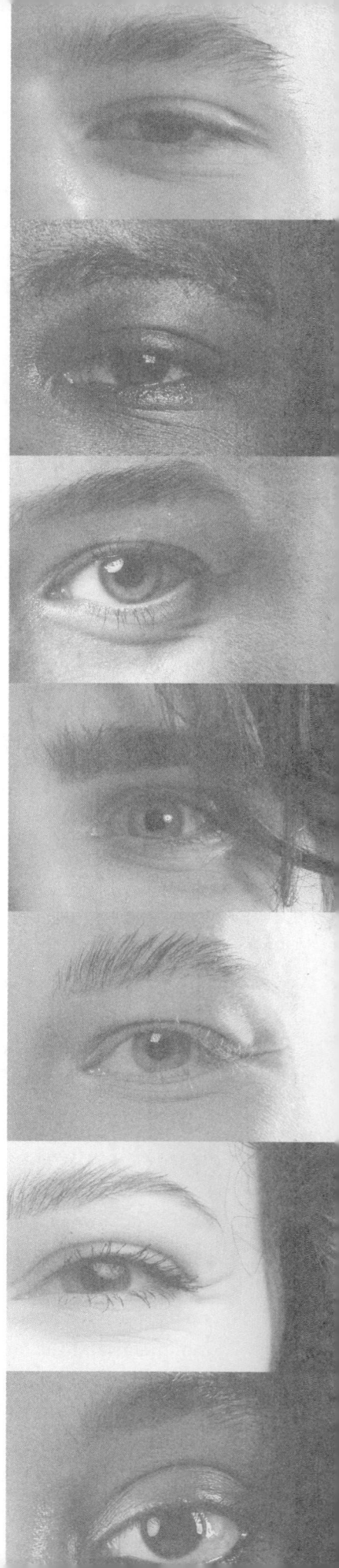

CHAPTER 6

INNOVATIVE

What does it mean to be innovative in education? Teachers are encouraged to use innovative instructional strategies. School leaders seek to find innovative methods to address challenges. Training programs and professional development offer innovative ways to streamline work for educators. Regardless of the focus, innovation is about doing things differently to improve outcomes (Ilomäki & Lakkala, 2018). Peter Serdyukov (2017) speaks of innovation as having two components: (1) an item or idea that is new or novel, followed by (2) a change that must occur because of the adoption of the object or idea. Therefore, introducing something new or novel for an individual, team, or the entire school in hopes of creating a positive difference is a key role for an administrator. Being an innovator in this context is as much about the process and getting others to follow as it is about the change itself. This is where the leadership comes in.

Robert J. Marzano, Timothy Waters, and Brian A. McNulty (2005) write about first- and second-order change when discussing school leaders driving for innovation. *First-order change* is incremental and in line with the current values of the school and the staff, whereas *second-order change* is driven by innovation and needs substantial change from current practices. This chapter explores the behaviors required for second-order change.

Innovative change within a system where a district rolls out training, materials, or resources often hits barriers based on lack of funds, not enough devices or inadequate technical support, and necessary repairs as reasons change did not take place long term. These are extrinsic factors and often limit the growth of first-order incremental change. Second-order change, however—the innovation this chapter discusses—is quite different. There is no time to wait for innovative change. Students only have one year in a particular grade. Some practices you might feel are harmful to student learning, and you know more effective ways to impact student learning. Substantial change can be held back because of intrinsic factors. Barriers to change occur because of staff beliefs, values, and discomfort in trying new things. Some staff members would rather continue operating the way things have always been done (Marzano, Waters, & McNulty, 2005). Administrators can reduce first-order barriers, but second-order barriers require administrators to be innovative—to challenge beliefs and practices and think deeply about what students are learning and doing.

Serdyukov (2017) explains that introducing something new or innovative into a classroom or in a school happens in three phases: the idea, implementation, and outcome.

1. **Idea:** An idea, tool, or resource is presented

2. **Implementation:** The new idea, tool, or resource is implemented

3. **Outcome:** A new way of operating has evolved that includes the innovation and results from implementation

Many who think of innovation think of the tools and programs that teachers use. In fact, although we do wish to advance teaching, we should actually be thinking about being innovative in order to improve learning. Innovation applies to any improvement in classroom practice and learning. Adjusting or changing a process to make things easier, more effective, more engaging or less stressful should, by definition, be considered an improvement rather than an innovation (Serdyukov, 2017); however, there's no need to get caught up in the distinction between an improvement and an innovation. Anything new to the school that has a significant impact and scale of change is innovative.

Allan M. Hoffman and John Holzhüter (2012) state that "Innovation resembles mutation, the biological process that keeps species evolving so they can better compete for survival" (p. 3). In schools, the outcome for innovation should always include improvement in student outcomes. Innovation in a school could include examination and change in methodologies, instructional tools, organizational structures, learning process, and teaching techniques.

As Serdyukov (2017) states, innovation can be directed to improve one or several aspects of teacher learning, school culture, teaching and learning, theory and practice, policy, technology, and curriculum, among others. School administrators can be innovative in their meeting structures, how they purchase and use resources, and how they budget. It can be in the way they organize and manage day-to-day operations. There are innovations in instructional techniques or the use of new technologies. A school can be innovative in how they welcome and organize students and families at arrival and dismissal times—the list goes on.

With innovation, new ideas, processes, and tools should be scalable, especially if they improve student learning. Teachers can demonstrate their creativity and innovation on their own, but to make a large-scale school impact, school leaders must find ways for innovators to share their talents and an opportunity for them to lead the change. Principal leadership has been shown to have a direct impact on the success of new initiatives. Change requires a belief among teachers that new methods, new ideas, and new tools will bring improvements to student outcomes, and these will be supported by their administration (Marzano, Waters, & McNulty, 2005).

The U.S. Department of Education (2024) recognizes the importance of innovation and requested funding amounting to 1.2 billion dollars to inspire state and local innovation. Within the budget is 269 million dollars for the following:

> The Education Innovation and Research program supports the creation, development implementation, replication, and scaling up of evidence-based, field-initiated innovations designed to improve student achievement and attainment for underserved students. The overall goal is to identify and support innovative and proven approaches that address persistent education challenges while also building knowledge of what works in education. (U.S. Department of Education, 2024, p. 14)

The Australian Institute for Teaching and School Leadership (2014) calls on current-day administrators to lead improvement, lead innovation, and lead change.

> Principals work with others to produce and implement clear, evidence-based improvement plans and policies for the development of the school and its facilities. They recognize that a crucial part of the role is to lead and manage innovation and change to ensure the vision and strategic plan is put into action across the school and that its goals and intentions are realized. (p. 16)

Not all staff members are innovators, so leaders must create a school community in which educators share knowledge and information about innovation. Leaders must be early adopters of innovation or be able to identify teachers or other staff members who can advocate for the innovation. Educators must understand that second-order change takes time and that there are barriers to second-order change. Innovation without concern for the process will be doomed to fail. For this reason, future leaders must understand how to do the following (Genlott, Grönlund, & Viberg, 2019).

- **Examine the quality of the innovation:** What does the research say? What will the innovation mean for students? Is there enough information and evidence to support the change? Does the state or province, district, or school board need to be involved in assessing the innovation?

- **Manage the process:** Who is doing the work? What are the timelines and budget? Are you meeting your key deadlines and check-in points? Is there follow through on commitments? How are you examining the process as it occurs?

- **Motivate staff:** Innovative leaders not only champion the idea, program, or resource; they also create an atmosphere that will allow for experimentation and collaboration (Genlott et al., 2019).

- **Communicate the vision:** School leaders understand that teacher learning to improve student outcomes is the driving factor for continuous improvement through innovation, and they communicate this vision to staff.

The second-order change that occurs when values and beliefs change can be accomplished with effective professional learning. It requires sustained attention and effort by the school administration if the innovation is to be adopted long term (Serdyukov, 2017). Implementing collaborative processes such as those advocated by the Professional Learning Communities (PLC) at Work® (DuFour, DuFour, Eaker, Many, Mattos, & Muhammad, 2024) are vital if school leaders want innovative practices to take hold in schools. School leaders must create the conditions for innovative ideas and for practices to multiply (Genlott et al., 2019).

Selecting who will attend professional learning sessions and who will share with staff the tools, activities, and ideas from their own classrooms needs to be done strategically. The content is important, but maybe more important is the messenger and how staff regard them. The most powerful learning and innovation occurs within the informal professional and personal relationships staff have with one another. Teachers are motivated to try new things, seek out new ideas, and look for change when they sense it will be good for their personal image. When teachers feel social support from their colleagues and administrators that innovative work is appreciated, innovation will flourish (Ilomaki & Lakkala, 2018).

When thinking about innovations in education, especially in the 21st century, technology is probably at the forefront. Technology has certainly been a driving force in schools. Many educators may become excited to grab the newest gadget and fit it into their classroom practice. It is up to administrators to help educators understand that just because a technological innovation is new, does not mean it will lead to better student learning. Innovative thinkers must be critical thinkers when implementing a new technology tool by examining how extensive and prominent the use of the technology is providing a better, more relevant learning experience. There is no stopping the revolution that is going on with technology in our classrooms. However, we must make sure that educational innovations embrace the complete child and ensure students are interacting with technology to enrich their learning experiences and provide better outcomes for all (Serdyukov, 2017).

Therefore, I think of those teachers who will become school leaders as the people who will innovate because it is necessary to create positive change for students. Students need constant innovation in the system in order to remain engaged in their learning, to move toward positive outcomes, and to be prepared for the world they will inherit.

KEY OBSERVABLE BEHAVIORS

Following are the behaviors that aspiring leaders who are innovative should exhibit. When rating a teacher in this way of being, think about the knowledge and skills involved with each behavior as well as the passion and motivation it requires. Consider providing the list of observable behaviors for this way of being to future leaders for self-evaluation and reflection prior to the mentoring planning meeting. (Visit **go.SolutionTree.com/leadership** for a free reproducible of this list.)

1. The teacher creates a classroom environment where students are involved in authentic and relevant learning, meaningful inquiry, and thinking outside the box. Creativity and self-directed learning are front and center.

2. The teacher has a strong leaning toward constructivist learning where students are active learners, not passive recipients of knowledge during teacher-dominated instruction.

3. The teacher sees the need for and seeks opportunities to grow their knowledge in information and communication technologies.

4. The teacher balances the use of technology in their classrooms and uses technology with purpose. They consider the tool, the task, and the amount of time that students are using technology.

5. The teacher uses a variety of teaching strategies. They interact and engage with students and the curriculum in a variety of ways and consider individual student needs.

6. The teacher provides a classroom where students are challenged and supported to take risks. They use positive language and have an encouraging attitude toward making mistakes, learning, and growing.

7. The teacher uses a variety of effective and appropriate resources that enhance learning for students. They find and work to acquire sufficient resources for all types of learners to support the curriculum.

8. The teacher helps students make connections that relate the learning to everyday life and students' prior knowledge. They challenge students to take what is known and consider possibilities.

9. The teacher works hard to find, learn about, and implement new teaching materials and techniques, and they adapt strategies for different classes and students. They find what is needed in the moment. They make in-year and in-time adjustments to look for new ways to assist students and bring to life the current unit of study.

10. The teacher has created a classroom learning environment where students use play, inquiry, and experiential learning to grow and reflect on their learning.

11. The teacher seeks out and shares new learning opportunities. They attend workshops, learning sessions, conferences, and so on. They are visibly engaged in their own professional learning.

12. The teacher reads professional journals and books. They visit reputable websites to learn. They look at research and policy. They share articles and resources related to education with peers.

13. The teacher takes on the leadership role of keeping students cyber safe by teaching students to use technology thoughtfully and responsibly.

14. The teacher understands that mistakes occur when trying new things. They therefore support student mistakes as a natural and valuable aspect of learning. These teachers have moved beyond only rewarding students for providing correct answers; they reward students for efforts and ideas. They have created a safe environment to take chances and fall short.

15. The teacher seeks out those who have more knowledge and information in areas that they do not, even if those individuals are less experienced educators. They are comfortable observing and being observed by other staff members to share and learn effective instructional strategies.

16. The teacher leads discussions and conversations and asks questions about the relative merits of new, current, or alternative practices. As a problem solver, they look for ways to be their best for each student.

17. The teacher suggests new ideas for staff learning. They encourage school leaders and others to try new practices or new ideas that align with the school's mission and goals.

18. The teacher stays current in the specific subject content. They evaluate and review their program for relevancy, looking for ways to increase student engagement and interest. They demonstrate their knowledge of research, trends, and new information relevant to their teaching assignment.

19. The teacher has developed and nurtured relationships with experts at other schools or at the district level.

20. The teacher looks for opportunities to integrate learning from their classroom with other subject disciplines.

SAMPLE TEACHER

This section presents an example using a fictional teacher and administrator. It shows the results when the administrator plots the future leader's observable behaviors from the way of being presented in this chapter; analyzes the data; plans the next steps; and conducts a meeting with the teacher.

Malik is a beginning teacher—within his first five years of teaching—who teaches ninth-grade mathematics. He is full of energy, smart, creative, and loves being in a classroom with students. Principal Bailey believes Malik should be a school leader one day as he is doing remarkable things within his classroom and is known to be innovative and engaging. Malik constantly seeks out new ideas, products, and resources and wants desperately to work with partners to provide a similar learning experience in other classrooms in the school. His enthusiasm and extroverted nature have caused some issues in the past with more traditional teachers in the school, so Malik is hesitant to work with those teachers as he is worried about how he is perceived. He has not come right out and said he is interested in administration, though Principal Bailey has shared that he should seriously consider it.

Step 1: Plot the Way of Being on the Leadership Action Matrix

Principal Bailey plots Malik's observable behaviors for the fifth way of being—an innovator—using the leadership action matrix. The results appear in figure 6.1.

Way of Being: Innovator

Administrator Name: Principal Bailey

Teacher Name: Malik Sample

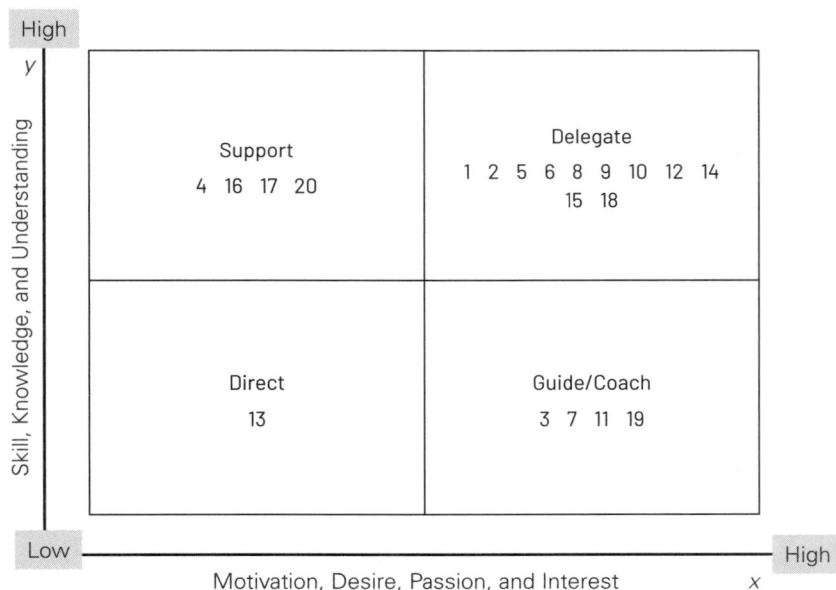

FIGURE 6.1: Malik's leadership action matrix for being innovative.

Step 2: Complete the Mentoring Planning Page

After plotting the observable behaviors for Malik on the leadership action matrix, Principal Bailey transfers the numbers to the mentoring planning page (see figure 6.2, page 98), adding comments about the behaviors she observed and her thoughts about the next steps. She bolds the items she wants to discuss further when she meets with Malik. Malik could use this tool for self-evaluation before the mentoring meeting as well.

Way of Being: Innovative

Teacher: Malik Sample

Administrator: Principal Bailey

Support		Delegate	
Behavior Number	**Notes**	**Behavior Number**	**Notes**
4	**Uses tech heavily. Is this heavy use always best for student learning? This is a good discussion topic since school administration is more traditional in tech use**	1	**Teaches content that is authentic and relevant using real-life math from students' world**
16	Has an innovative outlook in his classroom; would love to see him lead professional learning and development shoolwide	2	Ensures students are active learners by incorporating student interests and current events
17	Often discovers new strategies for instruction; should think about how to share or spread the knowledge	5	Shows evidence of differentiation for the variety of student needs in classroom
20	Focuses mostly on math; should look for opportunities for learning across subject disciplines	6	Uses encouraging words and positive comments about students' effort
		8	Uses real examples, such as from sports, business, and personal finance
		9	Uses new and differentiated strategies and often sources new and interesting materials
		10	Does a lot of exploring to find new and exciting opportunities for students
		12	Always seeking out new knowledge with wide, personal reading and a variety of interests; looks outside education for real-world connections
		14	Encourages experimentation and makes positive, uplifting comments
		15	Has a strong mentor relationship

		18	Continually updates program
			Recommendations for delegation: • **Participate in the Come on Over program**

Direct		Guide/Coach	
Behavior Number	**Notes**	**Behavior Number**	**Notes**
13	**Brings in new technology quickly without having it vetted; needs to consider board regulations on software and safe use and policies for students' personal information being entered and shared**	3	Shows that he is tech hungry as an early adopter; should check appropriateness of tech being used
		7	Always seeks effective and appropriate resources
		11	Wants professional development and to work with others. Seeks these out on his own.
		19	**Wants to identify other professionals or experts doing similar things in the classroom**

FIGURE 6.2: Sample mentoring planning page for Malik for being innovative.

Following are explanations of some of Principal Bailey's ratings for Malik and her rationale.

Behavior 13: *The teacher takes on the leadership role of keeping students cyber safe by teaching students to use technology thoughtfully and responsibly.*

Principal Bailey placed behavior thirteen in the direct quadrant because Malik is quick to bring new software and programs into his classroom without first checking that the technology is approved for use and meets the standards of confidentiality set out by the board of education. In his rush to be innovative and engage with students, he is not thinking of the big picture, which could cause significant problems in the future. For this reason, Malik is considered both low in skill and interest in this area. Principal Bailey will work directly with Malik to identify relevant policies and procedures.

Behavior 4: *The teacher balances the use of technology in their classrooms. They consider the tool, the task, and the amount of time that students are using technology. They notice effective use of technology that benefits student outcomes, so technology is used with purpose.*

Principal Bailey placed behavior four in the support quadrant because while Malik has great knowledge and skills with technology, Principal Bailey wants to be sure his motivation and desire to use the technology aligns with what is best for students. Principal Bailey observed Malik using lots of technology in his classroom but is uncertain if it is being used with a purpose. The fear is that the tool is the attraction and Malik is losing sight of the important teaching that must occur. Principal Bailey is concerned, however, that she may be too traditional about technology and will invite Malik to have a deeper conversation about his technology use to balance his interest in using technology while still focusing on effective pedagogy. Malik's knowledge and skills are strong, so Principal Bailey wants to find out more while supporting Malik's passion for teaching and technology.

Behavior 19: *The teacher has developed and nurtured relationships with experts at other schools or at the district level.*

Principal Bailey placed behavior nineteen in the guide/coach quadrant because Malik is high in motivation but lower in knowledge and needs assistance. Malik is an excellent candidate for guiding and coaching because he has expressed interest in learning more and working with others who have similar passions and interests. He does not see the same level of innovation in his own school and wants to reach out to others. Principal Bailey will assist with this by reaching out to other school leaders to find teachers with a similar high passion for teaching in a style similar to Malik. Possibly Malik can organize an online meeting group if face-to-face meetings are difficult to coordinate.

Behavior 1: *The teacher creates a classroom environment where students are involved in learning that is authentic and relevant and they engage in meaningful inquiry. Students are challenged to think outside the box, and creativity and self-directed learning are front and center.*

Principal Bailey placed behavior one in the delegate quadrant because Malik is both high in knowledge and high in passion and interest. Malik's students are highly engaged, involved in their learning, and using mathematics in real-world contexts. Principal Bailey will have some challenging conversations with Malik about some other behaviors, so delegating with behavior one reinforces Malik's extremely positive qualities. Principal Bailey has written, "Come on Over" (described later in this chapter in the school example section on page 103) as an activity she thinks would help Malik with his connections to staff as well as provide a worthwhile activity for other staff and students. Principal Bailey will discuss a modified example of Come on Over and suggest that Malik work with the ninth-grade English and science teachers to create a cross-discipline learning unit for students. Delegating this responsibility to Malik will give him practical experience working with other staff in an area of great passion prior to beginning his administrative role. Working with others is an innovative second-order change where staff examine their beliefs, values, and comfort with innovations so that change can happen. Principal Bailey hopes Malik can become the type of innovative administrator who can overcome second-order change barriers. This opportunity gives Malik the chance to work with others to challenge beliefs and practices and think deeply about what students are learning and doing.

Step 3: Use the Mentoring Meeting Planner

Principal Bailey fills in most of the information on the mentoring meeting planner tool in preparation for her meeting with Malik. Figure 6.3 shows the completed mentoring meeting planner including notes from the meeting.

Date: April 18

Administrator: Principal Bailey

Teacher: Malik Sample

Focus

Which way or ways of being will we discuss?

Innovator. Discuss what innovation in education means—the importance of adopting change and having others on board—and why it is important as a school administrator to champion the use of innovation as teaching practice. Ask Malik for input.

Agenda for Sharing and Discussion

- What specific points about the way or ways of being will we discuss?
- Discuss the many positives about Malik's classroom program and student engagement.
- Discuss the need to be well rounded in many aspects of leadership.
- Find out Malik's perspective on his strengths and needs in this way of being.
- Discuss notes from the twenty observable behaviors.
- Discuss notes from the mentoring planning page.

Key Points

For each of the following sections, list the bolded or circled items from the mentoring planning page.

- **Direct**
  - » It is important not to use every type of technology you find just because you can. It is necessary to determine board regulations on software and safe use and understand policies in relation to student personal information being entered and shared.
- **Support**
  - » Classes are tech heavy. Is this degree of technology use justified for the learning? Maybe I am too traditional, so this will be a good discussion topic for us.
  - » Would love to see you lead professional learning or professional development experiences to share the magic happening in your classroom.
- **Guide/Coach**
  - » Malik wants professional development opportunities and to work with others. He currently does a lot of professional learning on his own.
  - » Help Malik find other professionals doing similar things in the district or beyond.
- **Delegate**
  - » Get Mailk involved in the Come on Over program.

FIGURE 6.3: Sample mentoring meeting planner for Malik for being an innovator.

continued ▶

Teacher Plans, Comments, and Ideas

- What plans, comments, and ideas did the teacher have during the meeting?
- Malik is not interested in leading any schoolwide professional development or having others come into his classroom to observe at this point.
- Malik bookmarked the board policy, during the meeting, regarding appropriate software use and has been given the contact information of the board leader responsible for student freedom of information and cyber safety. He will check all resources he wants to use in class.
- Malik wants to show he is following policy. He is concerned about how others view him not having followed policy.
- Malik has invited administration to visit his classroom to see what students are doing with technology and discuss at any time the teaching behind the innovation.
- Malik would love to be in contact with other teachers from other schools doing similar things with instruction and technology.
- Malik wants to work with ninth-grade English and science teachers to develop a cross-discipline unit and has requested release time to begin planning.

Goal Setting

What is the teacher's goal related to this way of being?

- Malik will report back to the office the next time he introduces new technology into the classroom and the process he used to determine its compliance with policy.
- Malik will organize a few students to come to the office to demonstrate some of the programs they are using in the classroom. This is so the principal can see from a student perspective what they are learning with the tools. Malik will set up a schedule with students and get suggestions from them on what they would like to share.
- Malik will set up a learning group with teachers from other schools once he receives names from the principal. He will also share what he is learning with the principal and invite her to observe the learning taking place.
- Malik will be provided with time during the next staff learning day to work with the other ninth-grade staff to begin to develop an integrated cross-discipline unit of study. The team will share their work during the last half hour of the day with school administration.

Potential Resources

What are some potential resources to recommend to the teacher that address their areas of needed growth from the direct and guide/coach quadrants?

- Connect Malik with district leadership responsible for Freedom of Information/Information Technology/Safe Use of Technology.
- Suggest the following book:
  - » *Mathematics Unit Planning in a PLC at Work, High School* by Sarah Schuhl, Timothy D. Kanold, Bill Barnes, Darshan M. Jain, Matthew R. Larson, and Brittany Mozingo

Final Thoughts

What are your final thoughts about next steps and when to check back in?

Malik is full of energy and his classroom reflects this. He has great potential as a future leader. Closely monitor his work with teams to support him working with others. Continue to encourage his talents so he becomes more comfortable sharing. Work toward having him lead teams of colleagues.

BEING INNOVATIVE IN ACTION: SCHOOL EXAMPLES

The following—Come on Over and Shared Professional Library—are two examples of what being an innovator could look like in your school. I share them here to provide leadership opportunities for staff you have identified and plotted in the leadership action matrix who require experiences for further development in innovation. These examples also show staff and the larger community that the school values innovation and understands the importance of this behavior.

Come on Over

Come On Over is a districtwide program we created for schools to show off their innovations. The program invites individual schools to open their doors at the end of the school day during a designated week so that administrators from different locations can drop in on another school in their area. There was no formal presentation. Rather, school leaders would be available to share school goals, speak about what their school community valued, answer questions, and so on.

Most of the time during the program was spent with visitors wandering the school to see highlighted facilities and innovations. As educators, we know we can learn a lot about what is important and what a school emphasizes by having a look around. As Peter Serdyukov (2017) shares, innovation can be thought of as two parts. In the first part, a person is thinking about, developing, or introduced to an item or idea that is new or novel. The second part is when a change occurs. Our plan was to have school leaders witness something they have never seen before, ask questions about it, dig deeper, and then consider adopting it at their school.

The visiting leader may notice how the school is welcoming for parents and community members by how they have set up their front entrance and office area. They would travel into specialized rooms like the theatre, the technology room, shops, and science labs to look at equipment and learn what projects students were involved in. We wanted leaders to become curious and use this experience to consider a wide variety of ideas.

Teacher leaders in your building can answer questions as guests observe. This program is also an excellent opportunity for your teachers to meet other leaders in the system and begin to connect and network, to assist struggling teachers in another location, or to create mentoring opportunities. Malik, the sample teacher featured earlier in this chapter, would be an excellent teacher to include in the come on over program because of his innovative use of technology in the classroom.

Some schools created an opportunity for student leadership by having tour guides to walk administrators through the school. The administrators always appreciated hearing about the school from a student perspective, and the students were proud to speak about their schools. We quickly realized we have much that we can learn from each other. It was common for administrators to take photos of innovations they saw and wanted to incorporate in their own school.

Shared Professional Library

Building a shared professional library is an innovative idea that exposes staff members to new learning, which has the potential to positively impact student learning. Include a wide variety of resources so teachers and future leaders can make individual decisions about what they want to read and research. I have always noticed that when staff discover something new to them, an innovation, and they invest in learning more about it, there is a very good chance they will implement it in their classroom. In my experience leading teachers, I often found that teachers learned about a teaching practice, program, or initiative from a wide variety of sources. School leaders have an obligation to make sure teachers are being influenced by the most beneficial materials backed by current research and best practice. Allow staff to select professional learning resources that are going to benefit them and the students in your school. By doing so, you can increase the number and quality of professional resources in your school and the collaborative learning opportunities your staff organizes. Introducing new resources into your school is innovation.

My school had a section in the school library devoted to professional resources for staff. I began the shared library by including some of my favorite resources—books that I had on my shelf that I use often and have had an influence on me as an educator. We sought input from staff who we encouraged to submit a request for any resource they wanted. Teachers simply shared a link to a resource or the name of a book. I investigated to make sure the resource was from a reliable and trusted source. If necessary, I reached out to colleagues at the central office or elsewhere to determine if the resource aligned with the school and district's mission and vision. If your district requires teachers to complete an annual learning plan (ALP), include in the library any resources teachers reference there and any resources that support areas of development teachers' desire. When a staff member requests a resource, investigate to make sure the resource is from a reliable and trusted source. If necessary, reach out to colleagues at the central office or elsewhere to determine if the resource aligns with the school and district's mission and vision.

I created an expense line in our school budget to purchase books for the library. If the books were requested by a specific teacher, I included a note in the book with the teacher's name on it and the date ("This book was presented to staff by [name] in April 2024."). I would then purchase two copies of the book: one for the teacher to keep and one copy for the professional learning library. The book then went into the professional learning library. Administrators mentor and support teachers to one day become school leaders. As you notice the strengths and talents of your staff members, ask them where they gained their expertise. Are their books and resources that they have used? Have them be some of the first to participate in the initiative to get a professional library started in your school. Use the brilliance in your building to power up the professional reference section of your library.

CONCLUSION

Innovation introduces something new or different in the hopes that it will lead to better outcomes. No one is better positioned within the school to support innovation than the school leader. School leaders are a wealth of knowledge—they bring with them good ideas from their professional experiences, innovations they learn from colleagues, and new research and findings from district, state, or provincial sources. In addition, school leaders are uniquely positioned to see what innovations are working in a school and which teachers are implementing innovations with the most positive impact. School leaders have access to the budget and resources to bring in and introduce new programs, strategies, technology, initiatives, and ideas. Most importantly, school leaders are in a position to support second-order change. As Robert Marzano and colleagues (2005) share, second-order change requires a change in the people involved. For values, beliefs, thoughts, and actions to change, the people being introduced to the innovation must see the value of the change. Future leaders are capable of this "people work" to convert innovative initiatives into second-order change.

CHAPTER 7

KNOWLEDGEABLE OF EFFECTIVE TEACHING

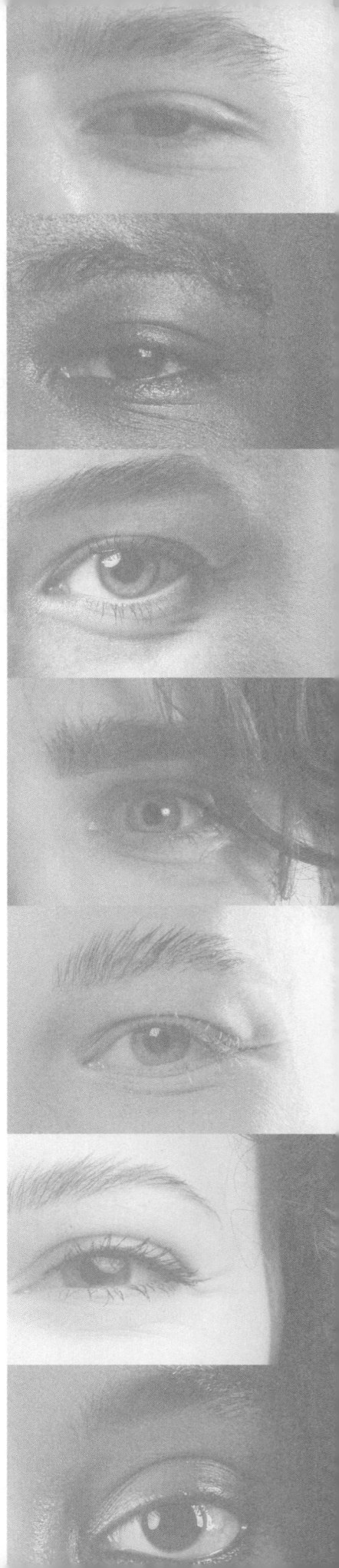

Earlier in this book, I asked you to picture a leader who has had a profound impact on you. Now, I want you to consider the best teachers you have come across in your experience and career. Who would you cast in a movie to illustrate to the world what effective teaching looks like and sounds like? Whose classroom would you want your own children, friends, or family members to spend time in? Which teachers fill you with hope knowing the difference they make in the life of students?

You might wonder: These teachers do extraordinary work in the classroom; doesn't it make sense for them to stay there where they can continue to work their magic? Research finds that principals who were the most effective teachers create higher achievement growth in their students when they become administrators (Goldhaber, Holden, & Chen, 2019). In addition, the best administrators are knowledgeable about learning conditions—the individual classroom and schoolwide factors that impact students (Leithwood, 2012)—and they have to know how to lead and develop effective instruction in others. Understanding what effective teaching looks like and creating the climate for that to happen enables others to develop to the point where there are schools full of teachers who are leaders in instruction (Fullan, 2014). The time spent by administrators directly coaching teachers on how they could improve their instruction and support student outcomes correlates positively with school improvement overall and with achievement gains by students—especially in urban and hard-to-serve locations (Donley, Detrich, States, & Keyworth, 2020; Grissom, Loeb, & Master, 2013).

In *Qualities of Effective Teachers*, James H. Stronge (2018) presents nine areas to consider when evaluating the effectiveness of teachers: professional knowledge, instructional planning, instructional delivery, assessment, learning environment, professionalism, dedication, reflective practice, and personal effectiveness. There is a positive association between a teacher's content knowledge and student learning at every grade level (Stronge, 2018). However, content knowledge is not sufficient on its own for teachers to be knowledgeable about effective teaching. The best teachers have subject knowledge, but they also understand how students learn. They utilize practices and skills that increase learning and can model, influence, and bring out the knowledge, skills, and passion in others. Importantly, the best teachers can translate their knowledge into improved student outcomes. To do this they must understand the context in which they work—the students they are teaching, their capabilities, their cultures, their interests, and more.

In my experience, our teachers who moved into administrative positions often began by taking on managerial tasks; however, it seems like an ineffective strategy to have the best teachers become school leaders and then not have an impact on instruction. Instructional leadership that begins in the assistant principal role, especially if the assistant principal is skilled with coaching and knowledge of effective teaching, will increase student achievement (Goldring, Rubin, & Herrmann, 2021).

Research does caution administrators from leaving the classroom too soon. Those who move into a leadership role within five years of teaching have less ability to understand, perform, and be successful as instructional leaders. They may not have the skills, knowledge, expertise, experience, or confidence to act as leaders who understand effective teaching—especially if working with older and more experienced teachers (Oleszewski et al., 2012).

A teacher who is knowledgeable of effective teaching can have a significant influence when given the opportunity to lead. The influence on student learning is different, however, with school leaders having an indirect influence on students in comparison to the more direct influence of teachers. Teachers are focused on one grade level, subject, or area whereas school leaders are focused on effective teaching across all grades. A dedicated push to improve the overall quality of teaching within the entire school is the goal of all effective administrators. To do this, leaders must be knowledgeable of effective teaching.

KEY OBSERVABLE BEHAVIORS

Following are the behaviors that aspiring leaders who are knowledgeable of effective teaching should exhibit. When rating a teacher in this way of being, think about the knowledge and skills involved with each behavior as well as the passion and motivation it requires. Consider providing the list of observable behaviors for this way of being to future leaders for self-evaluation and reflection prior to the mentoring planning meeting. (Visit **go.SolutionTree.com/leadership** for a free reproducible of this list.)

1. The teacher demonstrates profound assessment literacy, understanding that assessment must be connected to the curriculum. They understand the best assessment materials are developed collaboratively using common formative assessment as a major feature of their programs. They use assessment to inform the next steps in their instruction. They use assessment data in planning and show a clear connection between individual student assessment results and classroom lessons.

2. The teacher works with students to build a common understanding of what students are learning. They identify, share, and clarify learning goals

and success criteria with student involvement. They also communicate learning intentions and objectives with parents.

3. The teacher continually provides students with timely, ongoing, descriptive feedback about their progress.

4. The teacher takes action when students are not learning. They become curious, seek help, look for answers and possible solutions, and initiate the next steps when students struggle. They do not make excuses or cast blame on students.

5. The teacher effectively differentiates instruction so students can access all parts of the curriculum. They demonstrate this through their unit planning, daily lessons, instructional groupings, instructional strategies, reteaching plans, and accommodations to the program and the assessment.

6. The teacher shapes their instruction for students who learn in a variety of ways to the ages and stages of students. When one method of instruction does not work, they look for other ways to assist learners. Their constant response to student assessment feedback is directed at meeting individual needs.

7. The teacher carefully frames the context of the lesson by sharing how the content is relevant and important. They review concepts from the previous day's work. They build interest and motivation by providing a challenge or hook to increase student engagement. They utilize a variety of questioning techniques. They speak well in the classroom and use their voice to create interest and understanding. They make learning exciting.

8. The teacher has created with students a classroom environment that maximizes learning. They have structured their classroom so learning can begin quickly and easily. Students have learned the flow of the day or class, know where to find materials, and have developed structures and routines so learning can happen.

9. The teacher has created an environment of active and student-centered learning. When ready, students have appropriate opportunities for independent practice of new skills as well as working in flexible groupings with every student in their class.

10. The teacher has an extensive knowledge of the subject matter. They know the expected curriculum and have worked with others to identify essential outcomes and the learning expectations from their district or area. They use the curriculum, board guidelines, and documents to guide

their program. They are aware of the best and most current materials and resources that support student learning.

11. The teacher demonstrates a wide variety of teaching practices. They are aware of the research on effective practices and highly regarded teaching strategies and use them to move students to achieve outcomes. They use classroom data to create homogeneous instructional groups so students can receive just-in-time instruction.

12. The teacher manages a classroom where disruptions to the program are infrequent. They value instructional time. They effectively organize the instructional time by providing for the needs of all students. They use class time in a focused, purposeful way.

13. The teacher is proactive in developing classroom commitments and expectations for behavior. Together with students, they establish and maintain a positive classroom culture. The teacher works with the class to develop conflict resolution and problem-solving strategies to establish and maintain positive relationships. Students see themselves reflected in the classroom and have a sense of belonging.

14. The teacher knows their students' interests and dreams. They take advantage of data in all its forms and turn it into useful information and instructional actions.

15. The teacher has frequent conversations with and observes other teachers. They continually acquire best practices and effectively apply new information and techniques to enhance their own teaching. They create relationships with others where they are invited into classrooms and provide constructive feedback that is useful to others. They have become mentors for younger, inexperienced teachers.

16. The teacher uses their knowledge and experience about teaching and students to be flexible and adapt when necessary. They take lessons in a different direction or at a different pace based on feedback they are receiving from students. They make decisions in the moment that are required to pause, refresh, take a break, have some fun, and look after students when needed.

17. The teacher demonstrates the importance of continuous learning through engagement in their own professional learning. They read, attend learning sessions, and incorporate changes in their instructional practices if it will benefit students.

18. The teacher continually demonstrates competence when interacting with students by providing the appropriate response. They recognize when

students are upset and comfort them. When students are angry, they listen and problem solve. When students are proud, they celebrate.

19. The teacher shares their classroom with families. They have created a class community where parents are welcome, respected, and valued as partners in their children's learning.

20. The teacher learns with and from other excellent educators. They maintain connections with expert school and district leaders. They are knowledgeable about big-picture items such as policy and procedures. They keep abreast of changes and challenges in education.

SAMPLE TEACHER

This section presents an example using a fictional teacher and administrator. It shows the results when the administrator plots the future leader's observable behaviors from the way of being presented in this chapter; analyzes the data; plans the next steps; and conducts a meeting with the teacher.

Mike is a second-grade teacher who is new to the school after working as an instructional coach in literacy and traveling to many schools throughout the district to support teachers. He has come back to work in a school to move into administration, getting back into the classroom for a few years prior to becoming an assistant principal. He is extremely skilled, and Principal Williams knows Mike will have little difficulty moving forward. It is still early in the school year, and Mike is becoming established on the staff and in the community. The staff knows Mike since he supported some of the teachers in the past with their literacy program; some staff are somewhat intimidated by his knowledge and expertise in teaching. He is quick to establish relationships and is joining a large second-grade team, and so far the staff is getting along well. For being knowledgeable about effective teaching, Principal Williams knows Mike would not have been hired for a district position if he did not already have a strong knowledge of effective teaching; Williams is, therefore, using this way of being as a starting point for their mentoring relationship and to also build Mike's knowledge of effective mathematics instruction. Part of mentoring conversations will focus on how to move Mike forward into other ways of being as the school year progresses.

Step 1: Plot the Way of Being on the Leadership Action Matrix

Principal Williams plots Mike's observable behaviors for the sixth way of being—knowledgeable about effective teaching—using the leadership action matrix. The results appear in figure 7.1 (page 112).

Way of Being: Knowledgeable of Effective Teaching

Administrator Name: Principal Williams

Teacher Name: Mike Sample

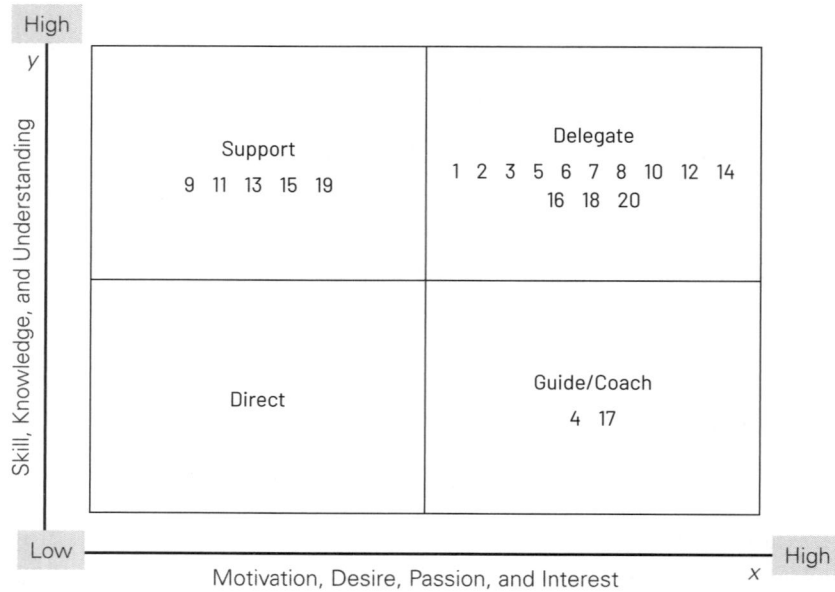

FIGURE 7.1: Mike's leadership action matrix for knowledgeable of effective teaching.

Step 2: Complete the Mentoring Planning Page

After plotting the observable behaviors for Mike on the leadership action matrix, Principal Williams transfers the numbers to the mentoring planning page (see figure 7.2), adding comments about the behaviors she observed and her thoughts about the next steps. She bolds the items she wants to further discuss when she meets with Mike. Mike could use this tool for self-evaluation before the mentoring planning meeting as well.

Way of Being: Knowledgeable of Effective Teaching

Teacher: Mike Sample

Administrator: Principal Williams

Support		Delegate	
Behavior Number	**Notes**	**Behavior Number**	**Notes**
9	Uses a lot of teacher-led learning instead of student led; would like to see more student-centered learning, but it is still early in the year and students are learning routine	1	Has strong assessment skills, a lot of plans, assessments, and essential outcomes
11	**Does not use small-group instruction in mathematics as much as in other subjects**	2	Displays learning goals with every lesson; makes sure students know learning goals

13	Has not shown evidence if or how he works with students to develop expectations; should discuss this	3	Uses success criteria charts in class that are developed with students
15	Has much to share with other staff, and they know his strengths; must determine how to increase staff comfort with him	5	Differentiates literacy instruction in particular
19	Has communication with families; was it successful at the start of the school year?	6	Has a real understanding of primary-age student abilities and offers a lot of variety of appropriate instruction
		7	Makes learning exciting and builds interest
		8	**Has a beautiful classroom set up that maximizes learning; should be shared with other staff—set up an internal field trip**
		10	Has extensive knowledge as a literacy specialist, held board and district positions in literacy; needs to acquire skills in mathematics as well
		12	Manages classroom well without much lost time and has quick transitions
		14	Learning student names and interests quickly; uses significant 72 strategy from start of the year
		16	Excellent lesson flow and instructional agility
		18	Cares for and supports students
		20	Has many connections with other schools and board staff
			Recommendations for delegation: • **Staff meeting coaching and internal field trips**

FIGURE 7.2: Sample mentoring planning page for Mike for knowledgeable of effective teaching.

continued ▶

Direct		Guide/Coach	
Behavior Number	Notes	Behavior Number	Notes
		4	Needs to learn school process for student support—the Tier 1, 2, and 3 interventions plan for this school
		17	**Has reached out for professional learning; has strong content and is knowledgeable in literacy—looking for resources in mathematics instruction and leadership**

Following are explanations of some of Principal Williams' ratings for Mike and the rationale for them.

Principal Williams has not placed any behaviors in the direct quadrant because based on her observations of Mike, she has determined that there are no observable behaviors that demonstrate that Mike is lacking knowledge and motivation or interest in becoming knowledgeable of effective teaching. This is a way of being for Mike that is a strength, and Principal Williams can see a bright future for Mike as an instructional leader. He is both knowledgeable and passionate about teaching and has much to share. Principal Williams still wants to ask some questions and get to know Mike's program better but realizes that it will be in other ways of being that she will spend her time preparing Mike for an administrator role.

Behavior 11: *The teacher demonstrates a wide variety of teaching practices. They are aware of the research on effective practices and highly regarded teaching strategies and use them to move students to achieve outcomes. They make excellent use of small-group instruction and have created a classroom where students can work independently at times so the teacher can pull small groups to an area of the room to work on needed skills at the students' current instructional level. They use classroom data to create these homogeneous instructional groups so students can receive just-in-time instruction.*

Principal Williams knew before Mike arrived at the school that he was an expert in assessment, evaluation, and literacy instruction. Mike spent years in a district office position coaching teachers in effective literacy instruction. Literacy is a major focus in his classroom, and it is clear how he integrates literacy knowledge into the instruction of other subjects, such as social studies and science. Recently, Mike's passion and desire to focus attention on all subject areas, mathematics in particular, has increased. Principal Williams added behavior eleven in the support quadrant (high knowledge/skill, low motivation) because Mike's knowledge of effective teaching is strong and his passion for literacy is extremely high. Principal Williams would like to support Mike in adding mathematics instruction to his already high skill set. She wants to be careful, however, with how this is phrased because she does not want Mike to believe there is any concern about his overall motivation or desire to be an effective teacher. Principal Williams simply wants to make the point of using Mike's knowledge and passion for literacy to motivate him to develop in his mathematics instruction.

Behavior 17: *The teacher demonstrates the importance of continuous learning through engagement in their own professional learning. They read, attend learning sessions, and incorporate changes in their instructional practices if they feel it will benefit students.*

Principal Williams placed behavior seventeen in the guide/coach quadrant because Mike is high in motivation but lower in knowledge. Principal Williams had difficulty deciding exactly where to place this observable behavior because of the broad teaching responsibilities of a primary teacher. Early grade teachers are responsible for all subject areas. Early in the year, Principal Williams discussed mathematics with Mike because she knew others on staff could assist him with his mathematics program. Principal Williams knows how Mike will benefit the school with assessment and evaluation in literacy; Mike's declaration that he wants to branch out from a singular focus on literacy is relatively new, as a similar observable behavior is also noted in the support quadrant focusing on mathematics. Regardless of what quadrant the behavior number is in, mentoring for Mike will remain the same. Principal Williams will guide Mike to resources to help develop his mathematics program and coach him on how to work with others in a school setting using his incredible knowledge of assessment, evaluation, and literacy. Mike's interest in learning is strong, and his desire to become an administrator is public, so Principal Williams will guide and coach Mike to develop the skills and knowledge he desires.

Behavior 8: *The teacher has created with students a classroom environment that maximizes learning. They have structured their classroom so learning can begin quickly and easily. Students have learned the flow of the day or class, know where to find materials, and have developed structures and routines so learning can happen.*

Principal Williams put behavior eight in the delegate quadrant because Mike is both high in knowledge and high in passion and interest. Mike has a classroom setup and arrangement that works for students and himself. The design and flow allow students to find materials quickly and start on a task. There are areas in the classroom for both large- and small-group instruction. Mike displays work samples and cocreated success criteria charts that students can reference to improve their work. The classroom is inviting, and students feel safe and comfortable inside. Principal Williams would like to have other teachers in the school see how the room is set up and have Mike speak about how he has been intentional in its design. During an upcoming staff learning day, teachers are going on an "internal field trip" to visit Mike's classroom (see page 120 to learn more about this strategy). The delegate quadrant allows the administrator to share all the extremely positive qualities Mike possesses and celebrate his abilities, particularly in literacy instruction. Delegating responsibilities to Mike, such as staff meeting coaching and the internal field trip, will provide Mike with some practical experience working with staff before beginning an administrator role.

STEP 3: USE THE MENTORING MEETING PLANNER

Principal Williams fills in most of the information on the mentoring meeting planner tool in preparation for her meeting with Mike. Figure 7.3 shows the completed mentoring meeting planner including notes from the meeting.

Date: November 5

Administrator: Principal Williams

Teacher: Mike Sample

Focus

Which way or ways of being will we discuss?

Knowledge of Effective Teaching. Discuss what it means to be knowledgeable of effective teaching and why it is important as a school administrator that you are knowledgeable about effective teaching in all subject areas. Draw on Mike's experience in his system role and ask about his experiences with coaching and mentoring teachers. Share positives about his literacy knowledge and discuss the need for mathematics and other subject areas having an increased focus this year. Ask Mike for input.

Agenda for Sharing and Discussion

What specific points about the way or ways of being will we discuss?

- Discuss many of the positives about Mike's classroom environment and relationships with students.
- Discuss the need to be well-rounded in many aspects of leadership.
- Find out Mike's perspective on his strengths and needs in this way of being.
- Discuss notes from the twenty observable behaviors.
- Discuss notes from the mentoring planning page.

Key Points

- **Support**
  - » Mike is excellent with small-group instruction in literacy; he should use small-group instruction in mathematics as well.
- **Guide/Coach**
  - » Mike wants to learn more. He has reached out, has strong content, is knowledgeable in literacy, and is looking for resources in mathematics instruction and leadership.
  - » Mike needs to learn school processes for student support—the Tier 1, 2, and 3 intervention plan.
- **Delegate**
  - » Mike has a beautiful classroom set up, which he should share with others. Organize an internal field trip to his classroom.
  - » Mike has potential to be a coach at staff meetings.

Teacher Plans, Comments, and Ideas

What plans, comments, and ideas did the teacher have during the meeting?

- Mike is excited to be back in the classroom and is positive about the start the students have had in his class.
- Mike knows he has a lot to learn since being out of the classroom for so long.
- Mike knows he focuses on literacy in his program and this is beneficial for primary-aged students. He also acknowledges his training in assessment and evaluation from his previous role could help others on staff.
- Mike wants to move carefully to integrate himself into the staff. He does not want to come across as an expert, but he does have a lot to share and has noticed that his skillset could assist in some areas of the school.
- Mike wants to balance what he can bring to the school with what he needs to learn from others.

- Mike is comfortable presenting on literacy, assessment, and evaluation at any time, but he has asked that there is an equal opportunity for him to be a participant. He is aware of his reputation with staff and does not want to come across in a negative way based on his experience.
- Mike wants feedback on how to navigate being knowledgeable and being a colleague with other staff members.

Goal Setting

What is the teacher's goal related to this way of being?

- Mike will present at staff meetings on literacy and assessment and evaluation, and be a participant in mathematics-focused professional development if there is an opportunity for him to do so.
- Mike will reach out to his colleagues at the district office to find out about the learning opportunities available to primary teachers in mathematics and sign up for as many as he can. Mike wants to go with another team partner each time so he can learn alongside others, and so they see he is not an expert in the area.
- Mike will participate in the internal field trip by sharing his classroom and how it functions for students.
- Mike will use this year to round out his knowledge in other subject areas and then would like to pursue an administration position the following year.

Potential Resources

What are some potential resources to recommend to the teacher that address their areas of needed growth from the direct and guide/coach quadrants?

- Mike has connections at the district office and will reach out for mathematics instructional resources and professional learning opportunities.
- Mike will work with Principal Williams through the other ways of being to identify areas for growth and delegation.
- Administration will purchase the book *Making Sense of Mathematics for Teaching the Small Group* by Juli K. Dixon, Lisa A. Brooks, and Melissa R. Carli.

Final Thoughts

What are your final thoughts about the next steps and when to check back in?

Mike is ready for administration. Taking time to return to the classroom is a wise decision to get a view from inside the school of teaching and administrative roles. In his previous district role, he did not really consider school administration, but now that it is a goal and a focus, he can use this year to concentrate on what it will take. He is interested in working through the other ways of being. He is concerned about how he comes across as a new staff member and wants to fit in and be accepted. At the same time, he does see some practices that concern him from other staff. We will have a lot of discussion on how to move staff without putting Mike in an uncomfortable position as a teacher colleague. His expertise will serve him well when he becomes an administrator. This is a good year to consider the people skills involved when an administrator has teachers examine their practice.

FIGURE 7.3: Sample mentoring meeting planner for Mike for knowledgeable of effective teaching.

KNOWLEDGEABLE OF EFFECTIVE TEACHING IN ACTION: SCHOOL EXAMPLES

The following—staff meetings reconsidered and an internal field trip—are two examples of what being knowledgeable of effective teaching could look like in your school. I share them here to provide leadership opportunities for staff you have identified and plotted in the leadership action matrix who require experiences for further development in this way of being.

These examples also show staff and the larger community that the school understands the importance of being knowledgeable about effective teaching.

Staff Meetings Reconsidered

When *The Ontario Leadership Framework* (Leithwood, 2012) was first published, one of the domains for effective administrators was "Lead the Instructional Program." Soon after publication, the domain title was changed to "Support the Instructional Program." This is an important change in wording; it is more important for an administrator to be knowledgeable of effective teaching—involved with curriculum, instruction, and teaching practices—than it is for the administrator to lead the learning.

Every staff meeting is a learning opportunity. Meeting content should never be left to chance; planning for them should start in advance of the scheduled date to make the most of these opportunities to make positive changes in your school.

The time staff spend together in meetings must add to the shared understanding of the important work staff does together or build relationships within the group. At the end of the meeting, if staff members do not have a deeper understanding of the work, purpose, rationale, or school mission, or if they do not have a deeper appreciation of the great people they are working with, then the time has been wasted (Grenny et al., 2022). A meeting should elevate both of these missions—deeper knowledge of the work or appreciation of people—or at least one of these purposes. If it does not, it may actually do more harm than good; too often meetings leave staff with less understanding about what they need to do and more confusion. Staff meetings should be professional learning meetings where staff learn together, have fun together, and learn to appreciate one another.

First, remove the "paperwork" from the meeting. Find a way to distribute passive information to staff in another way. There are ways staff can be held accountable for required content, especially if you find creative ways to provide them with time outside of the staff meeting to read and review it. Make staff meetings about learning together and building relationships by having a lot of interactions; communicate all announcements, due dates, and so on in a different format.

I set up a shared document to organize staff learning by meeting agenda and by month. I encouraged staff to add the ideas that they would like to share, the amount of time they desire, and the month in which they would like to present. In the example, our sample teacher Mike would present information about assessment and evaluation and his literacy program. He is too talented to keep that knowledge to himself. Praise your staff and nudge them to get involved. As you walk through the school and notice great things happening, ask staff members to share with others at the next meeting. Staff members will appreciate having someone notice their good work and acknowledge the benefit of sharing it with others.

Second, organize staff meetings like conferences. In the week heading into the staff meeting, create a "conference schedule" with all the options available at the upcoming meeting. Start together in a central gathering spot with staff then provide breakout session presentations in various locations. Those presenting can do quick thirty-second elevator speeches about their topic before asking staff to move into the different locations. If any announcements need to be done face to face, they can be done at this time.

There might be five different choices of presentations for the first half hour, and then shorter sessions in the next block of time (fifteen or twenty minutes, for example). Also, presenters could share their knowledge twice, so more of their colleagues can attend. Encourage members of the same teams to divide and conquer to attend as many different presentations as possible.

Some sessions were done by master teachers; others were done by beginning teachers trying new strategies and desiring feedback. Some sessions shared a resource or technology tool. It is important to note that as the administrator, you should be aware of the content and what is being shared. During our meetings, the English Language Learner Team presented almost every month, as well as the special education resource teachers. These sessions did not have extensive content, but instead, the staff noticed a few ideas or concepts in the classrooms that they wanted to highlight to benefit students. The goal was to present strategies that could be used the next day. We had classroom teachers present about community building, significant 72 (see chapter 5, page 76), or their program. When close to a reporting period, meetings would often include an open session where teachers could attend a facilitated discussion on reporting. Aspiring leaders can facilitate conversations if they are coached ahead of time and given a protocol to follow. Another option for sessions is a "train the trainer" model where a single teacher or pair of teachers receive professional development and then share with others during a staff meeting. As presented in the previous chapter (page 90), staff members would also present on an important book or resource they have implemented.

It is also possible to include community members with expertise. Some topics included days of significance that students and their families observe or celebrate. For example, every year we had conversations and presentations close to Ramadan. This is a great way to involve your community and provide much needed perspective for staff to understand the students they serve. Topics also included mental health and well-being, equity, the health curriculum, culturally responsive and relevant pedagogy, Indigenous education, discriminatory and harmful language protocols, and technology-enhanced learning and mathematics. In some districts, teachers are required to develop a yearly plan of personal learning. We utilized these plans to develop and find content for our meetings.

Michael Fullan (2014) has written that professional learning must be promoted within a school. It is important to have structured meetings and forums. Have teaching demonstrations and workshops conducted by instructional coaches and by internal staff. Create settings that will foster formal and informal professional discussions. The biggest difference in student learning will occur when professional learning is focused on the implementation of teaching strategies and techniques (Fullan, 2014).

Internal Field Trip

Mike has an amazing classroom; he is intentional in how it is set up. Most other staff members notice this while passing but do not understand the rationale for it. One of my favorite ideas for staff development of effective teaching strategies is to plan internal field trips. After initially gathering for staff learning, our first point of business might be to go on a field trip inside the building or somewhere on the grounds. Do kindergarten teachers even step out of the kindergarten area? Do middle school teachers ever observe a primary classroom? Have your teachers seen some of the amazing specialty rooms in the building?

Every staff learning opportunity is an opportunity for growth and learning new skills, and for staff to model best practices. During an internal field trip, I asked staff to silently observe the learning environment and how it serves students. Then, I lead them through the following three steps.

1. Ask teachers to share one thing they noticed or observed that was impressive to them and why. They should comment; there is no need for a response. The individual who works in the space gets to hear some compliments and positive affirmations.

2. Ask staff to say something about the room. Why has the teacher who is sharing done something, or what is the purpose of the observation? Allow the sharing teacher to respond.

3. Finally, the teacher shares a challenge or dilemma they have in their room, or with their materials, and so on. This is something that they are considering or want to change. The staff can help brainstorm answers to the challenge.

This strategy eventually allows best practices to start to blend into other locations in the school and for staff to find solutions to common roadblocks collectively, along with allowing future leaders to gain experience sharing their knowledge and acquiring more knowledge.

CONCLUSION

Teachers must be knowledgeable of effective teaching practices if they are going to one day be effective administrators. They must be able to cultivate understanding and desire for improvement when working with teachers as administrators. The teacher may be a leader in their curriculum area, but we should be encouraging those who are more universal in thought and application. Instructional methods that work in one school may not be effective in all schools. Understanding a subject is not the same as understanding students. It is not logical, given the many tasks, roles, and responsibilities that an administrator has in regard to learning, to have someone who was not an effective practitioner leading this work. Current leaders must identify future leaders who understand and have demonstrated effective teaching and value the importance of instructional leadership. Having expertise in understanding and describing high-quality instruction allows administrators to observe and evaluate their teachers and offer correct and actionable feedback to improve teaching and learning. It gives them credibility that they are coming from a place of experience by sharing what they did when they were teaching. They will be able to determine what is needed to move from low- to high-quality pedagogical practice. They will be able to recommend key professional development for their teachers (Grissom et al., 2021). Understanding what effective teaching looks like, sounds like, and feels like is a key way of being for future school leaders.

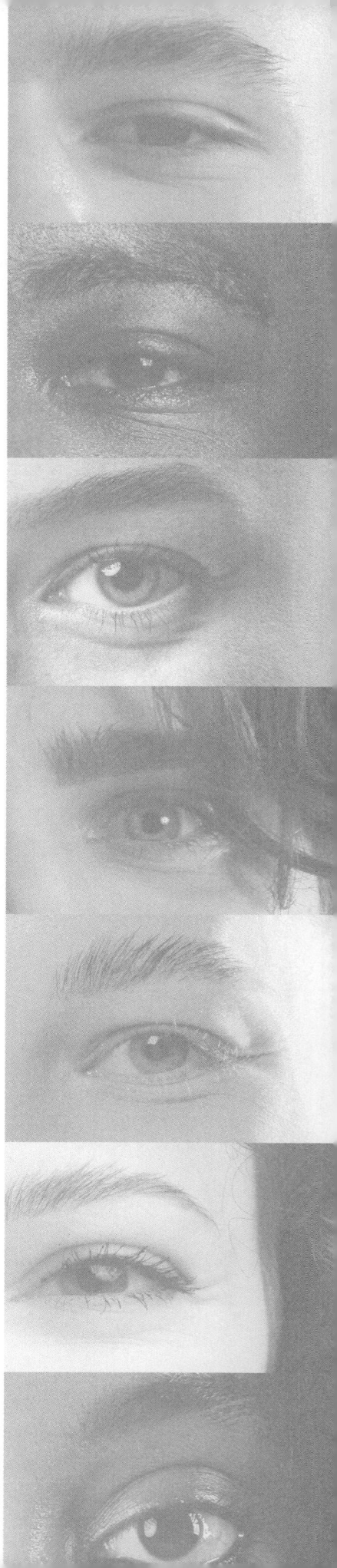

CHAPTER 8

OPTIMISTIC

I t would be difficult—if not impossible—to find many people who would argue that the expectations placed on school leaders are anything less than immense and the work some of the most complex. There is great uncertainty with what each new day will bring as well as a multitude of expectations from various stakeholders. The job is ambiguous because there are different expectations from staff, students, and the community on how the school should be run, not to mention at the state, province, or national level. As a school leader, taking risks and stress are a large part of a job that is filled with both joy and moments of sadness that can be quite significant. To be successful in such a position, teachers who move from the classroom into administration must be optimistic.

Leithwood (2012) defines *optimism* in an educational setting as "the habitual expectation of success in one's efforts to address challenges and confront change now and in the future" (p. 50). A leader with optimism expects good results. They are also realistic in understanding what is within their control and what is beyond their influence. The optimistic but realistic administrator realizes they have influence but not control over all outcomes; therefore, at times they have to accept outcomes that are not what they hoped for. Optimistic administrators do expect, however, to be successful in relation to goals and plans over which they have direct control and influence (Leithwood, 2012).

The optimistic school leader takes risks in areas where they can and should bring about positive changes. Closely related to optimism is efficacy, which is an administrator's belief in themselves that they have the skills to get the job done. Having self-efficacy as a school leader often means putting forth effort and persisting in the face of initial disappointment. Optimism involves believing in a goal or change so strongly that overcoming whatever problems or challenges are in the way is a nonnegotiable. The leader's belief in getting there, as well as their belief in their abilities to get there, means they will continually look for alternative means for achieving what they set out to do (Institute for Education Leadership, n.d.). We want our teachers to work on teams and believe in themselves. Our future school leaders must be teachers who have experienced teacher efficacy.

Teachers need to be optimistic about what they do and what they can accomplish together. A school staff with a collective belief that they can achieve incredible outcomes for students is essential for an effective school and to profoundly impact student learning (Hattie, 2023). A school administrator who is optimistic and understands the power of teacher efficacy can make it happen. The research is clear: together teachers can achieve more, especially if they collectively believe that they can do so! (Visible Learning, n.d.).

KEY OBSERVABLE BEHAVIORS

Following are the behaviors that aspiring leaders who are optimistic should exhibit. When rating a teacher in this way of being, think about the knowledge and skills involved with each behavior as well as the passion and motivation it requires. Consider providing the list of observable behaviors for this way of being to future leaders for self-evaluation and reflection prior to the mentoring planning meeting. (Visit **go.SolutionTree.com/leadership** for a free reproducible of this list.)

1. The teacher regularly engages with staff to analyze evidence about student learning progress. They participate in data-informed meetings looking at how to improve student outcomes. They believe in and demonstrate collective teacher efficacy.

2. The teacher uses assessment and evaluation to build students' optimism and hope. Their effective use of feedback builds students up, it does not tear them down. They provide opportunities for students to resubmit work. They assess in multiple ways so students can show, speak, and share what they know.

3. The teacher articulates the attitude that when given time and the right support, all students can learn. They have a "not yet" approach regarding student learning.

4. The teacher is positive and engaged when they are around other talented people. Their positive energy excites others. Their caring attitude supports others when needed.

5. The teacher looks for the good things in others, and when they find it, they acknowledge and praise it. They share feedback that identifies the positive as well as areas for growth. They show appreciation and recognize student and staff member accomplishments.

6. The teacher acknowledges student growth, their accomplishments, and when students display solid effort. They are supportive and build students up with a "you got this" attitude. They put faith in other people that goals can be met.

7. The teacher understands their strengths. They believe in their abilities; they know what they do well and what they should improve. They take on initiatives and activities that they know will help their skill set and benefit students.

8. The teacher takes appropriate risks. They try new things and allow themselves to be vulnerable to failure. They do this because they want to improve.

9. The teacher takes on new challenges with a mentor. They want to improve in some areas that they feel need attention and do not mind having others around for support or guidance. They seek out those who can assist them.

10. The teacher has "stick-to-it-ness": If at first, they do not succeed, they try, try again. They have self-efficacy. They believe they can achieve their goals and accomplish their tasks. They put in effort and persist when they have a goal worth pursuing. They look for multiple paths to success.

11. The teacher sets yearly goals to improve their practice. They put effort into their program to add to their already excellent teaching for student benefit.

12. The teacher is excited about working on a team and values the contribution of team members. They do not work in isolation and are willing to ask others for support in areas where they want to improve. They know they are not alone and reach out to others to make great things happen for students.

13. The teacher is focused on where they can make a difference with direct influence and control. They do not stay stuck thinking only about factors they do not control.

14. The teacher shows they are resilient, that they are able to bounce back and recover from setbacks. They understand that there will be change and misfortune but are ready to accept and move on with time.

15. The teacher demonstrates they can come through challenging circumstances. They learn and adjust when things do not go as planned. They focus on outcomes and make decisions concentrating on what is best for students. They always manage their emotions, displaying a positive and professional attitude when with students, staff, and families.

16. The teacher has a positive attitude toward parents and families. What they say and do regarding families in the community sends a powerful message that is positive and hopeful.

17. The teacher is a positive role model for students while in the classroom as evidenced by an enthusiastic and positive attitude toward learning. They promote and show joy in learning. The classroom is a vibrant, happy, engaging place.

18. The teacher encourages students to excel to the best of their ability. They acknowledge student success and accomplishments. They boost student confidence with encouraging words and gestures.

19. The teacher demonstrates a positive, professional attitude when communicating with parents, students, and colleagues on any issue. They speak highly about education and the direction of the school. They are mindful of their environment and audience when they discuss issues that are concerning or when they hold a strong opinion.

20. The teacher has frequent, meaningful interactions with teachers, students, parents, and families that further school goals. They are aligned with the school's direction and optimistic about achieving goals. They establish, with staff, students, and other stakeholders, an overall sense of purpose or vision for work in their schools to which they are all strongly committed.

SAMPLE TEACHER

This section presents an example using a fictional teacher and administrator. It shows the results when the administrator plots the future leader's observable behaviors from the way of being presented in this chapter; analyzes the data; plans the next steps; and conducts a meeting with the teacher.

James is a high school teacher who works in technology and the trades. He worked in industry before moving into education. He teaches multiple sections in the school and provides a program that is hands-on with construction, electrical, automotive, and manufacturing being his main passions. He has been described by others as an amazing teacher because he "loves the unlovable." School was difficult for James when he was a student, and he has a real soft spot for students who struggle. He seeks out and seems to attract students who have been underserved in the past or those who may have "an edge" to them but shine in the trades where work is practical and hands-on. He draws students in and shares his personal story so struggling students know they are not alone. He is optimistic with students and staff.

The community does not know much about the technology wing of the school and the wide variety of programs that are available for students; James is the perfect staff member to highlight to the community the good learning that is happening there. He would represent the school extremely well if given the opportunity to showcase the excellent programs it offers. Principal Lopez has been nudging James toward administration because of his optimism and passion for learning. His people skills are outstanding, he has strong management skills, and he believes in students. However, James was not successful the last time he applied for an administrative role; privately, when working with the current administration, he is feeling quite defeated and does not know whether he wants to continue to try to become an assistant principal.

Step 1: Plot the Way of Being on the Leadership Action Matrix

Principal Lopez plots James's observable behaviors for this way of being—optimistic—using the leadership action matrix. The results appear in figure 8.1.

Way of Being: Optimistic

Administrator Name: Principal Lopez

Teacher Name: James Sample

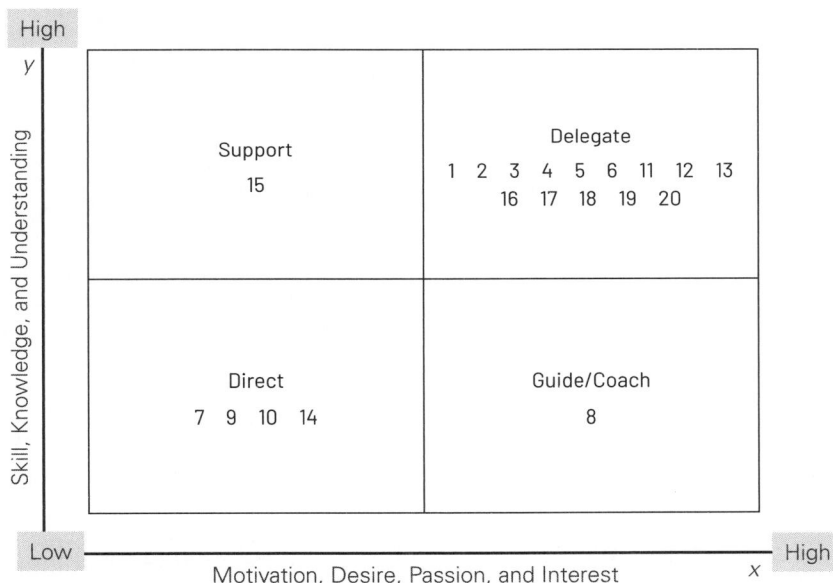

FIGURE 8.1: James's leadership action matrix for being optimistic.

Step 2: Complete the Mentoring Planning Page

After plotting the observable behaviors for James on the leadership action matrix, Principal Lopez transfers the numbers to the mentoring planning page (see figure 8.2, page 128), adding comments about the behaviors she observed and her thoughts about the next steps. She bolds the items she wants to discuss further when she meets with James. James could use this tool for self-evaluation prior to the mentoring meeting as well.

Way of Being: Optimistic

Teacher: James Sample

Administrator: Principal Lopez

Support		Delegate	
Behavior Number	**Notes**	**Behavior Number**	**Notes**
15	**Shows optimism with students and concern about their best interests; feels down on himself currently because of the administration process, and there is concern about him bouncing back**	1	Holds data meetings and shows he is a strong member of the team; cheerleader for the team
		2	Supports students' hope and optimism, provides many opportunities to redo work, assesses in multiple ways with performances, projects, practical applications, and so on
		3	**Advocates for students with a "they will get there!" approach**
		4	Has charisma and positive energy
		5	Connects with students, gives high-fives, praises, and shows enthusiasm for student accomplishments
		6	Supports students and makes them feel like they can do it
		11	Sets goals for program and curriculum, and makes needed changes
		12	Works collaboratively as part of a strong team with all members
		13	Always looking for ways to benefit and move students forward
		16	Has a positive attitude with parents, acts as a role model, and loved in the community
		17	Promotes learning and is a great model for students, has high enrollment in classes, and shares personal story

		18	Encourages students to excel
		19	Professional and optimistic about education, the school, and where education can take you
		20	Aligns with direction of school and has a sense of purpose
			Recommendations for delegation: • **Open house in tech wing of school**
Direct		**Guide/Coach**	
Behavior Number	**Notes**	**Behavior Number**	**Notes**
7	Does not recognize his strengths, how good he is; feels down about his abilities	8	**Needs to take risks in leadership; has lack of knowledge on leadership and hiring process; needs to get experience and start leading**
9	**Needs to find a mentor—perhaps another administrator who has taken a similar pathway**		
10	Has a "never give up" attitude with students he should adopt for himself		
14	Shows resilience in many ways; needs help bouncing back from failed experience		

FIGURE 8.2: Sample mentoring planning page for James for being optimistic.

The following are explanations of some of Principal Lopez's ratings for James and the rationale for them.

Behavior 9: *The teacher takes on new challenges with a mentor. They want to improve in some areas that they feel need attention and do not mind having others around for support or guidance. They seek out those that can assist them.*

Principal Lopez placed behavior nine in the direct quadrant because she wants to have a deep conversation about possibly finding a mentor outside the school as another source for James in his pursuit of an administrative position. Now, James is low in passion and interest for administration because he was not successful in his recent attempts at promotion. Principal Lopez is also worried about James's lack of having optimism about himself. He is always professional and invested with students. Principal Lopez would like to see this passion return for James as he reconsiders leadership roles. The administrator is confident that James will make a successful school leader and an excellent role model, advocate, and inspiration for many students. Principal Lopez will speak with James about finding another administrator in the district who may have a similar experience, someone who was not successful and continued to persevere to become a school administrator. Also, it would be helpful to connect James with someone who may have followed a similar pathway through business to education as a second career. Principal Lopez is questioning how she can best support James and wants his perspective on branching out to others for mentorship.

Behavior 15: *The teacher demonstrates they are able to come through challenging circumstances. They learn and adjust when things do not go as planned. They focus on the outcomes of children and make decisions concentrating on what is best for students. They manage their emotions always displaying a positive and professional attitude when with students, staff, and families.*

Principal Lopez placed behavior fifteen in the support quadrant (high knowledge/skill, low motivation) because, with the way James is feeling now, Principal Lopez believes that support is the key way of framing how to best assist James at this time. James has the knowledge and understanding about how to be optimistic with students and staff, but he is not feeling the same way about himself. Principal Lopez wants to assist James through this difficult time because James will be an excellent future leader and just needs to understand the district process around hiring leaders so as not to take his earlier rejection personally.

Behavior 8: *The teacher takes appropriate risks. They try new things and allow themselves to be vulnerable to failure. They do this because they want to improve and be better.*

Principal Lopez placed behavior eight in the guide/coach quadrant because James is overall high in motivation to become an administrator even though currently that passion and optimism have taken a hit. James is lower in understanding and knowledge about the importance of an optimistic outlook for his own self-care. Principal Lopez wants to coach him in bouncing back. Part of the mentoring plan will be providing James with a better understanding of the process of becoming an administrator—courses, paperwork, and interviewing. Principal Lopez believes a deeper understanding of leadership in general as well as the steps required to become an assistant principal will increase James's overall sense of optimism.

Behavior 3: *The teacher articulates the attitude that when given time and the right support all students can learn. They have a "not yet" approach in regard to student learning.*

Principal Lopez placed behavior three in the delegate quadrant because James is both high in knowledge and high in passion and interest. James is extremely supportive of all students and an extremely popular and inspirational teacher. Students sign up for his classes in large numbers. In addition, James runs a program where students have multiple opportunities to demonstrate their learning. He describes himself as a "late bloomer" and knows that certain academic aspects of school are not for all students. He models this "not yet" approach in everything he does. Principal Lopez appreciates this and wants James to see himself in the same way. Principal Lopez wants the community to see the work being done in the technology section of the school. James is the perfect choice to lead an open house in the tech wing. By delegating this responsibility to James, Principal Lopez celebrates his abilities, particularly in his optimism and view of students, while providing him with practical experience working as a leader.

Step 3: Use the Mentoring Meeting Planner

Principal Lopez fills in most of the information on the mentoring meeting planner tool in preparation for her meeting with James. Figure 8.3 shows the completed mentoring meeting planner, including notes from the meeting.

Date: February 26

Administrator: Principal Lopez

Teacher: James Sample

Focus

Which way or ways of being will we discuss?

Optimistic. Discuss how being optimistic relates not only to work with students, but also with learning in general—being optimistic about ourselves. Draw on James's background from his previous work and ask about his experiences with setbacks and moving forward. Why it is important as a school administrator that you demonstrate optimism and are optimistic about yourself as a school leader? Ask James for input. Share positives about his teaching. Move toward discussing his desire to become an administrator.

Agenda for Sharing and Discussion

What specific points about the way or ways of being will we discuss?

- Many of the positives about James, his teaching, his view of students, and how he shows optimism with staff
- The need to be well-rounded in many aspects of leadership
- James's perspective on his strengths and needs in this way of being
- Notes from the twenty observable behaviors
- Notes from the mentoring planning page

Key Points

- **Direct**
  - » Find a mentor for James so he can see positive experiences from another administrator—a mentor—who experienced a similar path to leadership.
- **Support**
  - » Express concern for James and his feelings after being rejected for a leadership opportunity. James is great with students, optimistic in their presence, but he is currently down on himself.
- **Guide/Coach**
  - » Help James take risks in seeking leadership; get him experience and help him understand that his negativity comes from a lack of understanding of leadership and the hiring process.
- **Delegate**
  - » James is an excellent advocate for students. Find ways for him to share his skills and knowledge.
  - » Hold an open house in the tech wing of the school.

Teacher Plans, Comments, and Ideas

What plans, comments, and ideas did the teacher have during the meeting?

- James is pleased with what is happening in the school and in the tech wing. He loves teaching and his students.
- James is disappointed he was not successful when he tried to become an assistant principal and is not sure he will attempt again.
- James would love to open up the shops in his wing and show the community what they are all about. He thinks it would be great for students to be in attendance and working on projects to show the community what the inside of the classrooms and shops look like.

FIGURE 8.3: Sample mentoring meeting planner for James for being optimistic.

continued ▶

- James sees the need to learn more about the process of becoming an administrator. He admits that he just "threw his hat in" the last time and really did not concentrate on the proper steps and best way to present himself. He went by personality, not substance (his words).

- James is uncertain at this time about connecting with another mentor. He likes working with me; however, he wants me to reach out and see if there are others.

Goal Setting

What is the teacher's goal related to this way of being?

- James will work with his department team as well as students to organize an open house after school and into the evening session for the community to see the work being done in the tech wing.

- James will reach out to the administrator when this committee work begins to get coaching and guidance on heading up this team and planning the event.

- James will consider another mentor to assist him with this process. He understands it will be a unique perspective and potentially beneficial to get assistance from someone with a similar pathway to leadership.

- James will take courses run by the district on leadership. He likes to learn and wants to think deeply about following a leadership path.

Potential Resources

What are some potential resources to recommend to the teacher that address their areas of needed growth from the direct and guide/coach quadrants?

- New potential mentor

- District courses on leadership for future leaders

- Resources to assist with resume writing, putting together a teacher portfolio, and developing interview skills

Final Thoughts

What are your final thoughts about next steps and when to check back in?

James started the meeting still feeling down about his recent setback; however, as the discussion progressed, he became more like himself. He was congratulated on always doing good work and not displaying his disappointment publicly with students or with staff. He is a true professional. James should be an administrator in our school system and should be continually supported and encouraged. Currently he is wavering on his interest, but it appears that with time he will make the decision to try again.

OPTIMISTIC IN ACTION: SCHOOL EXAMPLES

The following—public appreciation and student presentations and meetings—are two examples of what an optimistic teacher looks like in your school. These examples show how school staff are optimistic and understand the behaviors in this way of being. Programs such as these also provide leadership opportunities for staff you have identified for this way of being and plotted in the leadership action matrix who require experiences for further development in building optimism.

Public Appreciation

Praise is an essential leadership tool. The act of acknowledging someone's effort and contribution to the team is motivating and can increase staff effort and productivity (Kuczmarski & Kuczmarski, 2020). We used praise in our school to foster a culture of gratitude. It is a simple way of communicating to others the thankfulness we feel for their contributions. Praise rewards the giver as well as the receiver. Praise needs to be given properly with thoughtfulness and sincerity (Kuczmarski & Kuczmarski, 2020). Praise should be an ongoing leadership move that occurs often enough that it impacts the school culture and reaches everyone (Kuczmarski & Kuczmarski, 2020).

In my time as a school administrator, I have witnessed what occurs when we acknowledge some of the amazing, unknown, quiet brilliance that happens in a school and how it can have a profound effect on the overall climate and culture of a school. Public appreciation that is planned and incorporated into a routine—for example, done for a few minutes at the beginning or end of a meeting—is a way to deepen the connection and bring positive, uplifting messages to the forefront. When public acknowledgement is part of the rituals of a school, relationships and commitment are strengthened, and people are more willing to step forward and take on tasks. In my experience, I always felt it was important for staff to see and hear about the wonderful people they work with in the school yet may not know all that well; challenging staff conversations are easier when staff members have built respect for one another.

Implementing this strategy can be as simple as asking, "Does anyone have any appreciation they would like to make public?" at the start or end of a meeting, followed by a staff member acknowledging a colleague by sharing what the colleague did to deserve the acknowledgment. I know of some schools that implemented a more formal and detailed system that included sharing accomplishments online with their school community. Or leaders can plan more structured sharing of public appreciation, such as monthly Bravo awards published on the school's social media.

Appreciation can be for something that had a direct impact on the person sharing, or something they witnessed with a student, another staff member, or a parent. In our school, it was common for new staff to appreciate the mentorship of others. It was common for grade team partners to thank one another for taking on a higher workload during a difficult time. An educational assistant might thank a partner for stepping in and assisting during a tough moment. It was heartwarming to hear about someone performing continual random acts of kindness, or that someone appreciated a colleague's instruction or their interactions with students. In our experience, team members who did not enjoy speaking in public were more comfortable doing so when offering appreciation for others. In this case, both the individual sharing and the person receiving the praise received a boost of optimism, and the entire staff felt inspired.

Typically, there was time for two or three staff members to share during each meeting. If more staff members wished to share, I encouraged them to find time in the coming days to have a private conversation with the person they appreciated to thank them.

We all want to be acknowledged for the work we do, the care we provide, and the effort we show. Lack of recognition can have a significant impact on teacher retention. A report from McKinsey and Company (Bryant, Ram, Scott, & Williams, 2023, citing research by

Carver-Thomas, Darling-Hammond, & Sutcher, 2019) states that nearly one third of teachers in the United States are thinking of leaving their job. In addition, the report finds:

> Over the past decade, the annual teacher turnover rate has hovered around 8 percent nationally and is more than double that for schools designated for Title 1 funding. By comparison, the annual turnover rate in high-performing jurisdictions, such as Finland, Ontario, and Singapore, is approximately 3 to 4 percent. (Bryant et al., 2023)

Compensation, including benefits, is listed across all school types as the number one reason why educators are considering leaving. For the majority of school types, administration does not dictate salaries or employee benefits. Beyond compensation, there are some factors and working conditions that administrators do have influence over (Bryant et al., 2023). After compensation, the next most common reason for turnover is educators feeling overworked and undervalued (Bryant et al., 2023). About 75 percent of educators in the group considering leaving say that "they put more into their job than they receive in return."

Start a positive tradition in your school by incorporating appreciations. You will be modeling to future leaders the importance of building a school culture that acknowledges the contributions of everyone. Show them with your words and actions that you value your staff.

Student Presentations and Meetings

There is perhaps no better way to boost optimism than to feature students and their good work for staff, families, and the community to see. Sometimes, groups of adults in a school or parent or school board groups can lose sight of why they exist as an organization as they get bogged down with political issues or seemingly insurmountable tasks. Including students in meetings to do a short presentation or performance serves as a reminder about the real reason behind the meetings.

At first, it might be difficult to convince participants to give up time on the agenda; however, it is worth persisting because the exercise has so many benefits. Parents and teachers are proud of their students and the accomplishments being featured in the meeting. Parents of invited students often become interested in returning for future meetings or getting involved the following year. For students, this is an opportunity to share their good work or highlight an aspect of the school they are proud of.

In our school, staff would sometimes invite a group of students to come into the meeting to demonstrate learning from the classroom. This is the idea behind the Open House that sample teacher James has been delegated as an opportunity for growth. It gives students the chance to show their hard work and dedication and at the same time provides a leadership opportunity for James.

Student presentations can even include field trips to parts of the school participants may have never seen. Parents of young students can see the science lab, music room, or specialized learning programs and realize the resources available to students in the school. Meetings can feature team achievements, clubs, and extracurricular opportunities. The art program can have an art show. The possibilities are endless, but the results are the same—a renewed sense of pride, positive energy, and optimism for all who attend.

CONCLUSION

Students need positive adults in their lives. Every day, school leaders and teachers are in a unique position to provide a positive influence on students, and this positive influence should extend to families and the community. Working in schools can be a stressful job; future leaders must be able to do more than just cope and risk burnout. To get through challenging times, leaders must be optimistic, or schools can become stuck—stuck in their practices and stuck in their traditions. To create needed change, a school leader must be optimistic that there is a better way and marshal all their knowledge, skills, and passion to bring others along.

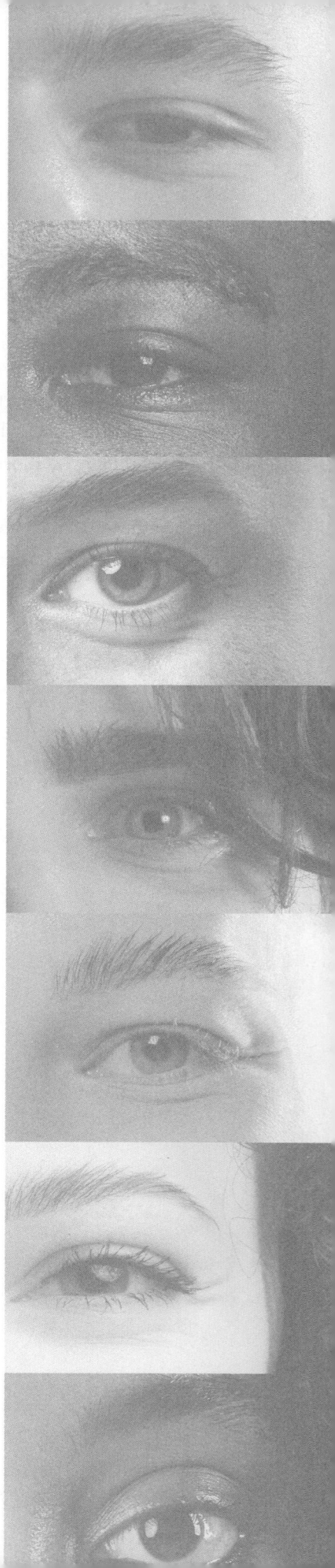

CHAPTER 9

PRESENT

A mentor of mine once told me that as a principal I should get used to the fact that 90 percent of the jobs are only going to get 75 percent done, and sometimes, the percentage did not even get that high! Most days, there is not enough time to get everything on the to-do list done. The time we invest as school leaders reflects our priorities; it indicates what we care about and what is seen as most important. As an administrator, it is important to remember what should be most important—it is the *people* that are important. Schools are a *people business*.

All stakeholders connected with a school want to know they have an administrator who is present and visible. When students see the school leader each day, it gives them feelings of security and belonging. Teachers will witness an individual who has passion and enthusiasm for being at school and know there is someone there that they can count on for support and advice. Parents gain confidence in the school when they see the administrator out and engaging with others. For the effective school administrator, presence is key.

School administrators must serve as role models for how students, staff, and families should be treated, and that requires being present—visible and authentic—for all stakeholders. James A. Autry (as cited in Marzano, Warrick, Rains, & DuFour, 2018) explains the need for administrators to be visible and authentic:

> Teachers can determine who you are only by observing what you do. They can't see inside your head, they can't know what you think or how you feel, they can't subliminally detect your compassion or pain or joy or goodwill. In other words, the only way you can manifest your character, your personhood, and your spirit in the workplace is through your behavior. (p. 20)

School leaders can show confidence, consistency, and optimism in their words and deeds. To do all of this, the administrator must be visible; the school leader must engage in positive, high-quality interactions with families, staff, and students (Leithwood, 2012). Administrators are the public face of the school. They have an opportunity each day to demonstrate the kind of relationships, communication, care, and dedication that are cornerstones of the school. Being present shows stakeholders that you are open for engagement, not shut off, and you welcome conversation and dialogue.

Administrators who are behind closed doors and not out within their school community, not engaging with staff and students, will find that the culture can quickly turn to one of distrust, disrespect, and the loss of important connections. However, simply showing up is not what it means to be present. With students this means an administrator is not just walking the halls like an officer on patrol. It is about engaging with students every day. Being visible sends the message that students matter, that they are safe, they are heard, and the people in the school are interested in what they have to share.

The best administrators are highly visible in the school and get into classrooms to witness student learning (Goldring et al., 2015), observing what they are doing and what they are learning. They get to know them in the hallways and care about their lives. Visible administrators build confidence and efficacy in teachers with their presence, support, and feedback. Being in the classroom with students and teachers builds trust with staff and is the avenue to improve teaching and learning (Joseph, 2019). As I visited classrooms, I would often carry a pack of sticky notes in my pocket, and as I left a classroom, I would write an encouraging statement, such as something I was impressed with in the lesson, and place it on the teacher's planner so they saw it later in the day. I always made sure the next time I saw the teacher to comment about something I observed so they knew that I noticed the good things that are happening. If I had a concern, there was a time and place to express that, but immediately following my time in the class, I wanted teachers to know I was present, aware, and appreciative.

Ask yourself, are you an administrator whose teachers are saying, "I can't wait to show them what my students are doing today" or do the teachers speak in fear and worry that something must be wrong when the administrator comes in the room because it is so infrequent and never for a positive reason? This is an important discussion to have with your teachers considering a role in administration. Visiting classrooms allows administrators to create opportunities for collaboration and connection. Because of scheduling, staff members do not often get the opportunity to be in their colleagues' classrooms, but administrators can do so, creating partnerships and support situations based on what they observe.

Frederick Buskey (2019) presents some interesting ideas to consider when thinking about devoting time to being present. How can you possibly do it? There are so many tasks that need to be done and the administrator is responsible and accountable for many of them. However, when thinking about the total amount of time in the day, consider that students and staff are only in the building together during the instructional day. Some tasks do not require that others be around; however, many tasks are dependent on students being in school. In reality, you don't have time to do everything you want to do at school—there will always be unfinished tasks.

The start of the day is an important time to be present and visible. Walk through the school and welcome staff and greet students and families outside. This is the perfect opportunity to check in with specific students and their support staff as needed, and it is also an opportunity to get a quick "temperature check" with how the day might go for certain individuals. I truly believe the first few hours of the day sets the tone for the rest of the day.

So, what do we teach our teacher leaders about presence? With everything that has to be managed in a school, being present is not always easy to do; it takes planning and the development of habits, like carving out time every day to visit classrooms, delegating tasks to others when possible, and scheduling parent meetings for before or after school to keep protected time during the day for staff and students. Be present and visible in the school and give staff your full attention when needed. Attend school events such as arts evenings, sports activities, concerts, and other activities when possible, and remember to greet and welcome families. Share a message about the gathering if you can. Administrators who thank staff, students, and families for making an event possible will be present and visible to all. The reputation of the school and the school administrator are built one interaction and conversation at a time.

KEY OBSERVABLE BEHAVIORS

Following are the behaviors that should be evident in aspiring leaders who are present. When rating a teacher in this way of being, think about the knowledge and skills involved with each behavior as well as the passion and motivation required. Consider providing the list of observable behaviors for this way of being to future leaders for self-evaluation and reflection prior to meeting to discuss. (Visit **go.SolutionTree.com/leadership** for a free reproducible of this list.)

1. The teacher is highly visible in the school, making it easy for students and staff to connect with them when needed.

2. The teacher does not minimize moments with students. They understand that for students, an interaction may be the best and most important moment of the day. The teacher is present in conversations with students, gives students their full attention, and engages with them in a situationally appropriate way.

3. The teacher demonstrates respect and caring with a cheerful, positive, and enthusiastic approach with students, and has a positive rapport with students.

4. The teacher has "with-it-ness," also called situational awareness. They know where they should have a presence in the school—when to be in the hallways, which classrooms to visit, and when to be in high-traffic areas where students gather and difficulties can occur.

5. The teacher performs supervision duties and additional responsibilities with care and consistency. They are where they should be, on time, present, and aware.

6. The teacher uses their visibility to set the tone in their classroom. They have routines and procedures in place so that students are

aware of expectations. They manage student behavior by being present and engaged.

7. The teacher is authentic in their interactions with students. They discuss interests outside the classroom, use students' names, and engage in a friendly manner with all students.

8. The teacher focuses on their responsibilities when supervising students in common areas, like hallways, rather than being engaged with other staff.

9. The teacher is involved in school events, for example, by attending extracurricular events to support students, cheer them on, and show school spirit.

10. The teacher is welcoming when students arrive at school or in the classroom. If students are late, the teacher does not admonish them publicly; rather, they express that they are happy to see the student, acknowledging their presence and following up later about attendance issues.

11. The teacher welcomes student voices in the classroom; students do most of the speaking and thinking. The teacher asks questions to solicit student voices and then uses instructional practices that put students at the center of the learning.

12. The teacher works with other teachers to expand their knowledge of curriculum and teaching practice. They are present and involved participants in learning. They show up and contribute during staff professional learning time. They model to others how valuable time is and use what they learn to improve their practice.

13. The teacher makes themselves available to other staff. They serve as a resource to colleagues, for example, in the effective use of technology, assessment strategies, and classroom management. They not only pursue learning themselves, but they effectively share new knowledge about current thinking, trends, and practices in education. They have designed and presented workshops during staff learning days.

14. The teacher makes their expectations known through their words and actions. They demonstrate to all stakeholders what they believe in the school's mission, vision, and goals. They exemplify, through their actions, the school's core values.

15. The teacher demonstrates respect for staff, students, and parents by listening to their ideas. They are open to the ideas of others and genuinely consider their value.

16. The teacher is welcoming. They smile and are warm to school guests and ask how they can help.

17. The teacher is present during arrival and dismissal times and engages with families in a warm and welcoming manner. In middle school and high school, the teacher will engage with parents when they are present at school events or around campus.

18. The teacher gives credit to others, shares successes, and speaks about accomplishments using words like *we, us*, and *the team*, rather than *I*.

19. The teacher is present for families—approachable, accessible, and welcoming. They have developed a communication system, or use the system authorized by the school, to be available to families. They have created a school environment that respects and values parents as partners in their children's learning.

20. The teacher provides ongoing feedback and information to parents; for example, they use websites, newsletters, messaging, and bulletins. They communicate with families about events, classroom learning, and other important information in ways that are convenient for families to access and find.

SAMPLE TEACHER

This section presents an example using a fictional teacher and administrator. It shows the results when the administrator plots the future leader's observable behaviors from the way of being presented in this chapter; analyzes the data; plans the next steps; and conducts a meeting with the teacher.

Rachel is a first-grade teacher early in her career. She is an enthusiastic staff member who is involved in many activities throughout the school. She directs clubs and intramural programs. She is still learning about teaching practices and curriculum. She is present and visible with students, and vocal and enthusiastic in the classroom, in the hallways, and outside. She is charismatic, has an infectious attitude, and always has a smile. She involves families, often greeting them at arrival and dismissal. She is confident in her abilities and has made it clear to many that one day she wants to be an administrator.

The one area Principal Linski has concerns about is Rachel's interactions with her teaching colleagues. They are beginning to view her as someone who is solitary and wants to be left to do her own thing. Although within her classroom, she is solid, Rachel requires assistance understanding the importance of her teaching colleagues and how working with others will be key for her as a future school leader.

Step 1: Plot the Way of Being on the Leadership Action Matrix

Principal Linski plots Rachel's observable behaviors for being present using the leadership action matrix. The results appear in figure 9.1.

Way of Being: Present

Administrator Name: Principal Linski

Teacher Name: Rachel Sample

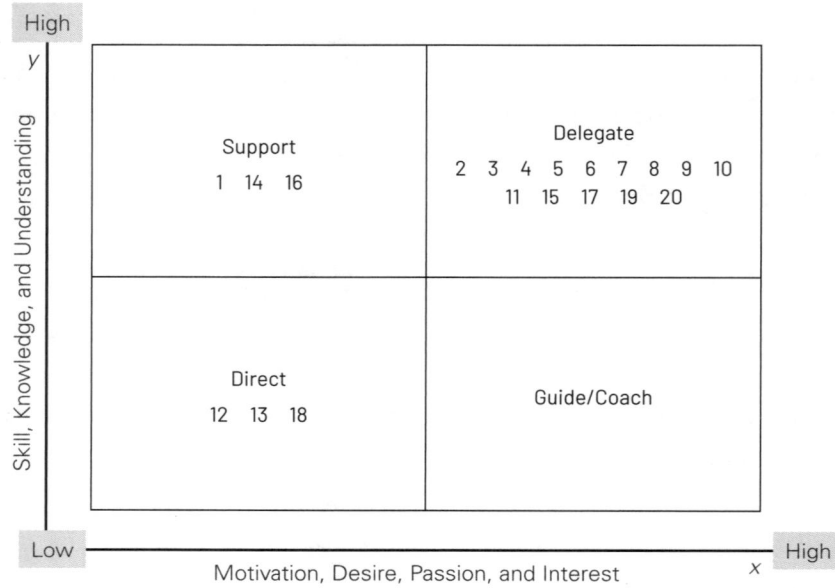

FIGURE 9.1: Rachel's leadership action matrix for being present.

Step 2: Complete the Mentoring Planning Page

After plotting the observable behaviors for Rachel on the leadership action matrix, Principal Linski transfers the numbers to the mentoring planning page (see figure 9.2), adding comments about the behaviors he observed and his thoughts about the next steps. He bolds the items he wants to discuss further when he meets with Rachel. Rachel could use this tool for self-evaluation prior to the mentoring meeting as well.

Way of Being: Present

Teacher: Rachel Sample

Administrator: Principal Linski

Support		Delegate	
Behavior Number	**Notes**	**Behavior Number**	**Notes**
1	**Always visible for students; needs to work on staff presence**	2	**Shows care and concern with students; always focused on them**

14	Does demonstrate belief in mission and vision to students and families; however, she is not aligned with our school direction in regard to staff collaboration	3	Has a positive rapport with students; is cheerful and enthusiastic
16	Welcoming to students and parents. There is concern about connections to staff	4	Has situational awareness and is responsive when sensing an issue or concern
		5	Performs supervision duties on time and with no issues
		6	Has routines and procedures in class, and is engaged when managing behavior issues
		7	Works to get to know students, is interested in their lives, and has a strong sense of community
		8	Has success with supervision and managing students in common areas
		9	Shows significant school spirit by attending many events, even for senior students
		10	Welcomes students when they arrive and is happy to see them
		11	Promotes active participation from students in class
		15	Listens well and is respectful of students and families
		17	Is always present to see parents at arrival and dismissal
		19	Communicates well with families
		20	Gives valuable information to parents, which is important in grade 1; is well informed

FIGURE 9.2: Sample mentoring planning page for Rachel for being present.

continued ▶

Direct		Guide/Coach	
Behavior Number	Notes	Behavior Number	Notes
12	**Needs to work with other teachers on curriculum or teaching practice; appears reluctant to participate during staff learning days**		
13	Appears to have closed herself off to staff who do not approach her for collaboration; she has a lot to share		
18	Focuses attention on self, with little mention of *the team* or *we*		

Following are explanations of some of the administrator's ratings for Rachel and the rationale for them.

Behavior 12: *The teacher works with other teachers to expand their knowledge of curriculum and teaching practice. They are present and involved participants in learning. They show up and contribute during staff professional learning time. They model to others how valuable time is and use what they learn to improve their practice.*

Principal Linski placed behavior twelve in the direct quadrant because, based on his observations of Rachel, when she is working with colleagues, she is low in both skill and passion in this observable behavior. He is concerned that there are times when Rachel can become disengaged in the conversation and contribute little input to the group as a whole. She has a lot to share because her classroom practice is strong. However, Rachel shows only mild interest in what the team is doing together, not sharing what she is doing with her students or learning from others. She is quick to invite administrators into the classroom to show what she is doing as a teacher but speaks little about the work of the entire team of teachers. Principal Linski must have a direct conversation with Rachel about her desire to become an administrator and how problematic it will be to focus only on herself in that position. It will be a difficult conversation because Rachel has so many other strengths in this area as well as other ways of being. However, she must develop skills in working with others and increase her passion for learning from and with other talented colleagues.

Behavior 1: *The teacher is highly visible in the school, making it easy for students and staff to connect with them if they are needed.*

Principal Linski observed that Rachel is doing great work in her classroom and throughout the school related to visibility and being present; however, she needs to improve when it comes to being available and working with other staff members. While her motivation and commitment are low in this area, her knowledge and skill could be considered strong because she has an understanding that presence is necessary and important with students and families. So Principal Linski put behavior one in the support quadrant (high knowledge/skill, low motivation). Principal Linski would like to support Rachel in seeing the parallels in this important way of being because if Rachel becomes an administrator, being present will require her commitment to all stakeholders.

The administrator did not place any behaviors in the guide/coach quadrant because Rachel did not demonstrate any observable behavior that could be considered high in motivation but low in knowledge. Rachel has the knowledge and skills to be a positive, present, and engaging educator. She demonstrates this constantly with students and their families. She knows being present is an important way of being for a teacher; she must extend this behavior, however, to connect with the other adults in the school. As an administrator, it is important to continually think of others and to consider "us" and "we" as more important than being a single individual who leads. This is not a guidance or coaching conversation; this is a directing conversation if Rachel is to move forward and gain the skills needed to succeed as an administrator.

Behavior 2: *The teacher does not minimize moments with students. They understand that for students, an interaction may be the best and most important moment of the day. The teacher is present in conversations with students, gives students their full attention, and engages with them in a way that is situationally appropriate.*

Principal Linski put behavior two in the delegate quadrant because Rachel is both high in knowledge and high in passion and interest. This is a quadrant with a lot of observable behaviors to celebrate with Rachel. To give a more direct message about working with other staff, Principal Linski can utilize all the observable observations in this quadrant to compliment and elevate Rachel. She is talented with students and good with parents, which should be acknowledged and appreciated. As a relatively young teacher, she has this way of being firmly entrenched. Principal Linski must use these positive attributes in this way of being to help Rachel make connections with staff. Rachel needs experience with the curriculum and can benefit from experienced staff sharing lessons, assessments, and evaluation plans. Rachel can share with them about relationship building and being present for students.

Step 3: Use the Mentoring Meeting Planner

Principal Linski fills in most of the information on the mentoring meeting planner tool in preparation for his meeting with Rachel. Figure 9.3 (page 146) shows the completed mentoring meeting planner, including notes from the meeting.

Date: January 25

Administrator: Principal Linski

Teacher: Rachel Sample

Focus

Which way or ways of being will we discuss?

Being Present. Discuss what it means to be present. Why it is vital as a school administrator that you are present? Who are all the stakeholders that an administrator must interact with? What does it mean to be present with each of them? How is an administrator present for students? For staff? For the community? Ask Rachel for input.

Agenda for Sharing and Discussion

What specific points about the way or ways of being will we discuss?

- The positives about Rachel's classroom environment and relationships with students
- The need to be well-rounded in many aspects of leadership, and the need to focus on many different groups of individuals as an administrator—staff and well as students and families
- Rachel's perspective on her strengths and needs in this way of being
- Notes from the twenty observable behaviors
- Notes from the mentoring planning page

Key Points

For each of the following sections, list the bolded or circled items from the mentoring planning page.

- **Direct**
  - » Needs to work with other teachers on curriculum and teaching practice.
  - » Needs to participate during staff learning days.
- **Support**
  - » Although highly visible for students, she needs to work on staff presence.
- **Delegate**
  - » Is excellent with student relationships, shows care and concern, and is always focused on them; can share this knowledge and skill with others.

Teacher Plans and Comments, and Ideas

What plans, comments, and ideas did the teacher have during the meeting?

- Rachel was excited to be speaking about leadership and wants to move in that direction.
- Rachel is focused on her classroom and likes to share with the administrator what is happening. She likes showing that she is doing good work with students.
- Rachel does not seem to realize that it is important for others to see the good work that is happening in the classroom. She commented that other teachers are too busy or doing their own thing, so they do not want to see her teaching.
- Rachel commented that she is working really hard on what she is doing now and concentrating on doing those things well. She indicated that when she does staff learning with others it "stresses me out" because she just keeps thinking about all the things that others are doing that she is not doing.
- Rachel is willing to share some of the things that she does that contribute to her positive student presence, but she is concerned that the veteran teachers will not see her contributions as important, or new, or relevant because they are doing more complex things. She thinks what she is doing is not that impressive.
- Informed Rachel that what she is doing in the classroom is impressive and does make a difference for students and the school, and that together with the administration, they will find a way for Rachel to exchange ideas with other staff. Staff at different stages of their career may be sharing different things that are working for them in the classroom; it is all valuable. In fact, many experienced teachers should be doing the relationship building, community building, and being there for students that Rachel demonstrates every day.

Goal Setting
What is the teacher's goal related to this way of being?

- » Rachel will demonstrate more commitment to the team and professional learning with others starting immediately.
- » Rachel will implement what she is learning when working with other staff and invite the administrator to the classroom to see the strategies in action.
- » Rachel will share with the administrator what the new addition to her classroom instruction is, who she learned it from (what resource or person), and then go back to the individual to let them know she tried the strategy in class and how it went.
- » Rachel will create a list of the behaviors she does as a teacher to show students and parents that she is present and visible and share it with administration. Working with administration, Rachel will share those behaviors with others on the team during a staff professional learning day.
- » Rachel will read *Unlocking Group Potential to Improve Schools* and discuss her thoughts and ideas with administrators.

Potential Resources

What are some potential resources to recommend to the teacher that address their areas of needed growth from the direct and guide/coach quadrants?

We will purchase *Unlocking Group Potential to Improve Schools* by Robert J. Garmston with Valerie von Frank for Rachel and discuss how the book will assist her with her first-grade team as well as in the future if she becomes an administrator.

Final Thoughts

What are your final thoughts about next steps and when to check back in?

Rachel is a relatively new teacher who brings a lot of energy into the school and her classroom. She is interested in administration but still has a lot to learn. Being present is only one way of being, and aspects of this are not difficult at all for her. The big lesson for Rachel in this way of being is working with colleagues, which she must develop skill in to be an administrator. These difficult conversations may make future discussions about the other ways of being easier to have, as she does show great potential.

FIGURE 9.3: Sample mentoring meeting planner for Rachel for being present.

BEING PRESENT IN ACTION: SCHOOL EXAMPLES

The following—kindergarten friendships and double-clicking—are two examples of what being present could look like in your school. I share them here to provide leadership opportunities for staff you have identified and plotted in the leadership action matrix who require experiences for further development in being present. These examples also show staff and the larger community that the school advocates for the importance of being present and visible.

Kindergarten Friendships

The bell to signal the end of the day is a happy time in any school, for both students and staff. As principal, one of my favorite activities to do to finish the school day was to interact with students in the kindergarten bus lines—a way of being present for students.

Our youngest learners lined up in the hallways of the school to wait for their buses. Each day, I picked a line to sit with students for five minutes, rotating groups so I would be with each line at least once in three weeks for our sixteen bus lines. This was exciting for students.

I asked students about what they were learning, and they asked me important questions like, "Do you know there is a Marshall on Paw Patrol?" and "How come you don't have hair on your head?" We were able to talk about all kinds of things, and I found out so much about what was happening in our kindergarten program.

This was an important way to be present since our school went from preK to grade 8—kindergarten students are just starting their journey in the school. This is a critical time for adults to influence, teach, inspire, and support students. This activity also sent an important message to staff members about our values—that students come first.

Double-Clicking

Like clicking on an app on your phone or computer, double-clicking allows you to go deeper or further—it's a way to be present; when someone makes a comment about the school or a staff member, instead of offering a thank you, I "double-clicked" to find out more. When a parent says something like, "We love this school," ask, "What do you love about it?" If I received a compliment like, "You are awesome," I asked why, and often the answer was, "Because we see you," "You are always outside saying hello," or "Because you are always happy and interacting with students." It was always a comment about being visible. Parents did not see the interactions with staff and students inside the building. They did not attend staff learning days. They did not see all the paperwork. They did not get an in-depth look at my leadership. What they did see was me being present, available, and visible.

The idea of double clicking shows others that you want more information, that you are interested in what they have to say, and in that moment, they come first. It's often possible to notice when someone is having a tough day, even if they say everything is fine. Double clicking with a simple reply like, "Are you sure you're good? You look like you have lots on your mind" or "Please let me know if there is anything I can do for you" goes a long way in being present. When working with aspiring leaders, answer their questions or respond to their comments with additional questions. I've asked aspiring leaders I've worked with how they felt when I used that strategy. Did it frustrate them? The response was that this double clicking made the aspiring leaders feel heard when speaking with me. This strategy is a way to consciously focus on being present.

Others cannot see inside your head; they do not know what you are thinking or how you feel, but they can see what is important to you based on your actions. It is such a simple idea, yet so powerful: Get out of your office. Be present.

CONCLUSION

Being present and the practice of having face-to-face interactions with students, families, and staff is a leadership way of being that the best administrators employ. These connections with people establish trust and send the message, "I am here for you, and I will listen" (Tyler, 2016). An administrator cannot serve the needs of their students and families if they are not present. Not only is it important to move throughout the campus to observe, it is also equally important that staff and others see you engaged in doing just that. Being present during transition times, recess times, in eating areas, and in play areas provide the administrator the opportunity to make connections. Model for your teachers the importance of being present, mentoring aspiring leaders to understand they must get out from behind the office door, get away from the paperwork, and be seen. It is a leadership way of being that is very much worth the time invested.

CHAPTER 10

A PROBLEM SOLVER WITH SITUATIONAL AWARENESS

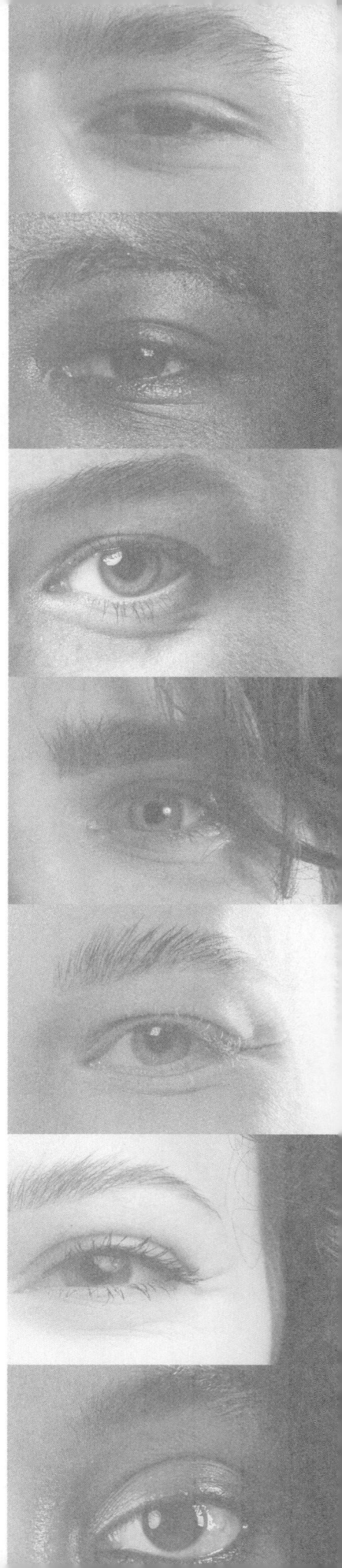

Every week, school administrators make hundreds of decisions, involving changes in direction, adapting to new information, mediating conflicts, and negotiating positive outcomes for students. The thought patterns involved in decision making do not change when teachers move into leadership roles; however, the volume and magnitude of the decisions increase greatly. In addition, many of the outcomes of administrator decision making will be public and open to criticism and debate. Problem solving becomes much more complex when teachers become school leaders.

Problem solving is a skill and requires a deep understanding of context, people, and situations as well as a desire to create outcomes that are best for students. According to Leithwood (2012), effective school leaders work through a decision-making process that consists of six components.

1. **Problem interpretation:** Expert problem solvers have many things in common when interpreting puzzles, conflicts, and challenges. They understand that each problem could have many potential issues attached to it, and they can consider many angles and then prioritize which one they will choose to work on in the moment. Effective administrators are optimistic and see difficult problems as challenges that are manageable. They rely heavily on evidence and facts instead of assumptions. They involve others in helping to get successful outcomes, and they are willing to take whatever time is needed to develop clarity and understanding (Leithwood, 2012).

2. **Goals:** Problem solvers determine what everyone involved is trying to achieve in response to the problem. For expert administrators, this is almost always tied back to student outcomes.

3. **Principles and values:** Problem solvers determine the longer-term purposes that guide the thinking. The best administrators rely on a more consistent set of values, and they can speak to these clearly and confidently.

4. **Constraints:** What are the barriers, the obstacles, or the factors that may narrow the range of possible outcomes the administrator has available? Talented administrators can identify what those are, are quick to problem solve around them, and rarely consider the challenge to be insurmountable.

5. **Solution processes:** These are the carefully planned actions taken to implement decisions. Effective administrators consider who else needs to be involved and include them.

6. **Mood:** This is the administrator's emotional response to the problem or issue. Effective administrators can work on complex issues, remain confident and calm, and show this disposition to others involved.

While in teaching positions, future administrators should demonstrate that they are good problem solvers. Breaking down problem solving into parts is a complex task that requires future leaders to be coached and mentored in this important way of being.

When administrators are confident in their problem-solving skills, it shows. Principal ratings of their own organizational management skills (managing budgets, hiring) are predictive of higher student achievement, parental ratings of the school are higher, and teacher satisfaction improves (Grissom & Loeb, 2011). The administrator's ability to problem solve and make good decisions is good for student outcomes; most important is the ability to hire well (Grissom et al., 2021). Some administrators struggle in this area of decision making. Schools that hire well and acquire more high-performing teachers have larger student achievement growth (Grissom et al., 2021).

A major task for school administrators is to make sure resources and materials are in place, and schedules exist to make the functioning of the school coordinated and beneficial for student learning. Schools are better places when the people inside feel they are led instead of managed; however, do not lose sight of the importance of the administrator's ability to manage activities and materials that are central to effective leadership (Huber & West, 2002). In addition to an administrator's problem-solving skills, they need to allocate time for resource management, to hire and make teacher assignments, allocate the budget, create schedules, do inventory, and more.

Problem solving can be seen as consisting of three elements: (1) preventive, (2) predictive, and (3) corrective (Tiddens, Braaksma, & Tinga, 2021).

1. **Preventive:** These are actions that occur well in advance of the problem. Asking questions such as the following are part of preventive problem solving. What can I do as a school administrator to put in place the values of caring, respect, and dignity to prevent problems from occurring? What systems and processes do I have in place for safety and emergencies?

2. **Predictive:** These are actions that occur immediately before any problem. Asking questions such as the following are part of predictive problem solving: How do I use my experience as an administrator to understand that certain times of the year are more stressful for staff, students, and maybe our school community? What areas of my school are "hot spots" for problems? How do I use my sense of situational awareness to feel when something is about to happen?

3. **Corrective:** These are actions that occur after a problem has occurred. Asking questions such as the following are part of corrective problem solving: How do I investigate situations that occur to determine fair, restorative, and dignified consequences? How do I make learning part of my corrective action?

Ideally, school administrators should not be thinking about problems only as they occur as there is much that can be done to decrease the overall number and the overall complexity of issues that arise. While we always need to be responsive and reactive to solve problems, leaders should also be working hard to be in a position of prevention rather than always reacting.

Administrators should emphasize preventive and predictive strategies so they do not spend all their time in corrective repair. Classroom teachers who understand this build classroom community, are present and check in with students, and are positive in their comments to students to prevent issues from arising in the classroom. They have situational awareness. They can predict when something troubling may be about to occur and move to that area of the classroom, hallway, or playground. They understand that if it is predictable, it is preventable (Weber, 2020). How does a teacher correct students when things do go off course? When a student has had a challenging moment or entire day, how do they handle things? Future leaders should be the teachers who understand that when they solve a problem with a student, they do it from the perspective of, "It's you and me versus the problem. Let me help you be a problem solver so that you do not continue to be a problem maker. We have a decision to make, let me help you. This is not you versus me."

For example, one area where effective problem solving has a significant impact on student outcomes is related to teachers' class assignments. Research shows that often the most experienced teachers are assigned to the more advantaged students (Grissom, Egalite, & Lindsay, 2021). This suggests that administrators are not using their decision-making skills to pursue equity as higher concentrations of low-achieving students are taught by novice teachers. Unfortunately, this is also true of English learners. When interviewed, school leaders suggest that this preferential treatment for more senior teachers getting easier-to-serve classrooms is based on the "micro political dynamics" among teachers, administrators, and even parents (Grissom et al., 2021). School leaders must use their influence and awareness to improve this inequity. Unfortunately, not all administrators have control over hiring decisions. Taking away school leaders' ability to hire has been shown to be a major factor leading to administrator departures (Grissom et al., 2021). Administrators want to make hiring decisions; when given the opportunity to hire, they must do it well.

Future leaders are teachers who are making decisions that are best for all students. They problem solve in a careful, thoughtful manner. They place an emphasis on making sure that students who require the most love and care, those who have been marginalized, and those who need adult advocates in their lives, are front and center in the decisions that are made. If a teacher is strong in these behaviors, they are well on their way to becoming an effective administrator.

KEY OBSERVABLE BEHAVIORS

Following are the behaviors that should be evident in aspiring leaders who are problem solvers with situational awareness. When rating a teacher in this way of being, think about the knowledge and skills involved with each behavior as well as the passion and motivation needed. Consider providing the list of observable behaviors for this way of being to future leaders for self-evaluation and reflection prior to meeting to discuss. (Visit **go.SolutionTree.com/leadership** for a free reproducible of this list.)

1. The teacher demonstrates that they are comprehensive in their problem-solving ability in three areas: preventive, predictive, and corrective (Tiddens et al., 2021).

2. The teacher is more curious than reactive when an issue arises. They ask questions. They find out information by speaking with and listening to students. They do not rush to judgment; instead, they take time to discover all necessary information. They think of all involved: students, families, staff, and others.

3. The teacher is determined to find out why a student is struggling with academics. Are students having difficulty with the content or are other personal factors involved. The teacher does not just assume student difficulties are simply related to motivation. They want to find the reason for poor performance and change their teaching if it contributes to the student's struggle. The teacher is reflective in their practice and considers what is working and not working for every individual in their class.

4. The teacher spends time and energy problem solving important issues rather than becoming weighed down by minor annoyances. They have the awareness to turn their focus to the issues that truly need their attention. They are aware of problems occurring in the classroom, even if they are impacting some students more than others, such as inequities and bullying situations.

5. The teacher displays an understanding of using consequences and knows that punishing does not change behavior; sending students to the office or the hallway is a short-term solution that removes students from learning. The teachers understand that students have trauma, deeper stories, and reasons for their behavior. The best teachers help students by looking for the purpose behind the behavior to prevent the undesirable behavior, not simply punish.

6. The teacher has situational awareness. Also called "withitness." They can see potential problems before they arise and immediately address them.

7. The teacher uses problem-solving strategies that are appropriate and respectful, honor each individual, involve student input, and utilize restorative practices.

8. The teacher is a person who gets others in the group to focus, slowing down to think deeply about a concern or issue. They ask good questions and question assumptions. They may take the lead in working through a procedure, template, or protocol, but not necessarily the lead in deciding for the group.

9. The teacher is a good communicator about a situation after it has occurred or been resolved. They communicate with families where appropriate, during all stages of the problem-solving process. They share necessary information with the administration and with others impacted by the problem being solved.

10. The teacher successfully brings issues and concerns to a positive solution. They do not inflame issues and make them worse. They have a positive outlook on the future and next steps.

11. The teacher's actions are aligned with the school's core values and beliefs. They use their class commitments and the school's mission as a guide when speaking with students. They use the school's common language to address how students are expected to behave while in school. They demonstrate to students that everyone is part of the community.

12. The teacher understands the importance of emergency procedures. They carry out their responsibilities during emergency and safety procedures. They communicate with students in an age-appropriate way about the need for having these procedures in school.

13. The teacher demonstrates instructional agility (Erkens et al., 2017). This is the ability to make real-time decisions during instruction using emerging evidence. They can change direction on the fly when students show a lack of understanding and try something else.

14. The teacher utilizes the school behavior code consistently. They create common commitments with their classes and hold students accountable for these agreements made together. The teacher involves the entire class in the creation of their class commitments using age-appropriate words. Students can articulate what is expected of them. The teacher understands that classroom management is about creating a community

and being proactive in their relationships with students, not reactive when class does not go well.

15. The teacher manages classroom resources well. They problem solve around issues having to do with time, schedules, materials, learning spaces, and other operations.

16. The teacher works with other staff members on school issues and demonstrates proper attention, listening, and participation behaviors. They involve themselves in discussions with staff about overall student behavior, what is going well, and what requires attention schoolwide.

17. The teacher remains calm when working through classroom and school issues. They are professional when questioning, debating, or providing answers. When students are agitated, the teacher remains respectful and productive and uses a clear and calm voice.

18. The teacher discusses student issues with others and is always respectful of the students in their choice of language. They stay away from assumptions and stick with facts. They treat students and the choices they make with dignity and are optimistic about future pathways for students. They are never hurtful or angry when sharing information about students. They speak about students as they would if a parent were in the room.

19. The teacher makes notes when a situation is serious, checking with the student to make sure they have captured accurately what the student has shared. They note facts, not assumptions or stories. They make sure to capture accurately what they saw and what they heard. They keep their notes private and do not share aspects of the situation with others unless they are part of the problem-solving team.

20. The teacher may question a school decision, however, they do so in a respectful way, looking for more information or a rationale. They do not speak negatively about a school decision in public. During staff meetings, they ask clarifying questions candidly. If troubled by a school decision, they will try to work with the administration in a professional way, meeting in private, and seeking clarification instead of issuing blame.

SAMPLE TEACHER

This section presents an example using a fictional teacher and administrator. It shows the results when the administrator plots the future leader's observable behaviors from the way of being presented in this chapter; analyzes the data; plans the next steps; and conducts a meeting with the teacher.

Saira is an experienced eighth-grade teacher who has been at the school for her entire teaching career of thirteen years. She was given the role of division lead teacher by the previous administrator. This is Principal Ahmad's first year at the school, and Saira stands out for numerous reasons. She is an excellent instructor, she understands when students struggle with academics, and she knows how to support students who require accommodations and reteaching. She has strong teaching practices and adapts quickly in the class when students struggle with content. Where she has difficulty is when students struggle with behavior. She is quick to send students to the main office. She reacts strongly in class when students misbehave and can become quite loud in her tone with students. She comments to others that students are "not like they used to be" and that this is the "worst group of students" she has seen in her time at the school. The entire middle school team seems to follow Saira's lead; there is a steady stream of students being sent to work in hallways, the resource room, or the office with no communication about what has occurred. Saira has been told by others in the past that she would make an excellent administrator one day and has asked for feedback and mentoring.

Step 1: Plot the Way of Being on the Leadership Action Matrix

Saira's administrator, Principal Ahmad, plots her observable behaviors for the tenth way of being—a problem solver with situational awareness—using the leadership action matrix. The results appear in figure 10.1.

Way of Being: A Problem Solver With Situational Awareness

Administrator Name: Principal Ahmad

Teacher Name: Saira Sample

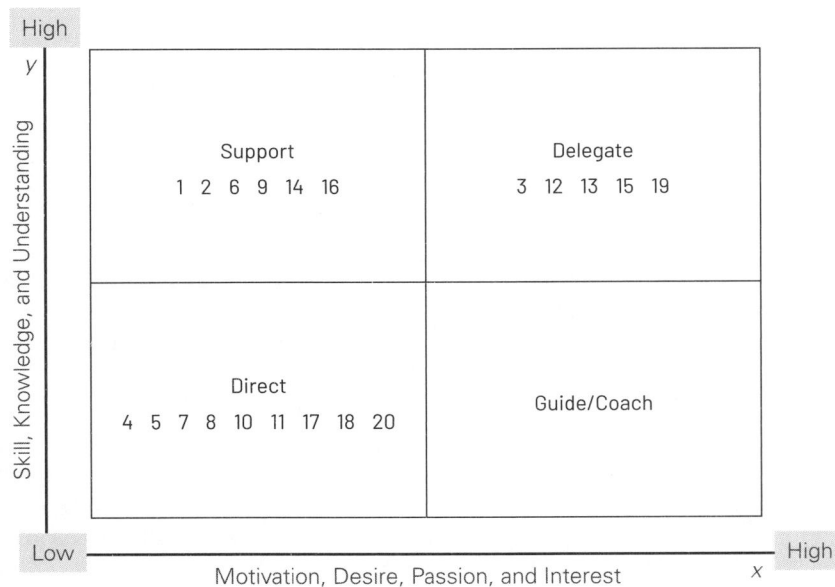

FIGURE 10.1: Saira's leadership action matrix for a problem solver with situational awareness.

Step 2: Complete the Mentoring Planning Page

After plotting the observable behavior s for Saira on the leadership action matrix, Principal Ahmad transferred the numbers to the mentoring planning page (see figure 10.2), adding comments about the behaviors he observed and his thoughts about the next steps. He bolds the items he wants to discuss further when he meets with Saira. Saira could use this tool for self-evaluation prior to the mentoring meeting as well.

Way of Being: A Problem Solver With Situational Awareness

Teacher: Saira Sample

Administrator: Principal Ahmad

Support		Delegate	
Behavior Number	**Notes**	**Behavior Number**	**Notes**
1	Displays preventive and predictive problem solving; need to discuss corrective actions	3	Shows excellence with classroom modification and accommodations, reteaching, and academic problem solving
2	Has the ability to be more curious, but is sometimes reactive	12	Appears organized and does duties well
6	**Has situational awareness for academics, but awareness for behavior needs improvement**	13	**Has agility while teaching—makes real-time instructional changes for academic success**
9	Shares and communicates information about problem, but context and manner of communication needs discussion	15	Serves as a division leader for an organized team and does well with resources and time management
14	**Provides collective commitments to students rather than creating them collaboratively**	19	Documents everything, separates fact and opinion from stories, gets details after initial reaction
16	Participates as part of a team, has the ability to work with others, seeks solutions; needs to be positive when discussing students		**Opportunities to Delegate:** • **Fair chance program** • **School directions program**

Direct		Guide/Coach	
Behavior Numbers	Notes	Behavior Numbers	Notes
4	Responses to situations are equal, but responses are elevated with students		
5	**Uses punishment rather than consequences**		
7	Wants corrective action taken rather than using problem-solving strategies with students		
8	Often makes assumptions about students rather than thinking deeply		
10	**Reacts negatively in front of students, which inflames issues**		
11	Actions not always in alignment with mission		
17	Has issues managing emotions; needs to consider if offense is dangerous or annoying		
18	Comments negatively about students with others; makes blanket statements about all students		
20	Shows a lack of support of some school decisions and has influence with group, which can be a problem		

FIGURE 10.2: Sample mentoring planning page for Saira for a problem solver with situational awareness.

Following are explanations of some of the administrator's ratings for Saira and the rationale for them.

Behavior 5: *The teacher displays an understanding of using consequences and knows that punishing does not change behavior; sending students to the office or the hallway is a short-term solution that removes students from learning. The teachers understand that students have trauma, deeper stories, and reasons for their behavior. The best teachers help students by looking for the purpose behind the behavior to prevent the undesirable behavior, not simply punish.*

Principal Ahmad placed behavior five in the direct quadrant because Saira must improve her understanding and motivation about student behavior if she wishes to move into administration one day. Principal Ahmad recognizes that Saira understands problem solving regarding academics in the classroom and what students need to be successful. As long as students show they are trying and have a positive attitude, Saira supports them in multiple ways. Where she struggles is when students do not behave in the ways she expects. When students do not conform to her rules and expectations, there are conflicts in front of other students, and she removes students from her class. Students are compliant in her class to prevent a blowup—not because they are comfortable and feel a sense of community. Principal Ahmad wants to have Saira start to look at student behavior in the classroom from two viewpoints: behavior that is dangerous or behavior that is annoying. Most of the student behavior that gets Saira upset are actions that annoy her but are not dangerous or impacting other students. While it is difficult, Saira must compartmentalize the behavior and not treat every misbehavior as a major offense. Saira will find it extremely difficult both professionally and personally if she tries to run a school with very little tolerance for misbehavior. Principal Ahmad will not support her in her desire to become a school leader until there is a change in her attitude toward student behavior and knowledge and skill improvement. Principal Ahmad knows this will be a difficult conversation, but it needs to occur for the sake of the students.

Behavior 6: *The teacher has situational awareness. Also called "withitness." They can see potential problems before they arise and immediately address them so they never come to the surface.*

The administrator observed that Saira is doing great work in her classroom related to gaps in student knowledge in academic subjects. She is quick to notice when students are having difficulty and changes her instruction, resources, and timing to help students when they struggle—but only if they are demonstrating their misunderstanding in what she perceives as an appropriate manner. Saira demonstrates she has the knowledge and skills to notice and then change directions based on student feedback during the lesson. Where there is a concern is her desire to assist students who struggle with behavior, or are having a difficult day, or any of the countless reasons that a student is not behaving to her standards. She has not demonstrated interest in closing the gaps in behavior. This is why Principal Ahmad placed his observations in the support quadrant (high knowledge/skill, low motivation). He wants to support Saira by acknowledging her situational awareness of academics and encouraging her to use this sense when situations are becoming tense with student behavior.

Principal Ahmad did not place any behaviors in the Guide/Coach quadrant because Saira is not demonstrating any of the observable behaviors with high motivation, passion, or desire. This is a quadrant usually reserved for those who want to learn more, improve their skills, and have the desire and interest to put in the work to do so. To become an administrator, Saira must develop an interest in learning and understanding student behavior. Her current views are hurtful to students. Her current attitude is unacceptable for a classroom teacher as well. Principal Ahmad knows this will be an important focus of his work with Saira in their first year. He cannot in good conscience allow Saira's missteps regarding student behavior to continue if the school is working to build community.

Behavior 13: *The teacher demonstrates instructional agility (Erkens et al., 2017). This is the ability to make real-time decisions during instruction using emerging evidence. They can change direction on the fly when students show a lack of understanding and try something else.*

The delegate quadrant is where Principal Ahmad notes all the extremely positive qualities that Saira possesses and celebrates her ability to help students academically. He put behavior thirteen in the delegate quadrant because Saira is both high in knowledge and high in passion and interest. She has situational awareness when students struggle with academic lessons. She senses when she needs to slow down instruction, pull instructional groups for additional support, use other materials and resources, or reteach a lesson. She uses formative assessments well to determine groups for reteaching and redirection. Principal Ahmad is looking for something to delegate to Saira so she can practice her leadership skills; however, he does not want Saira to have a negative influence on her teaching partners related to Saira's lack of skill in dealing with student misbehavior and her opinions about students. At this time, he will not be suggesting any leadership initiatives for Saira to lead. Instead, Principal Ahmad will focus on directing change in both Saira's attitude and knowledge while building school culture with two initiatives: fair chance and administrator-led school directions meetings. Both of these initiatives are described in the school examples section of this chapter (page 163).

Step 3: Use the Mentoring Meeting Planner

Principal Ahmad fills in most of the information on the mentoring meeting planner tool in preparation for his meeting with Saira. Figure 10.3 shows the completed mentoring meeting planner, including notes from the meeting.

Date: March 3
Administrator: Principal Ahmad
Teacher: Saira Sample
Focus
Which way or ways of being will we discuss?
A Problem Solver With Situational Awareness. Why it is important as a school administrator that you problem solve well? What have I noticed? What are the positive aspects Saira brings to the school? Ask Saira her view on student behavior. What needs to change and how can I assist? Ask Saira for input.

FIGURE 10.3: Sample mentoring meeting planner for Saira for a problem solver with situational awareness.

continued ▶

Agenda for Sharing and Discussion

What specific points about the way or ways of being will we discuss?

- Saira has excellent classroom situational awareness surrounding academics.
- Saira view of students' behavior must change if she is to be a school leader.
- Saira needs to be well-rounded in many aspects of leadership.
- Review Saira's perspective on her strengths and needs in this way of being.
- Review notes from the twenty observable behaviors.
- Review notes from the mentoring planning page.

Key Points

For each of the following sections, list the bolded or circled items from the mentoring planning page.

- **Direct**
  - » Seeks punishment for students, not consequences
  - » Wants to take corrective action
  - » Makes assumptions about students
  - » Reacts negatively in front of students
- **Support**
  - » Has situational awareness for academics, but not for student behavior
  - » Gives commitments to students instead of creating collaboratively with students
- **Guide/Coach**
  - » None
- **Delegate**
  - » Is excellent with classroom modifications, accommodations, and reteaching; academic problem solving superb
  - » No delegation of initiatives until situational awareness and problem solving of student behavior improves
  - » Participate in fair chance initiative
  - » Participate in school directions initiative

Teacher Plans, Comments, and Ideas

What plans, comments, and ideas did the teacher have during the meeting?

- Saira is aware that she has not started the year well with this way of being. She acknowledges she has complained about students to her colleagues and has not been positive.
- Saira would like to be an administrator one day and is disappointed she does not have the support of current administration.
- Saira would like to join school directions meetings.
- Saira is willing to read suggested books and will try to achieve a better attitude toward students.

Goal Setting

What is the teacher's goal related to this way of being?

- Saira will read the suggested books and share her thoughts in upcoming conferences with her administrator. She is happy to discuss content and application.
- Saira will begin to jot down the behaviors in her classroom that are disturbing to her and classify them as "dangerous," or "annoying."
- Saira will share her list and have discussions with the administrator one time each week.
- Saira will join every upcoming school direction meeting.
- Saira will discuss with the class the assembly on fair chance and start to use that terminology with students to try to avoid sending students out of class.

Potential Resources

What are some potential resources to recommend to the teacher that address their areas of needed growth from the direct and guide/coach quadrants?

- Give Saira the Employee Assistance Program contact information so she may speak to someone about managing emotions and get recommendations on resources or programs.
- Suggest the following books:
  - » *Lost & Found: Unlocking Collaboration and Compassion to Help Our Most Vulnerable, Misunderstood Students (And All the Rest)* by Ross W. Greene
  - » *Why Has Nobody Told Me This Before?* by Julie Smith

Final Thoughts

Saira was upset about the meeting but understood it was necessary for improvement in this important way of being. She believes she can make a change and get administrative support as a future leader. I will have to find quick wins to show I am invested in her. I have invited her to be part of school directions initiative so I can model how we speak about students and begin to show her the importance of team and school culture. There will be a lot of check-in conversations. I am hopeful that over time I will see a transformation.

A PROBLEM SOLVER WITH SITUATIONAL AWARENESS IN ACTION: SCHOOL EXAMPLES

The following—fair chance and school directions—are two examples of what being a problem solver with situational awareness could look like in your school. I share them here to provide opportunities for staff you have identified and plotted in the leadership action matrix who require experiences for further development with problem solving and situational awareness. These examples also show staff and the larger community that the school values problem solving with situational awareness and understands the importance of this behavior.

Fair Chance

Fair chance is a way to strengthen the school climate by giving students the skills to problem solve and work through issues with classmates. Fair chance is a problem-solving process that students can use to begin to solve issues and concerns with their peers prior to staff involvement. By helping students understand their behaviors, giving them the skills to problem solve, and developing a common language that the entire student body understands and uses, fewer students with behavior problems or conflicts end up in the office. Fair chance works well when presented to classrooms or in large assemblies, with teachers then reinforcing and reteaching the concepts.

Fair chance is for small-scale conflicts that occur during student interaction. It prevents the misrepresentation of these daily occurrences as being conflicts that are intentional offensive behaviors. Note that bullying behavior, hurtful comments, physical violence—behavior of a much more harmful nature—requires more than someone pointing out to a student that it is unacceptable and giving them a "fair chance." Bullying and other harmful behaviors have lifelong impacts on students. More serious situations require adult intervention. Students should always be held accountable to school rules and district policies about bullying, harassment, and harmful language. Fair Chance helps students understand the distinction between bullying and conflict, and teaches them skills for getting along, negotiating, apologizing, and caring for each other.

Fair Chance uses scenarios to teach students about speaking up and trying to solve issues on the playground, in the locker areas, in hallways, and classrooms on their own. For example, while playing a game or walking quickly in the hallway, one student bumps into another. The student who causes the collision does not acknowledge the contact. The student who was bumped into then makes an insulting comment to the person who collided with them. After students act out the scenario, we pause and talk about what could happen next.

The performance continues with the students acknowledging the accidental physical contact or insult by saying to the other person, "I didn't like it when you . . .," "Please be careful," or something similar that is kind but appropriate in the circumstance. The performance pauses again so the students can answer a question like, "What would a kind person, a student at our school who understands the school mantra and what it means to Work Hard, Be Nice, Make a Difference, do at that point?" If it truly was an accident or a mistake, or an event that occurred because of the game or sport, what would a good person do when their behavior is pointed out to them? At this point, students agree the right thing to do is to give the offending student a fair chance, allowing all to pause, reflect, and think, and for the offending student to provide an apology or for the students to work toward a resolution.

Fair chance teaches students to give a person with whom they have a conflict a polite fair-chance comment, prompting the offending student to reply. The goal is to have the offending student pause, realize the error, and apologize in the moment for the mistake. If they reply with an unkind comment or harassing behavior and continue to escalate, even after being given the opportunity to acknowledge and correct their behavior, the first student reminds the offending student, "Remember fair chance?" or "I'm giving you fair chance, was that on purpose?" If the person continues to escalate the problem, the receiver of the comment then looks around for others in the area and asks, "Did you hear me give them fair chance?" When others have heard the offer of fair chance it provides positive peer pressure. The student also learns that in the school community, others are there to help make good decisions and we have a collective agreement that we are going to treat each other with respect. Our school culture is stronger because we share the same language of problem solving. Students also have the language to explain the situation to an adult: "I gave (offending student) fair chance and they didn't listen to me." A teacher or administrator still needs to investigate the event, but there are not layers of statements to wade through. When problem solving after an issue, we are always trying to find the moments where a situation escalated and when and how a student in the moment could have de-escalated the situation. Fair chance gives students a chance to be problem solvers as they consider if, in the moment, were they a problem maker or a problem solver?

Parents appreciate fair chance common language. When they hear that their child was given fair chance and continued to bother or upset another child, they understand more clearly the behavior as bullying or harassment; they can reinforce the idea of students being problem solvers or problem makers. Many parents have said they use fair chance at home with siblings after students explain the process and common language. If there are some students who are resistant to fair chance, then teachers and administrators address this issue on an individual basis.

You are now probably thinking about a student who receives fair chance constantly—getting fair chance comments every day from other students. This is a separate issue to address with the student and their family.

The payoff of this program is the high number of students who share, "I gave (student name) fair chance when we were playing and now we are friends again." When teachers discuss fair chance in the classroom and add it to their lessons on being part of the classroom community, they reinforce the teaching aspect of building healthy relationships. Our teacher Saira takes on every issue in the classroom and any difficulty between students interrupts the lesson and the learning because of her reaction to it. When teachers teach students the tools to solve conflict, to treat others with kindness and respect, then more time can be devoted to teaching and learning instead of corrective actions. Having teachers understand that time spent in preventative and predictive problem solving is well worth the effort.

School Directions

School directions is a short meeting about one important topic for the school. It includes administrators and any staff who are interested in participating in the problem solving and decision making for the school. Instead of having a leadership team that makes many of the school decisions, our school used a school directions meeting open to anyone interested in a specific topic. In some of the meetings, participants provided opinions and thoughts about an upcoming event and shared decisions and rationale. This group shares their leadership skills and uses their talents to help the whole school, not just a select group of individuals, solve problems.

School directions meetings cover one topic in one hour. Everyone is invited to attend a meeting if they are interested. Administrators can nudge those teachers interested in leadership to attend specific meetings. Some examples of topics include the following:

- Planning a professional activity day
- Planning an assembly
- Sharing the school budget and how it has been allocated and how any budget lines could be further divided
- Planning outside supervision of students and what areas should be closed during inclement weather
- Getting updates on student behavior during lunch or outside at break times
- Scheduling changes in the use of high interest areas of the school
- Sharing new guidelines for the staff (such as with social media)
- Purchasing mathematics materials for shared resources

When staff arrive for the meeting, thank them for their time and introduce the topic in more detail. Meetings are an excellent way to showcase to staff how to speak about students, the school, and the community appropriately, which is a reason why this activity was suggested for sample teacher Saira.

Meeting attendees can be either consultants or decision makers, depending on the focus of the meeting. For example, when planning content for a school assembly, attendees are decision makers, and when determining budget allocation, they may be consultants. The administrator should be up front about how much of the decision-making process staff will control for each topic. Provide the rationale and explain what will happen after the meeting. It is important to review norms and expectations for the meetings, such as strategies for raising hands, monitoring the amount of talk time for each individual, and how to make final decisions.

If there were any topics or events that were causing stress or concern among staff, I called a School Direction meeting to address it instead of allowing it to instigate negative talk and incorrect assumptions. The aspiring leaders on staff who are starting to consider administration could suggest topics. They become a set of extra eyes and ears in the school, sharing with the administrator when it might be time for a school directions meeting on different topics.

Have you ever been in a meeting where at the end you felt like the leader had their mind made up from the start or participants did not give their honest opinions because they were worried about how they would be perceived? A helpful strategy to use in school directions meetings is loud listening (Scott, 2018). To be a *loud listener* is to state a point of view strongly from the beginning. It prevents people from wasting time trying to figure out what I am thinking of doing. Right from the start, I state that I am thinking of the following action or decision and I want to hear from everyone about what I may be missing in my logic. Therefore, a sentence starter could be, "I'm thinking of (doing this) because . . ." and then ask for views, counterarguments, and other pieces of information that will help with the decision. If you are open and transparent at the start and respectful of people's views, you will receive high-quality conversation.

School directions meetings are helpful for future leaders when they see modeling of decision making, problem solving, and appropriate group dynamics. The meetings help build leadership skills and also give administrators a deeper perspective on staff personalities.

CONCLUSION

At times, the administrator's job seems like a jigsaw puzzle with professional, social, and political pieces. School administrators must examine pieces closely, make decisions to solve problems, and move forward in ways that are beneficial to students, staff, and school. Administrators love the days when the problems are relatively small and easy to solve; however, the reality of the role is that rarely does a day go by that does not include needing expert problem-solving ability to tackle a complicated issue. Being a poor problem solver can create negative reputations and ruin relationships.

Teachers who are good problem solvers and excellent decision makers in the classroom can learn to be equally effective as school leaders by slowing down, considering numerous perspectives, and by prioritizing decisions that are best for students. They must also have the motivation to use problem solving and decision making as an opportunity to create and sustain community, build relationships, advocate for every student, and develop the reputation that they are a school leader who is thoughtful, considerate, kind, and reliable. Future leaders must be coached and mentored to understand the far-reaching impact and consequences their decision-making ability has for an entire school community, making decision making and being a problem solver with situational awareness a key way of being.

CHAPTER 11

A RELATIONSHIP BUILDER

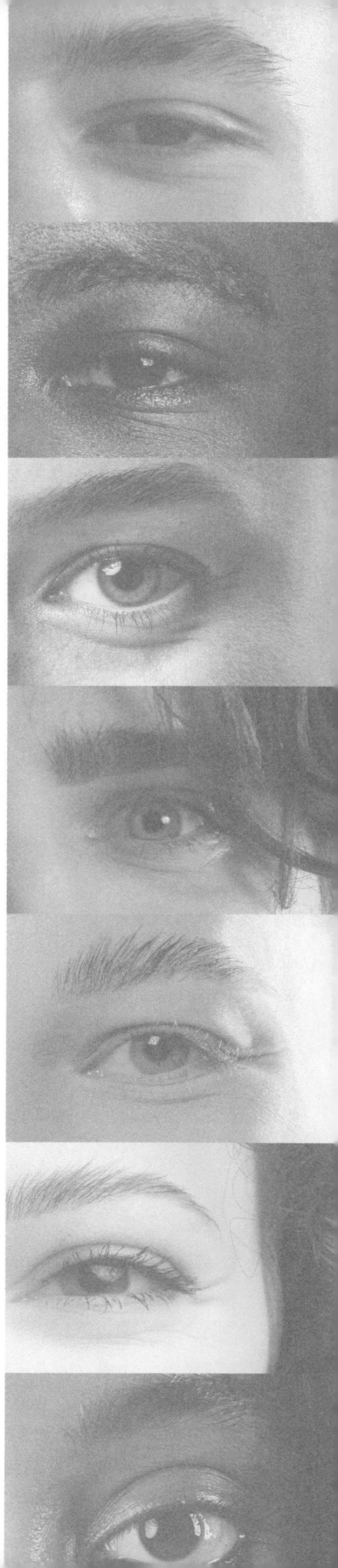

In my work with schools, I often ask administrators what they consider the key attribute in a teacher who wants to move into administration. The answer I get more than any other is the teacher must be a relationship builder. This tenth and final way of being is closely connected to all the others. If an administrator is advocating for all students, they are building relationships. If they are an effective communicator, they are going to build relationships. If they are optimistic, they build relationships. The same can be said for each of the ways of being; they all have a need for the behaviors within relationship building. You build your relationships, develop a reputation, and create a story about the school and about yourself by all the connections you have. All the relationships in a school must be cared for and considered.

As educators, we are all familiar with the three Rs in education: reading, writing, and arithmetic. There is a fourth as well: relationships (Rieg & Marcoline, 2008). If real estate is all about location, location, location, then education is all about relationships, relationships, relationships. As Tom Hierck, Charlie Colman, and Chris Weber (2011) state, "if effective teaching had to be summarized in one word, that word would be relationships" (p. 8).

When becoming an administrator, a teacher will be expected to create a family-like atmosphere for everyone connected to the school. Effective school leaders understand that relationships are fundamental and create a sense of who we are; we cannot separate who we are from our relationships. Administrators who focus too much on the bureaucratic aspects of the role or have a singular focus on test scores are missing what should be considered the most important aspect of education and the key for achieving positive school outcomes. As current administrators, we must mentor our teachers to make clear that as they become administrators, spending time building relationships with students, staff, and families will reward them with higher academic achievement, a beneficial school climate, and lower discipline referrals (Reig & Marcoline, 2008).

While we may understand the importance of relationships, we have to consciously put time and effort into building them; relationship building must be intentional and planned. With the large number of complex tasks an administrator has to handle, there are fewer opportunities to concentrate on relationship building in our modern educational landscape, so when given the chance, the effective administrator prioritizes relationships. The Canadian Association of Principals &

The Alberta Teachers' Association (2014) found that principals perceived relationship building to be "the most meaningful and effective use of their time" (p. 11).

An administrator needs to consider several layers of relationships. First and foremost are relationships with students. Children and adolescents depend on relationships the most. They seek out and desire strong social bonds, which are critical for healthy growth and development. Students look to others for support, approval, problem solving, and acceptance (Sethi & Scales, 2020). When students feel a connection with their teacher, their engagement and motivation increases. This makes sense when we consider the importance that relationships play in our lives as adults to drive our passions, our enjoyment, and dedication to a task (Sethi & Scales, 2020). Not only do strong relationships increase motivation and engagement, but students who can identify connections with teachers and school staff learn more (Roehlkepartain et al., 2017; Roorda, Jak, Zee, Oort, & Koomen, 2017), have stronger social skills, and demonstrate more positive behavior than the students who have difficulty identifying relationships with adults in the school (Roehlkepartain et al., 2017). Students of all ages in our schools and from all backgrounds benefit from strong school relationships with staff (Sethi & Scales, 2020).

Culture building creates a sense of belonging for students (Allen et al., 2021), and administrators and teachers who prioritize this put processes in place to consistently check in on and monitor how students are feeling and what they are thinking. The importance of learning about each student's DNA (dreams, needs, and abilities) to create connections can't be emphasized enough (Hierck, 2017). Hierck (2017) explains that the more educators "can tap into what motivates students and what students bring to the classroom each day, the more they can target instruction to those needs" (p. 41). Curriculum and student learning is important, and relationships are important; however, the order that you focus on these two factors is most important. Relationships must be prioritized. Not relationships *instead* of learning; rather, relationships to *allow* for learning.

Administrators must also consider the relationships with staff and with students' families, and the need to reach out beyond the school to nurture connections with other schools, the district, and the school community. Parents put trust in schools when they know they are part of the decision making, when the administrator is easily accessible, and when their concerns are dealt with in a respectful and timely manner (Reig & Marcoline, 2008). The hard work in schools is done through teams, and teams are connected by relationships. Our teachers should not be independent contractors, left on their own to do things in a way that only they examine, monitor, and approve. They work on teams, in partners, and with others to provide the best learning opportunities for students. Getting along with all the adults in the building is sometimes hard work, but a factor that administrators must consider when thinking about future leaders. Teachers, like students, must feel a personal connection to the school and the individuals within it.

Building trust with the adults in the school aids in developing the relationships students need to be successful in all aspects of their education (Berger, Berman, Garcia, & Deasy, n.d.). Schools are able to retain teachers at higher rates because of relationships. Effective administrators are proactive in their support of new teachers and are committed to the relationships and success of both their new and veteran teachers (Grissom et al., 2021). Being an administrator who understands the importance of teaming and staff relationships is one of the four key principal practices from a large synthesis of qualitative and quantitative studies positively linked to increased outcomes for students (Grissom et al., 2021). The best administrators understand the needs of their teachers, and they can recall their time as a teacher. They are supportive and sincere in their feedback and assistance. They utilize their relationship with teachers to facilitate growth and suggest professional development. Effective school leaders build relationships by recognizing and celebrating the accomplishments of their staff (Rieg & Marcoline, 2008).

KEY OBSERVABLE BEHAVIORS

Following are the behaviors that should be evident in aspiring leaders who are relationship builders. When rating a teacher in this way of being, think about the knowledge and skills involved with each behavior as well as the passion and motivation needed. Consider providing the list of observable behaviors for this way of being to future leaders for self-evaluation and reflection prior to meeting to discuss. (Visit **go.SolutionTree.com/leadership** for a free reproducible of this list.)

1. The teacher notices students when they are on their own, away from the group, and becomes curious to find out why and if by choice. They check in with students to show they care.

2. The teacher is welcoming and excited when receiving a new student, creating a positive first impression for the student and their family. They set up the student for some immediate success.

3. The teacher makes connections with students in less structured moments. They offer the valuable resource of their time and give it freely to students when needed. The teacher is available to students and spends time speaking and engaging with students in hallways, outside, between classes, and during lunch and recess.

4. The teacher is interested in learning about students—their abilities, their needs, what they enjoy, and what motivates them.

5. The teacher helps students through hard times and helps build their confidence to achieve and tackle difficult things.

6. The teacher reaches out and creates relationships with parents. Parents are well-informed and understand what is happening in the classroom. The teacher understands that parent involvement with their child's school life has a positive impact on students.

7. The teacher understands their relationship with students, sets boundaries, and establishes limits to keep students focused and on task. They use positive classroom management that promotes polite and respectful exchanges. They establish a sense of belonging in the classroom and monitor student interactions to make sure they are healthy and beneficial. They recognize, label, and correct inappropriate behavior between students.

8. The teacher catches students being good, doing things well, and putting in effort. They notice when a student is positively contributing to the lesson, the class, and the school, and recognize this behavior.

9. The teacher includes student voice. They involve students (based on age and stage) in decisions that affect them and make an effort to gain students' perspectives on matters that impact them. Students receive opportunities in class to lead, make decisions, and get involved.

10. The teacher works on building a community with students, making time in class for regular activities and learning that create a sense of belonging.

11. The teacher creates connections. They know people and places that can help. They foster relationships for students and families to create success for students. They make sure students are getting the assistance they need.

12. The teacher gives tangible support to other staff when needed. They have strong relationships with the adults in the school that involve trust and confidence. They are collegial, friendly, courteous, and treat others fairly.

13. The teacher shares in the appreciation and recognition of other staff. They are quick to share the good news of team accomplishments and represent their team in a positive way. They do not take individual credit for the work.

14. The teacher works with other staff members to expand their knowledge of curriculum and teaching practice. They participate as an effective team member and share their expertise with others. The work they do with other staff is frequent, meaningful, and about creating positive outcomes for students.

15. The teacher shows respect when dealing with students, staff, and families. They take concerns seriously and make others feel that they have been heard and understood.

16. The teacher collaborates with individuals when working on an issue or a task, sometimes as a leader and other times as a participant. They understand group dynamics and the roles they play within a group.

17. The teacher is dependable and trustworthy. They pay attention and listen to build trust. They respond to others in a respectful and truthful way.

18. The teacher is encouraging. They show their belief in others and praise the efforts others make. They are excited when things go well and supportive when things do not go as planned.

19. The teacher is inspiring. They speak and behave in a way that projects belief in a better future. They broaden the perspective of others by speaking about new experiences and ideas to improve the lives of students.

20. The teacher demonstrates relationship-building actions that are done with an equity lens. The teacher supports positive racial, cultural, and ethnic identity development.

SAMPLE TEACHER

This section presents an example using a fictional teacher and administrator. It shows the results when the administrator plots the future leader's observable behaviors from the way of being presented in this chapter; analyzes the data; plans next steps; and conducts a meeting with the teacher.

Bryan is a fifth-grade teacher who has been teaching for six years and is interested in administration. Principal Waller sees a future for Bryan as an administrator and has agreed to mentor him. This is the first year for the new school, which was built in a new and quickly developing part of town and staffed with expert teachers from within the district. The community of students is diverse, filled with families who have moved to the area from across the country and the world.

Bryan taught at one other school, which was quite different demographically from his current location. Bryan's previous school was predominantly white; the student population did not represent the diverse ethnicities of his new location. He participates well as a team member and is a leader on his team. Others look to him to organize and structure their time together. He is an effective teacher who enjoys working with students, and they enjoy their time with him. He builds strong, healthy relationships with them. Principal Waller has not encountered many teachers who are as talented this early in their career; however, Principal Waller does have one area of concern: Bryan's view of parents and their involvement in school. In Bryan's previous school, staff made it clear they wanted parents at the school only when called upon to participate—that parents should "just let us do our job." Principal Waller must work with Bryan to change his perspective on the importance of parent involvement in his classroom and the school.

Step 1: Plot the Way of Being on the Leadership Action Matrix

Principal Waller plots Bryan's observable behaviors for being a relationship builder using the leadership action matrix. The results appear in figure 11.1.

Way of Being: A Relationship Builder

Administrator Name: Principal Waller

Teacher Name: Bryan Sample

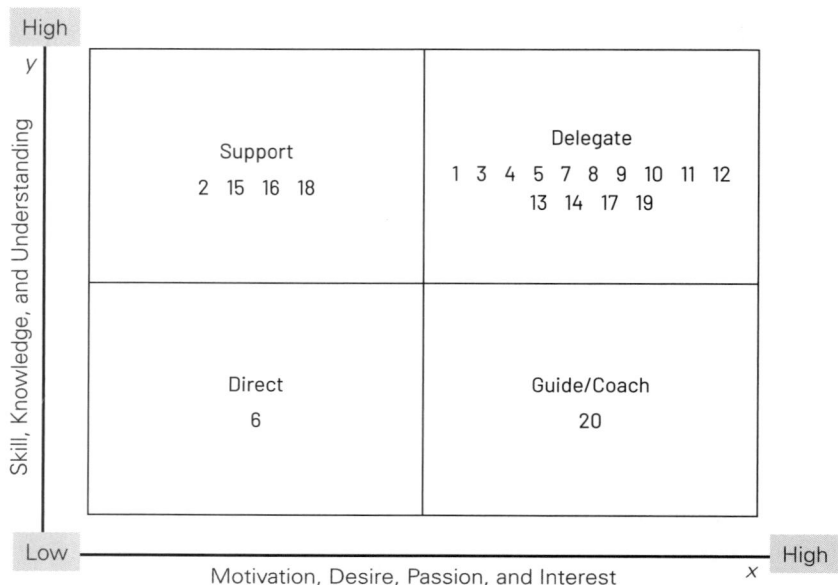

FIGURE 11.1: Bryan's leadership action matrix for being a relationship builder.

Step 2: Complete the Mentoring Planning Page

After plotting the observable behaviors for Bryan on the leadership action matrix, Principal Waller transfers the numbers to the mentoring planning page (see figure 11.2), adding comments about the behaviors she observed and her thoughts about the next steps. She bolds the items she wants to discuss further when she meets with Bryan. Bryan could use this tool for self-evaluation before the mentoring meeting as well.

Way of Being: A Relationship Builder

Teacher: Bryan Sample

Administrator: Principal Waller

Support		Delegate	
Behavior Number	**Notes**	**Behavior Number**	**Notes**
2	Welcomes new students; as an administrator, needs increased focus on parents	1	Notices students' moods and behaviors and acts on them

15	**Respects students; must also respect parents and their concerns**	3	Has talent at engaging students and making connections with them
16	Collaborates with staff and students; must use those skills with parents and families	4	Does a lot of activities with students to get to know them, for students to know each other, and for students to know him
18	Encourages students and staff; should assume positive intentions with parents as well and encourage them	5	Supports students and builds their confidence; notices opportunities to acknowledge and recognize things to celebrate about students
		7	Makes sure students know expectations, makes the classroom student focused and positive, and manages the classroom well
		8	Has positive tone and approach, is happy in class, and recognizes positive student behavior
		9	Includes student voice by creating many avenues for student involvement
		10	**Includes many opportunities for community building in the classroom, including regular check-ins with students, community circles, and significant 72**
		11	Teaches students about making and keeping friends and appropriate behavior, and gets them the assistance they need
		12	Has strong relationships with staff, is friendly, popular, and a leader with staff
		13	Is part of a strong team, values the team, and is focused on working as a team
		14	Does strong work at staff meetings, grade meetings, and data meetings, and keeps the focus on students
		17	Shows he is trustworthy—does what he says he will do
		19	Has excitement for teaching, shares with others, and has enthusiasm
			Recommendations for delegation: • **Could we use significant 72 with parents? What can this look like?**

FIGURE 11.2: Sample mentoring planning page for Bryan for being a relationship builder.

continued ▶

Direct		Guide/Coach	
Behavior Number	**Notes**	**Behavior Number**	**Notes**
6	**Needs to increase skills in building relationships with parents so there is positive student involvement; change habit of speaking about desire for no parent involvement**	20	**Identifies having an equity lens with relationship building as a needed growth area; reviewing chapter 2 (An Advocate for All Students, page 28) and assessing his behaviors in that way of being will support growth**

Following are explanations of some of the Principal Waller's's ratings for Bryan and her comments.

Behavior 6: *The teacher reaches out and creates relationships with parents. Parents are well-informed and understand what is happening in the classroom. The teacher understands that parent involvement with their child's school life has a positive impact on students.*

Principal Waller put behavior six in the direct quadrant because Bryan must improve his view and beliefs about parents and families if he wishes to move into administration one day. His previous school did not welcome or invite parent's voices and that suited the needs of the staff as they were not eager to involve parents. Principal Waller wants her school to be a safe and welcoming space for families—a community hub. Other observable behaviors show that Bryan is a relationship builder with staff and students. However, Bryan has been overheard making comments about appreciating that parents "stay out of the way." Principal Waller wants Bryan to understand his influence with staff and work with him to change this perspective. Waller plans to be direct about this behavior with Bryan, and she does not expect any pushback. Bryan shows high skill and desire to demonstrate strong relationships with students. This difference in lack of motivation between parent relationship building and student relationship building cannot exist if Bryan is to move into a career in administration.

Behavior 15: *The teacher shows respect when dealing with students, staff, and families. They take concerns seriously and make others feel that they have been heard and understood.*

Principal Waller observes that Bryan shows a high level of success and dedication in his classroom and with staff when it comes to relationship building. However, once again, Bryan needs to apply the same dedication to his work with parents and families. Bryan acts professionally with parents and families. He listens well and solves problems that emerge. Parents feel that they have been heard and that their concerns will receive attention. Behavior fifteen is in the support quadrant (high knowledge/skill, low motivation), however, because of Bryan's opinions about parents that he has shared with other staff members—how he does not reach out and involve them. He has relationship-building skills but has little motivation to involve parents in his work with students. Before becoming an administrator, he must improve this belief and see the value of parental involvement for students.

Behavior 20: *The teacher demonstrates relationship-building actions that are done with an equity lens. The teacher supports positive racial, cultural, and ethnic identity development.*

The administrator placed behavior twenty in the guide/coach quadrant because Bryan recognizes he is now working in a different school from his previous position, where the student body was less diverse and there was little parent involvement. Although in his previous school, he was exposed to professional development involving diversity, equity, and inclusion, Bryan paid little attention as he did not believe it was necessary, missing out on important learning and skill development. It is commendable that he recognizes this is an area requiring his attention. Although he knows he is strong at building relationships, he understands he must put that in the context of positive racial, cultural, and ethnic identity development for his own learning, to better match his new location, to assist him in his growth as a leader, but most importantly to make him a better teacher for his students. This is a quadrant usually reserved for those who want to learn more and improve their skills and have the desire and interest to put in the work to do so. This is exactly the situation for Bryan—to become an administrator in the future he must develop an interest in learning and understanding what it means to be an educator with an equity lens.

Behavior 10: *The teacher takes time in class with specific, regular activities and learning that create a sense of belonging for the students. They work on building a community with the students.*

The delegate quadrant allows the administrator to share all the extremely positive qualities that Bryan possesses and celebrate his ability to build relationships with students. Principal Waller put behavior ten in the delegate quadrant because Bryan is both high in knowledge and high in passion and interest. Bryan is top-notch in the classroom with building a respectful, engaging, and productive community of learners. He is aware when students are sad and withdrawn and steps in to make sure students are feeling better about themselves. He has a strong program and is learning more about curriculum, assessment, and evaluation. He prioritizes relationships at this point in his career and Principal Waller knows the other parts will fall into place. Principal Waller is pleased Bryan demonstrates a passion and understanding that relationships come first because he will improve his teaching practices and knowledge with time. Having a core belief in building relationships with students and demonstrating observable behaviors at a high rate indicates that this will be Bryan's strongest way of being. Principal Waller does want to use Bryan's strengths to assist him with relationship building with parents and has indicated delegating using significant 72 with parents as a possibility on the mentoring planning page (see figure 11.2, page 175) to give Bryan some leadership opportunities in an area where he shows strength. Bryan is personable and charismatic and has been doing significant 72 (see A Relationship Builder: School Examples for an explanation).

Step 3: Use the Mentoring Meeting Planner

Principal Waller fills in most of the information on the mentoring meeting planner in preparation for the meeting with Bryan. Figure 11.3 (page 178) shows the completed mentoring meeting planner including notes from the meeting.

Date: March 2

Administrator: Principal Waller

Teacher: Bryan Sample

Focus

Which way or ways of being will we discuss?

A Relationship Builder. Why it is important as a school administrator that you are a relationship builder with all the stakeholders? Who are all the stakeholders that an administrator must consider when thinking of building relationships? What is Bryan's view on building relationships? What needs to change and how can administration assist? The positive aspects does Bryan bring to the school. Ask Bryan for input.

Agenda for Sharing and Discussion

What specific points about the way or ways of being will we discuss?

- Bryan is excellent at building relationships with students, he cares deeply about each student, and he wants them to do well, feel connected, and be involved.
- How do Bryan's views of relationships with parents need to change in order to be a school leader?
- Why is there a need for Bryan to be well-rounded in many aspects of leadership?
- What is Bryan's perspective on his strengths and needs in this way of being? He has identified work on inclusion, diversity, and equity, which is another way of being (an advocate for all students).
- Review notes from the twenty observable behaviors.
- Review notes from the mentoring planning page.

Key Points

- **Direct**
  - » Bryan needs to be aware of how he talks about parents who advocate for their own children.
- **Support**
  - » Bryan's skills with students are excellent; he needs support respecting concerns of parents.
- **Guide/Coach**
  - » Being an advocate for all students is an area Bryan has identified for growth. He will review chapter 2: An Advocate for All Students and the observable behaviors.
- **Delegate**
  - » Regular check-ins with students, community circles, significant 72
  - » Delegate significant 72 with parents—what can this look like?

Teacher Plans, Comments, and Ideas

What plans, comments, and ideas did the teacher have during the meeting?

- Bryan is excited to be thinking about becoming an administrator one day and wants to receive feedback and support.
- Bryan is surprised to hear that his work with students is considered so good. He feels he is just doing what he should do. He thinks all teachers prioritize relationships like he does.
- Bryan wants to learn about the students and families that do not look like him. He realizes that the school is diverse and becoming more diverse. He is excited about this and wants to learn about different cultures.
- Bryan realizes that his previous school and this school are different in their perspectives on parent involvement. He wants to work on building relationships with parents and involving them more.
- At first, Bryan appeared to want to build relationships with parents and learn more because of how it will assist him with becoming an administrator. As the conversation deepened, he started to see the benefit for students, parents, and the school as a whole. Bryan will learn and is eager to learn. He is willing to look at significant 72 in connection to parents and building relationships. He wants to know what this could look like for the entire school. He is interested in this leadership opportunity.

Goal Setting

What is the teacher's goal related to this way of being?

- Bryan will work next on chapter 2: An Advocate for all Students with the administrator.
- Bryan will begin and lead a staff committee to look at significant 72 for the parent community and what it would look like for the first 72 hours of the year.
- Bryan will have regular meetings with the administration to go through other ways of being as well as give regular updates on the parent significant 72 committee.

Potential Resources

What are some potential resources to recommend to the teacher that address their areas of needed growth from the direct and guide/coach quadrants?

- Give Bryan the list of observable behaviors (Visit **go.SolutionTree.com/leadership** for a free reproducible of the list.)
- Suggest the following books:
  - » *Parentships in a PLC at Work®: Forming and Sustaining School-Home Relationships with Families* by Kyle Palmer
  - » *Significant 72: Unleashing the Power of Relationships in Today's Schools* by Greg Wolcott

Final Thoughts

What are your final thoughts about next steps and when to check back in?

Bryan was really excited about meeting to begin discussions about his administration journey. He knew improving his view and relationships with parents was a real need for him but also that it would benefit students and the school as a whole. Hopefully, he understands it is really all about parents deserving a strong relationship with their child's school. He is interested in beginning a committee to look at a project to do with the parents in the community. He wants to look at the other ways of being and because of his age and experience we both believe this may be his strongest way of being. I am glad that it is a strong aspect in his teaching because relationships are key. Other parts to his program will come in time. He does understand the school is different from his previous school and he wants to learn and develop in his understanding and skills working with an equity lens. He is eager to learn more about equity, inclusion, and diversity. He is excited to be at the school and knows it is a great opportunity for him to grow and become a better educator.

FIGURE 11.3: Sample mentoring meeting planner for Bryan for being a relationship builder.

A RELATIONSHIP BUILDER IN ACTION: SCHOOL EXAMPLES

The following—Significant 72 and Thank You Thursday—are two examples of what a relationship builder in action and what they could look like in your school. I share them here to provide leadership opportunities for staff you have identified and plotted in the leadership action matrix who require experiences for further development in relationship building. These examples also show staff and the larger community that the school supports relationship building and understands the importance of this way of being.

Significant 72

I introduced the significant 72 strategy in chapter 5, A Goal Setter Who Uses Data, for the fourth way of being. I shared a school's use of significant 72 for 72 minutes each month to give students a voice and gather their opinions. Significant 72 can also be used to focus specifically on relationships: student to student, staff to student, student to staff, and school to families. At our school, the first 72 hours (the first three days) of school were all about relationships—building our classroom and school community. Our priority was on having staff learn each student's story by using activities that helped educators focus on what each student would need during the year to be successful.

Activities focused on what makes each individual unique and how our differences make us stronger as a unit. What are the gifts others have to offer? How are we going to function as a community for the next ten months? We formed classroom agreements and commitments using our motto: "Work Hard, Be Nice, Make a Difference." Teachers adjusted the activity for the age and stage of the learners, but every classroom displayed their agreements by the end of the first week. School assemblies brought the entire school population together to share in this relationship building to determine how our commitments translate to common areas such as the playground, fields, washrooms, library, gymnasium, and so on. What does it mean to work hard in the library? What does it mean to be nice in the playground? What does it mean to make a difference while eating our lunches?

Students needed to leave each day excited to come back, sharing the positive energy with family members at home; teachers contacted families early in the school year to further strengthen parents' belief that their child was in a warm, welcoming, accepting classroom.

To build relationships within the homeroom, students did not travel through the school to meet all their teachers. Homeroom teachers used the significant 72 hours to form relationships with families. On the second and third day, students met their specialty teachers, but no curriculum was taught. Specialty teachers continued to work on relationships and commitments.

Teachers develop and share many creative, engaging activities to implement during the significant 72 for use in individual homerooms, grade teams, and for culminating activities for the whole division or school. One of my favorite memories was seeing our graduating grade 8 classes begin their final year at the school in celebration, together as a group. After we started implementing significant 72 in this way, I noticed the number of requests from parents to ask for their child to be placed in a different class with another teacher all but disappeared.

Before they talk about the curriculum or create long-range plans, grade-level teachers meet for their first planning session of the new school year together to talk about how they are going to make their classrooms places where students feel safe, feel heard, feel represented, and will thrive. They discuss building relationships!

Significant 72 also refers to 72 seconds each day. The idea of this strategy is to make a difference for a student in 72 seconds. What actions can every adult in the school take for 72 seconds each day to profoundly impact the lives of students? Positive interactions that last approximately 72 seconds, done consistently, day after day, have a huge impact on the mental health, well-being, and sense of connection students have to schools. Every student needs to know they are seen (Wolcott, 2019).

Many schools have programs where staff identify students who would benefit from a caring adult taking an interest and connecting with them each day, such as SOS (Save One Student), Playground Buddies, Teacher's Little Helpers, and so on. These programs that focus on connecting with students are valuable; however, all students need to feel connected to the school. It is not good enough to target only some students. If every student has an advocate in the school, their chances of success are much greater (Margolius et al., 2020). When every adult gives students significant 72 seconds each day—in the hallways, outside on the fields, entering the school, coming into our classrooms—students know staff are glad to see them, are happy they are in school, and that today will be a good day.

We asked every adult in the building to make sure they had multiple significant 72 moments with students in a day. Significant 72 has a definite beneficial impact on both the giver and the receiver. The overall school climate feels different when staff commit to speaking and interacting with students in this way. The atmosphere is positive, and staff want to join in and do all they can to maintain and participate in that culture. Significant 72 is contagious. It was not uncommon for visitors to our school to comment about the feel or the vibe in the school.

Thank You Thursday

As an administrator, you do many things to show staff you appreciate them. I always believed it was the daily interactions, done consistently, that showed I valued all staff and their contributions to our students and school. While grand gestures are nice, and they have a place in the way we celebrate; it is the day-in, day-out connections that make the bigger difference.

A habit I picked up early in my career came after a professional learning experience with Todd Whittaker, an author and staff motivation expert. I do not remember what he called the strategy; I came to call it Thank You Thursday. It is a practice I did for more than twenty years.

Every week, my work calendar included an appointment called Thank You Thursday. Every Thursday, I wrote three handwritten thank you cards. Most times they were for staff members, but, every once in a while, I would write one for a parent, the crossing guard, a bus driver, and even a student. During the week I jotted in my notebook things that I had seen or heard about a staff member going above and beyond. On Thursday I wrote a note and placed it on their desk or in their mailbox. I also write notes to new staff members to welcome them, or to say goodbye, but most of the time it was for a small, yet powerful random act that they had done. For example, a positive interaction I witnessed between them and a student, a particularly strong lesson I saw in their classroom, an interaction they had with parents during drop off or pick up, their use of break time to run a club. I always connected my thanks to our motto Work Hard, Be Nice, Make a Difference to connect back to school beliefs.

Thank You Thursday is an easy way to build relationships with staff and other stakeholders. It takes less than five minutes to show others you value them.

CONCLUSION

Effective administrators spend time developing, improving, and investing in relationship building. Positive relationships really are the heart of the school; they can make a good school a great school. An administrator focused on relationships is building an environment of learning, caring, respect, compassion, professionalism, and trust.

Who is leading a school is a major part of teacher ratings of the school environment and where they want to work, independent of other district and school factors (Burkhauser, 2017). In an era with significant concerns about teacher shortages, having effective administrators in schools not only keeps teachers at the school, but also keeps them in the profession (Podolsky, Kini, Bishop, & Darling-Hammond, 2016). When teachers have high satisfaction with their school and in their role, they are less likely to leave—especially in high-poverty schools where excellent teachers are most needed (Grissom, 2011). The school leader plays a major role in motivating and keeping effective teachers to ensure that multiple years of students benefit from their instruction (Hughes, Matt, & O'Reilly, 2015). One way to keep the best teachers in hard-to-serve schools is to make sure that there is an effective administrator in the office (Grissom, 2011).

Education is a people business with relationship building at the forefront of the work of an administrator. Teachers who are considering a move into an administrative role spend time building relationships with students—this is still the most important relationship to consider in a school—but they also recognize the importance of interactions with other stakeholders to establish connections and build relationships.

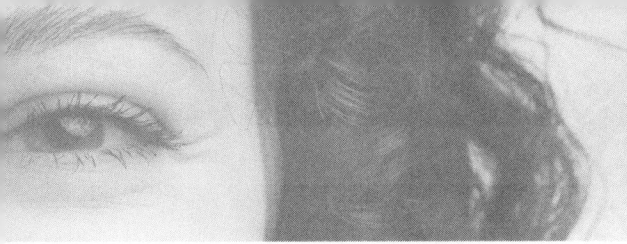

EPILOGUE

It is a cold day in the middle of February and the morning bell to end classes has just rung. Students and staff are putting on their warm winter clothing to head outside for a recess break; the administrator is no exception. Closing his computer, he leaves the office and heads down the hall.

During his walk outside, he passes students and staff who are happy, engaged, and full of joy. There is an infectious and exciting energy in the hallways. He exchanges pleasantries, smiles, and nods, giving students high-fives and fist bumps as he makes his way through the crowds of students. He notices a new pair of running shoes being taken off so boots can be put on. He comments about a bright new jacket and a comical winter hat. The administrator talks to a few students about the hockey game the night before and how his favorite team was able to pull off a victory. He is excited to see students, calls them by name, and asks them how they are going to play in the snow today. He is heading outside just as he has done for the past twenty-two years, but today is different because that morning he wrote and sent his retirement letter into the district office.

While outside, a young second-grade student named Zaynab approaches him and starts a conversation. Zaynab looks him in the eyes and asks, "Can I tell you something?" Without waiting for a reply, she continues, "You remind me of home."

The administrator is taken aback for a moment. What a lovely thing to say, and after all the years of working hard with staff, students, and the community to create a climate and culture where everyone feels welcome and safe, today the comment meant even more. Zaynab has made his heart light up.

"That is so wonderful, Zaynab. Thank you. What made you say that?"

She smiles and says, "Cause you kind of look like my grandfather!" and runs off.

Zaynab's statement did not end up being the profound commentary on his life's work that he had first thought; rather, it meant he was old. Smiling to himself, he made his way back inside as the bell rang.

When he got back to his desk, he saw that someone left him a warm cup of coffee from the local bakery with a chocolate chip cookie sitting on top of the lid (so the cookie would stay warm—just the way he liked it). Leaning against the cup was an envelope. The note inside read:

> It's Thursday, so I just had to write to you. Thank you so much. I cannot begin to tell you how much I love my new job. Being a vice principal is the best thing I have ever done in education. Some days are a challenge, but I love the students, the staff are great, and I am in a lovely community. You have given me so much to get me to this point. During the course of my day, I often hear your voice in my head and think, "I wonder what he would do in this situation." Just wanted you to know you have been a big influence on me. Thank you for showing me how to Work Hard, Be Nice, and Make a Difference. I appreciate you.

The administrator put down the card, smiled, and took a deep breath.

While it is gratifying to see the research that confirms the importance of a school administrator and the ten ways of being this book presents, it is experiences such as the one described here that say the most. Schools are better places when an administrator possesses certain ways of being.

As a current school leader, you have a role to play in making sure the best candidates become administrators so they can impact, influence, and make a difference for students, staff, and the communities they serve. Are you ready to do your part and mentor the next generation of effective leaders? Take a look around because there are leaders among us!

REFERENCES AND RESOURCES

Allen, K.-A. (2022, January 28). *The power of relationships in schools* [Blog post]. Accessed at https://www.psychologytoday.com/ca/blog/sense-belonging/202201/the-power -relationships-in-schools on February 15, 2024.

Allen, K.-A., Slaten, C. D., Arslan, G., Roffey, S., Craig, H., & Vella-Brodrick, D. A. (2021). School belonging: The importance of student and teacher relationships. In M. L. Kern & M. L. Wehmeyer (Eds.), *The Palgrave handbook of positive education* (pp. 525–550). New York: Palgrave Macmillan.

Alphonso, C. (2023, March 20). Toronto schools see rise in difficult student behaviour, report says. *The Globe and Mail.* Accessed at https://www.theglobeandmail.com/about/ on February 15, 2024.

Armstrong, D. E. (2014, April). *Transition to the role of principal and vice-principal study.* Paris, Ontario, Canada: The Institute for Education Leadership. Accessed at https://www .education-leadership-ontario.ca/application/files/1914/9452/4574/Principal_and_Vice _Principal_Transition_to_the_Role.pdf on February 15, 2024.

Australian Institute for Teaching and School Leadership. (2014). *Australian professional standard for principals and the leadership profiles*. Melbourne, Australia: Author. Accessed at https://www.aitsl.edu.au/docs/default-source/national-policy-framework /australian-professional-standard-for-principals-and-the-leadership-profiles on February 15, 2024.

Bagwell, J. L. (2013). *Exploring the leadership practices of elementary principals in program improvement schools through a distributed leadership framework* [Doctoral dissertation, California State University, Northridge]. ScholarWorks. https://scholarworks.calstate.edu /concern/theses/n009w548k

Barajas-López, F., & Ishimaru, A. M. (2020). "Darles el lugar": A place for nondominant family knowing in educational equity. *Urban Education*, *55*(1), 38–65.

Barber, R. S. (2020). *A case study of communications between school administrators and teachers in an urban middle school* [Doctoral dissertation, Indiana University, Bloomington]. ScholarWorks. https://scholarworks.iu.edu/iuswrrest/api/core/bitstreams/8fd431e3 -73af-4bd9-9fc7-32dbdebb73e9/content

Bartanen, B. (2020). Principal quality and student attendance. *Educational Researcher*, *49*(2), 101–113.

Bastian, K. C., & Henry, G. T. (2015). The apprentice: Pathways to the principalship and student achievement. *Educational Administration Quarterly*, *51*(4), 600–639.

Berger, R., Berman, S., Garcia, J., & Deasy, J. (n.d.). *National Commission on Social, Emotional, and Academic Development: A practice agenda in support of how learning happens*. Washington, DC: The Aspen Institute. Accessed at https://www.aspeninstitute. org/wp-content/uploads/2023/02/aspen_practice_final_web_optimized.pdf on February 15, 2024.

Blanchard. (2024). *SLII*. Accessed at www.blanchard.com/our-content/programs/slii on October 30, 2024.

Blanchard, K., & Johnson, S. (1982). *The one minute manager*. New York: Morrow.

Blazar, D., & Lagos, F. (2021). *Professional staff diversity and student outcomes: Extending our understanding of race/ethnicity-matching effects in education*. (EdWorkingPaper: 21-500). Annenberg Institute at Brown University: https://doi.org/10.26300/bz9t-7640.

Boyce, J., & Bowers, A. J. (2016). Principal turnover: Are there different types of principals who move from or leave their schools? A latent class analysis of the 2007–2008 Schools and Staffing Survey and the 2008–2009 Principal Follow-Up Survey. *Leadership and Policy in Schools*, *15*(3), 237–272.

Branch, G. F., Hanushek, E. A., & Rivkin, S. G. (2012, February). *Estimating the effect of leaders on public sector productivity: The case of school principals* [Working paper 17803]. Cambridge, MA: National Bureau of Economic Research.

Bronk, K. C., & McLean, D. C. (2016). The role of passion and purpose in leader developmental readiness. *New Directions for Student Leadership*, (149), 27–36.

Brown, C., & Militello, M. (2016). Principal's perceptions of effective professional development in schools. *Journal of Educational Administration*, *54*(6), 703–726.

Bryant, J., Ram, S., Scott, D., & Williams, C. (2023, March 23). *K–12 teachers are quitting: What would make them stay?* McKinsey & Company-Education. Accessed at www.mckinsey.com/industries/education/our-insights/k-12-teachers-are-quitting-what -would-make-them-stay on August 3, 2024.

Burkhauser, S. (2017). How much do school principals matter when it comes to teacher working conditions? *Educational Evaluation and Policy Analysis*, *39*(1), 126–145.

Buskey, F. (2019). 6 strategies to become a present principal. *Communicator*, *42*(10).

Can, M. H. (2016). Use of mobile application: Means of communication between parents and class teacher. *World Journal on Educational Technology: Current Issues*, *8*(3), 252–257.

Canadian Association of Principals & The Alberta Teachers' Association. (2014). *The future of the principalship in Canada: A national research study*. Edmonton, Alberta, Canada: The Alberta Teachers' Association. Accessed at https://legacy.teachers.ab.ca/SiteCollection Documents/ATA/Publications/Research/The%20Future%20of%20the%20 Principalship%20in%20Canada.pdf on February 15, 2024.

Canadian Mental Health Association. (n.d.). *Mental health*. Accessed at https://ontario.cmha .ca/mental-health/ on February 15, 2024.

Carver-Thomas, D., Darling-Hammond, L., & Sutcher, L. (2019). *A coming crisis in teaching? Teacher supply, demand and shortages in the U.S.* Annenberg Institute at Brown University working paper, EdWorkingPaper series, number 19-184.

Centers for Disease Control and Prevention. (n.d.). *Safe and supportive environments*. Accessed at https://www.cdc.gov/healthyyouth/safe-supportive-environments/index.htm on February 19, 2024.

Corporate Finance Institute. (n.d.). *Hersey-Blanchard Model*. Accessed at https://corporate financeinstitute.com/resources/management/hersey-blanchard-model/ on February 15, 2024.

Chiang, H., Lipscomb, S., & Gill, B. (2016). Is school value added indicative of principal quality? *Education Finance and Policy*, *11*(3), 283–309.

Clayton, G., & Bingham, A. J. (2018). The first year: Assistant principals in Title I schools. *Journal of Educational Leadership and Policy Studies*, *1*(2).

Collado, W., Hollie, S., Isiah, R., Jackson, Y., Muhammad, A., Reeves, D., et al. (2021). *Beyond cnversations about race: A guide for discussions with students, teachers, and communities*. Bloomington, IN: Solution Tree Press.

Couros, G. (n.d.). *Four attributes of a great assistant principal* [Blog post]. Accessed at https://georgecouros.ca/blog/4-attributes-of-a-great-assistant-principal-2/ on February 15, 2024.

Darling-Hammond, L., & Bransford, J. (Eds.). (2005). *Preparing teachers for a changing world: What teachers should learn and be able to do.* San Francisco: Jossey-Bass.

de Bruin, L. (2020, March 28). *Hersey and Blanchard Situational Leadership Model: Adapting the leadership style to the follower.* Accessed at https://www.business-to-you.com/hersey-blanchard-situational-leadership-model/ on February 15, 2024.

Deci, E. L., Olafsen, A. H., & Ryan, R. M. (2017). Self-determination theory in work organizations: The state of a science. *Annual Review of Organizational Psychology and Organizational Behavior, 4,* 19–43.

Dhuey, E., & Smith, J. (2018). How school principals influence student learning. *Empirical Economics, 54*(2), 851–882.

Di Lucia, D. C. (2014). The quest for increased student achievement and well-being: Inspiring learning: Mobilizing sustainable improvement. Education and communication in the 21st century. *The Quest Journal*, Volume 8. Access at chrome-extension://efaidnbmnnnib pcajpcglclefindmkaj/https://www.yrdsb.ca/Programs/PLT/Quest/Documents/2014DiLuciaArticle.pdf on August 3, 2024.

Diamanti, K., Duffey, T., & Fisher, D. (2018). *Creating a safe and respectful environment in our nation's classrooms* (2nd ed.). Washington, DC: National Center on Safe Supportive Learning Environments.

Dixon, J. K., Brooks, L. A., & Carli, M. R. (2019). *Making sense of mathematics for teaching the small group.* Bloomington, IN: Solution Tree Press.

Donlan, R. (2022). *All other duties as assigned: The assistant principal's critical role in supporting schools inside and out.* Bloomington, IN: Solution Tree Press.

Donley, J., Detrich, R., States, J., & Keyworth, R. (2020). *Principal retention overview.* Oakland, CA: The Wing Institute. Accessed at https://winginstitute.org/quality-leadership-principal-retention on February 15, 2024.

DuBois, D. L., Holloway, B. E., Valentine, J. C., & Cooper, H. (2002). Effectiveness of mentoring programs for youth: A meta-analytic review. *American Journal of Community Psychology, 30*(2), 157–197.

DuFour, R. (2015). *In praise of American educators: And how they can become even better.* Bloomington, IN: Solution Tree Press.

DuFour, R., DuFour, R., Eaker, R., Many, T. W., Mattos, M., & Muhammad, A. (2024). *Learning by doing: A handbook for Professional Learning Communities at Work* (3rd ed.). Bloomington, IN: Solution Tree Press.

DuFour, R., DuFour, R., Eaker, R., Many, T. W., Mattos, M., & Muhammad, A. (2024). *Learning by doing: A handbook for Professional Learning Communities at Work* (4th ed.). Bloomington, IN: Solution Tree Press.

DuFour, R., & Eaker, R. (1998). *Professional Learning Communities at Work: Best practices for enhancing student achievement*. Bloomington, IN: Solution Tree Press.

Dunbar, M. (2020). *Morning meetings and closing circles: Classroom-ready activities that increase student engagement and create a positive learning community*. Berkley, CA: Ulysses Press.

Dweck, C. S. (2008). *Mindset: The new psychology of success*. New York: Ballantine Books.

Dweck, C. S. (2016). *Mindset: The new psychology of success* (2nd ed.). New York: Ballantine Books.

Erkens, C. (2019). *The handbook for collaborative common assessments: Tools for design, delivery, and data analysis*. Bloomington, IN: Solution Tree Press.

Erkens, C., Schimmer, T., & Dimich-Vagle, N. (2017). *Essential assessment: Six tenets for bringing hope, efficacy, and achievement to the classroom*. Bloomington, IN: Solution Tree Press.

Erkens, C., Schimmer, T., & Dimich-Vagle, N. (2017). *Instructional agility: Responding to assessment with real-time decisions*. Bloomington, IN: Solution Tree Press.

Evers-Gerdes, B., & Siegle, R. (2022). *Establishing a lasting legacy: Six steps to maximize your leadership impact and improve teacher retention*. Bloomington, IN: Solution Tree Press.

Fairholm, G. W. (1994). *Leadership and the culture of trust*. Westport, CT: Praeger.

Ferriter, W. M. (2020). *The big book of tools for collaborative teams in a PLC at work*. Bloomington, IN: Solution Tree Press.

Fields, L. J., & Egley, R. J. (2005). Assistant principals in Florida rank first-year challenges: Study's results highlight areas of need for professional development. *ERS Spectrum, 23*(1), 4–10.

Fink, D., & Brayman, C. (2006). School leadership succession and the challenges of change. *Educational Administration Quarterly, 42*(1), 62–89.

Freeman, D. (2016). *Lack of skill or lack of will? Adapt your call coaching method accordingly!* Accessed at https://qatc.org/summer-2016-connection/ on February 15, 2024.

Fullan, M. (2013). *Stratosphere: Integrating technology, pedagogy, and change knowledge*. Toronto, Ontario, Canada: Pearson.

Fullan, M. (2014). *The principal: Three keys to maximizing impact*. San Francisco: Jossey-Bass.

Fullan, M. (2019). *Nuance: Why some leaders succeed and others fail*. Thousand Oaks, CA: Corwin Press.

Gardner, J. W. (1990). *On leadership*. New York: Free Press.

Garmston, R. J. (2012). *Unlocking group potential to improve schools*. Thousand Oaks, CA: Corwin Press.

Gates, S. M., Baird, M. D., Master, B. K., & Chavez-Herrerias, E. R. (2019). *Principal pipelines: A feasible, affordable, and effective way for districts to improve schools*. Santa Monica, CA: RAND Corporation.

Genlott, A. A., Grönlund, Å., & Viberg, O. (2019). Disseminating digital innovation in school—leading second-order educational change. *Education and Information Technologies, 24*, 3021–3039.

Goldhaber, D., Holden, K., & Chen, B. (2019, January). *Do more effective teachers become more effective principals?* [Working paper no. 215-0119-1]. Washington, DC: National Center for the Analysis of Longitudinal Data in Education Research. Accessed at https://caldercenter.org/sites/default/files/CALDER%20WP%20215-0119-1.pdf on February 15, 2024.

Goldring, E., Grissom, J. A., Neumerski, C. M., Murphy, J., Blissett, R., & Porter, A. (2015). *Making time for instructional leadership: Volume 1: The evolution of the SAM process*. New York: The Wallace Foundation. Accessed at https://wallacefoundation.org/sites/default/files/2023-10/Making-Time-for-Instructional-Leadership-Vol-1.pdf on February 15, 2024.

Goldring, E., Rubin, M., & Herrmann, M. (2021, April). *The role of assistant principals: Evidence and insights for advancing school leadership*. New York: The Wallace Foundation. Accessed at https://wallacefoundation.org/sites/default/files/2023-10/the-role-of-assistant-principals-evidence-insights-for-advancing-school-leadership.pdf on February 15, 2024.

Good, R. (2008). Sharing the secrets. *Principal Leadership, 8*(8), 46–50.

Grafwallner, P. (2021). *Not Yet . . . and That's Ok: How Productive Struggle Fosters Student Learning*. Bloomington, IN: Solution Tree Press.

Grant, A. (2013). *Give and take: A revolutionary approach to success*. New York: Viking.

Grant, A. (2016). *Originals: How non-conformists move the world*. New York: Viking.

Grant, A. [@AdamMGrant]. (2023, August 9). *When considering a new role, the most important question isn't 'can I do it?' It's 'do I want it?' It's up to the employer to decide whether you're qualified. Only you can gauge whether you're motivated. Values should align with the job. Skills can be learned on the job* [Post]. X. Accessed at https://twitter.com/AdamMGrant/status/1689307327248183296 on February 15, 2024.

Greene, R. W. (2021). *Lost and found: Unlocking collaboration and compassion to help our most vulnerable, misunderstood students (and all the rest)* (2nd ed.). San Francisco: Jossey-Bass.

Greenfield, W. D. (1985). The moral socialization of school administrators: Informal role learning outcomes. *Educational Administration Quarterly, 21*(4), 99–119.

Grenny, J., Patterson, K., McMillan, R., Switzler, A., & Gregory, E. (2022). *Crucial conversations: Tools for talking when stakes are high* (3rd ed.). New York: McGraw Hill.

Grissom, J. A. (2011). Can good principals keep teachers in disadvantaged schools? Linking principal effectiveness to teacher satisfaction and turnover in hard-to-staff environments. *Teachers College Record, 113*(11), 2552–2585.

Grissom, J. A., & Bartanen, B. (2019). Principal effectiveness and principal turnover. *Education Finance and Policy, 14*(3), 355–382.

Grissom, J. A., Egalite, A. J., & Lindsay, C. A. (2021, February). *How principals affect students and schools: A systematic synthesis of two decades of research.* New York: The Wallace Foundation. Accessed at http://wallacefoundation.org/principalsynthesis on February 15, 2024.

Grissom, J. A., Kalogrides, D., & Loeb, S. (2015). Using student test scores to measure principal performance. *Educational Evaluation and Policy Analysis, 37*(1), 3–28.

Grissom, J. A., & Loeb, S. (2011). Triangulating principal effectiveness: How perspectives of parents, teachers, and assistant principals identify the central importance of managerial skills. *American Educational Research Journal, 48*(5), 1091–1123.

Grissom, J. A., Loeb, S., & Master, B. (2013). Effective instructional time use for school leaders: Longitudinal evidence from observations of principals. *Educational Researcher, 42*(8), 433–444.

Grissom, J. A., Mitani, H., & Blissett, R. S. L. (2017). Principal licensure exams and future job performance: Evidence from the school leaders licensure assessment. *Educational Evaluation and Policy Analysis, 39*(2), 248–280.

Grissom, J. A., Mitani, H., & Woo, D. S. (2019). Principal preparation programs and principal outcomes. *Educational Administration Quarterly, 55*(1), 73–115.

Grissom, J. A., Woo, D. S., & Bartanen, B. (2020). *Ready to lead on day one: Predicting novice principal effectiveness with information available at time of hire* [EdWorkingPaper no. 20–276]. Providence, RI: Annenberg Institute. Accessed at https://edworkingpapers.com/sites/default/files/ai20-276.pdf on February 15, 2024.

Hargreaves, A., Moore, S., Fink, D., Brayman, C., & White, R. (2003). *Succeeding leaders? A study of principal rotation and succession.* Toronto, Ontario, Canada: Ontario Principals' Council.

Hartzell, G. (1993). The assistant principal's office: What message does it convey? *NASSP Bulletin, 77*(552), 68–76.

Hattie, J. (2009). *Visible learning: A synthesis of over 800 meta-analyses relating to achievement.* New York: Routledge.

Hattie, J. (2023). *Visible learning: The sequel: A synthesis of over 2,100 meta-analyses relating to achievement.* New York: Routledge.

Hausman, C., Nebeker, A., McCreary, J., & Donaldson, G., Jr. (2002). The worklife of the assistant principal. *Journal of Educational Administration, 40*(2–3), 136–157.

Henderson, A. T., Mapp, K. L., Johnson, V. R., & Davies, D. (2007). *Beyond the bake sale: The essential guide to family-school partnerships.* New York: The New Press.

Hersey, P., & Blanchard, K. H. (1993). *Management of organizational behavior: Utilizing human resources* (6th ed.). Englewood Cliffs, NJ: Prentice-Hall.

Hierck, T. (2017). *Seven keys to a positive learning environment in your classroom.* Bloomington, IN: Solution Tree Press.

Hierck, T. (2019). *Managing unstoppable learning* (D. Fisher & N. Frey, Eds.). Bloomington, IN: Solution Tree Press.

Hierck, T., Coleman, C., & Weber, C. (2011). *Pyramid of behavior interventions: Seven keys to a positive learning environment.* Bloomington, IN: Solution Tree Press.

Hoffman, A. M., & Holzhüter, J. (2012). The evolution of higher education: Innovation as natural selection. In A. M. Hoffman & S. D. Spangehl (Eds.), *Innovations in higher education: Igniting the spark for success* (pp. 3–15). Lanham, MD: Rowman & Littlefield.

Huber, S. G., & West, M. (2002). Developing school leaders: A critical review of current practices, approaches and issues, and some directions for the future. In K. Leithwood & P. Hallinger (Eds.), *Second international handbook of educational leadership and administration* (pp. 1071–1101). New York: Springer.

Hughes, A. L., Matt, J. J., & O'Reilly, F. L. (2015). Principal support is imperative to the retention of teachers in hard to staff schools. *Journal of Education and Training Studies, 3*(1), 129–134.

Ilomäki, L., & Lakkala, M. (2018). Digital technology and practices for school improvement: Innovative digital school model. *Research and Practice in Technology Enhanced Learning, 13*(1), Article 25.

Institute for Education Leadership. (n.d.). *Strengthening your psychological personal leadership resources (PLRs): Reflective manual for self-discovery for Catholic school leaders.* Accessed at https://www.education-leadership-ontario.ca/application/files/6216/1955/5441/RM _Psychological_PLRs_Catholic.pdf on February 19, 2024.

Institute for Education Leadership. (2013, September). *The Ontario Leadership Framework: A school and system leader's guide to putting Ontario's leadership framework into action.* Toronto: Queen's Printer for Ontario.

Ishimaru, A. M. (2019). From family engagement to equitable collaboration. *Educational Policy, 33*(2), 350–385.

Jacob, B. A., & Lefgren, L. (2008). Can principals identify effective teachers? Evidence on subjective performance evaluation in education. *Journal of Labor Economics, 26*(1), 101–136.

Joseph, M. X. (2019, December 24). *Leadership: 7 ways to increase your visibility.* Accessed at https://districtadministration.com/leadership-7-ways-to-increase-your-visibility/ on February 16, 2024.

Karlgaard, R. (2009, July 23). Purpose-driven leadership. *Forbes.* Accessed at https://www.forbes.com/2009/07/23/bmw-hy-vee-karlgaard-intelligent-technology-leadership.html?sh=41e8b28865c3 on February 16, 2024.

Keesor, C. A. (2005). Administrative visibility and its effect on classroom behavior. *NASSP Bulletin, 89*(643), 64–73.

Koch, A. R., Binnewies, C., & Dormann, C. (2015). Motivating innovation in schools: School principals' work engagement as a motivator for schools' innovation. *European Journal of Work and Organizational Psychology, 24*(4), 505–517.

Kouzes, J. M., & Posner, B. Z. (2002). *The leadership challenge* (3rd ed.). New York: Wiley.

Kraft, M. A., & Gilmour, A. (2016). Can principals promote teacher development as evaluators? A case study of principals' views and experiences. *Educational Administration Quarterly, 52*(5), 711–753.

Kruse, K. (2019, September 23). *Situational leadership theory in plain language: The landmark model from Paul Hersey and Ken Blanchard.* Accessed at https://leadx.org/articles/situational-leadership-theory-model-blanchard-hersey on August 3, 2024.

Kuczmarski, S. S., & Kuczmarski, T. D. (2020). How to create a culture of praise and recognition. Accessed at https://podiatrym.com/pdf/2020/3/Kuczmarski420web.pdf on August 3, 2024.

Kutsyuruba, B., Klinger, D. A., & Hussain, A. (2015). Context and implications document for: Relationships among school climate, school safety, and student achievement and well-being: A review of the literature. *Review of Education, 3*(2), 136–137.

Kyzar, K., & Jimerson, J. B. (2018). Bridging the school-home divide in the middle grades: A process for strengthening school-family partnerships. *Middle-School Journal, 49*(1), 13–23

Laing, D., Rivkin, S. G., Schiman, J. C., & Ward, J. (2016, March). *Decentralized governance and the quality of school leadership* [Working paper no. 22061]. Cambridge, MA: National Bureau of Economic Research. Accessed at https://www.nber.org/system/files/working_papers/w22061/w22061.pdf on February 16, 2024.

Leithwood, K. (2012, March). *The Ontario Leadership Framework 2012 with a discussion of the research foundations.* Paris, Ontario, Canada: The Institute for Education Leadership. Accessed at https://www.education-leadership-ontario.ca/application/files/2514/9452/5287/The_Ontario_Leadership_Framework_2012_-_with_a_Discussion_of_the_Research_Foundations.pdf on February 16, 2024.

Leithwood, K., Louis, K. S., Anderson, S., & Wahlstrom, K. (2004). *How leadership influences student learning.* New York: The Wallace Foundation. Accessed at https://wallace

foundation.org/sites/default/files/2023-07/How-Leadership-Influences-Student-Learning .pdf on February 16, 2024.

Leithwood, K., Harris, A., & Hopkins, D. (2008). Seven strong claims about successful school leadership. *School Leadership and Management*, *28*(1), 27–42.

Leithwood, K., Harris, A., & Strauss, T. (2010). *Leading school turnaround*. San Francisco: Jossey-Bass.

Levin, S., & Bradley, K. (2019). *Understanding and addressing principal turnover: A review of the research*. Reston, VA: National Association of Secondary School Principals & Learning Policy Institute. Accessed at https://learningpolicyinstitute.org/media/326/download ?inline&file=NASSP_LPI_Principal_Turnover_Research_Review_REPORT.pdf on February 16, 2024.

Margolius, M., Lynch, A. D., Hynes, M., Flanagan, S., & Jones, E. P. (2020, September). *What drives learning: Young people's perspectives on the importance of relationships, belonging, and agency: Results from a 2020 survey of high school youth*. Washington, DC: America's Promise Alliance. Accessed at https://files.eric.ed.gov/fulltext/ED617364.pdf on February 16, 2024.

Marshall, C. (1985). Professional shock: The enculturation of the assistant principal. *Education and Urban Society*, *18*(1), 28–58.

Marshall, C., Mitchell, B., Gross, R., & Scott, D. (1992). The assistant principalship: A career position or a stepping-stone to the principalship? *NASSP Bulletin*, *76*(540), 80–88.

Marzano, R. J., Warrick, P. B., Rains, C. L., & DuFour, R. (2018). *Leading a High Reliability School*. Bloomington, IN: Solution Tree Press.

Marzano, R. J., Waters, T., & McNulty, B. A. (2005). *School leadership that works: From research to results*. Alexandria, VA: ASCD.

Mascall, B., & Leithwood, K. (2010). Investing in leadership: The district's role in managing principal turnover. *Leadership and Policy in Schools*, *9*(4), 367–383.

Mascareñaz, L. (2021). *Evident equity: A guide for creating systemwide change in schools*. Bloomington, IN: Solution Tree Press.

Mayer, J. E. (2007). *Creating a safe and welcoming school: Educational practices series-16*. Geneva, Switzerland: International Bureau of Education.

McCray, C. R. (2022). *Equitable instruction, empowered students: A teacher's guide to inclusive and culturally competent classrooms*. Bloomington, IN: Solution Tree Press.

Meirovich, G., & Gu, J. (2015). Empirical and theoretical validity of Hersey-Blanchard's contingency model. *Journal of Applied Management and Entrepreneurship*, *20*(3), 56–73.

Mental Health America. (2024). Key findings 2024. Accessed at https://mhanational.org /issues/state-mental-health-america on August 3., 2024.

Mertz, N. T. (2006). The organizational socialization of assistant principals. *Journal of School Leadership, 16*(6), 644–675.

Miller, A. (2013). Principal turnover and student achievement. *Economics of Education Review, 36*, 60–72.

Mitgang, L. (2012, June). *The making of the principal: Five lessons in leadership training.* New York: The Wallace Foundation. Accessed at https://wallacefoundation.org/sites/default /files/2023-09/The-Making-of-the-Principal-Five-Lessons-in-Leadership-Training.pdf on February 16, 2024.

Moyle, K. (2010). *Building innovation: Learning with technologies.* Camberwell, Victoria, Australia: Australian Council for Educational Research.

Natale, K., & Lubniewski, K. (2018). Use of communication and technology among educational professionals and families. *International Electronic Journal of Elementary Education, 10*(3), 377–384.

National Policy Board for Educational Administration. (2015). *Professional standards for educational leaders.* Reston, VA: Author. Accessed at https://www.npbea.org/wp-content /uploads/2017/06/Professional-Standards-for-Educational-Leaders_2015.pdf on February 16, 2024.

Oelschlager, F. (2021, April 27). *The skill-motivation matrix.* Accessed at https://tenmilesquare .com/resources/technology-strategy-innovation/the-skill-motivation-matrix/ on February 19, 2024.

Oleszewski, A., Shoho, A., & Barnett, B. (2012). The development of assistant principals: A literature review. *Journal of Educational Administration, 50*(3), 264–286.

Ontario Human Rights Commission. (n.d.a). *Creating a welcoming environment.* Accessed at https://www.ohrc.on.ca/en/guidelines-accessible-education/creating-welcoming-environment on February 19, 2024.

Ontario Human Rights Commission. (n.d.b). *Racial discrimination, race and racism (fact sheet).* Accessed at https://www.ohrc.on.ca/en/racial-discrimination-race-and-racism-fact-sheet on February 19, 2024.

Ontario Ministry of Education. (n.d.). *Human rights, equity, and inclusive education.* Accessed at https://www.dcp.edu.gov.on.ca/en/program-planning/considerations-for-program -planning/human-rights-equity-and-inclusive-education on February 16, 2024.

Ontario Ministry of Education. (2010). *Growing success: Assessment, evaluation, and reporting in Ontario schools: First edition, covering grades 1 to 12.* Toronto, Ontario, Canada: Queen's Printer for Ontario.

Ontario Ministry of Education. (2013). *School Effectiveness Framework: A support for school improvement and student success, K–12*. Toronto, Ontario, Canada: Queen's Printer for Ontario.

Ontario Ministry of Education. (2020, July 9). *Ontario taking bold action to address racism and inequity in schools*. Accessed at https://news.ontario.ca/en/backgrounder/57542/ontario -taking-bold-action-to-address-racism-and-inequity-in-schools on February 19, 2024.

Ontario Ministry of Education. (2022a, February 24). *Promote a positive school environment*. Accessed at https://www.ontario.ca/page/promote-positive-school-environment on February 19, 2024.

Ontario Ministry of Education. (2022b, July 11). *Creating safe and accepting schools*. Accessed at https://www.ontario.ca/page/creating-safe-and-accepting-schools on February 19, 2024.

Ontario Ministry of Education. (2022, June 29). Creating safe and accepting schools: addressing inappropriate behavior. Accessed at https://www.ontario.ca/page/creating -safe-and-accepting-schools-addressing-inappropriate-behavior.

Ontario Principals' Council. (2011). *The principal as leader of challenging conversations*. Thousand Oaks, CA: Corwin Press.

Ontario Principals' Council. (2023, September 28). Equity, diversity, inclusion workshop. Self-directed online module and virtual workshop led by Irfan Toor, OPC's director of equity, diversity, and inclusion.

Orta, D., & Gutiérrez, V. (2022). *Improving school-family communication and engagement: Lessons from remote schooling during the pandemic*. Chicago: University of Chicago Consortium on School Research.

Ovando, M. N., & Ramirez, A., Jr. (2007). Principals' instructional leadership within a teacher performance appraisal system: Enhancing students' academic success. *Journal of Personnel Evaluation in Education, 20*(1–2), 85–110.

Palmer, K. (2022). *Parentships in a PLC at Work: Forming and sustaining school-home relationships with families*. Bloomington, IN: Solution Tree Press.

ParentSquare. (April 2022). *Communications future survey: Perspectives on what works to reach families and what should change*. Accessed at www.parentsquare.com/engage /communications-future-survey on August 3, 2024.

Podolsky, A., Kini, T., Bishop, J., & Darling-Hammond, L. (2016, September). *Solving the teacher shortage: How to attract and retain excellent educators*. Palo Alto, CA: Learning Policy Institute. Accessed at https://learningpolicyinstitute.org/media/180 /download?inline&file=Solving_Teacher_Shortage_Attract_Retain_Educators _REPORT.pdf on February 19, 2024.

Pollock, K. (2014). *The changing nature of principals' work: Final report, September 2014.* Accessed at https://www.principals.ca/en/professional-learning/resources/Documents/Changing-Nature-of-Principals-Work---K-Pollock---2014.pdf on February 19, 2024.

Pollock, K. (2017, June). *The changing nature of vice-principals' work: Final report.* Accessed at https://www.principals.ca/en/professional-learning/resources/Documents/Changing-Nature-of-Vice-Principals-Work---K-Pollock---2017.pdf on February 19, 2024.

Pratt, S. M., Imbody, S. M., Wolf, L. D., & Patterson, A. L. (2017). Co-planning in co-teaching: A practical solution. *Intervention in School & Clinic, 52*(4), 243–249.

Retelle, E. (2010). Promotion of the assistant principal to the principalship: Good work is no guarantee. *International Journal of Educational Leadership Preparation, 5*(1).

Rieg, S. A., & Marcoline, J. F. (2008, February 20–23). *Relationship building: The first "R" for principals* [Conference paper presentation]. Eastern Education Research Association Conference, Hilton Head Island, SC, United States.

Roehlkepartain, E., Pekel, K., Syvertsen, A., Sethi, J., Sullivan, T., & Scales, P. (2017). *Relationships first: Creating connections that help young people thrive.* Minneapolis, MN: Search Institute. Accessed at https://www.search-institute.org/wp-content/uploads/2017/12/2017-Relationships-First-final.pdf on February 19, 2024.

Roorda, D. L., Jak, S., Zee, M., Oort, F. J., & Koomen, H. M. Y. (2017). Affective teacher–student relationships and students' engagement and achievement: A meta-analytic update and test of the mediating role of engagement. *School Psychology Review, 46*(3), 239–261.

Salamondra, T. (2021). Effective communication in schools. *BU Journal of Graduate Studies in Education, 13*(1), 22–26.

Schaefer, B. (2015, October 12). On becoming a leader: Building relationships and creating communities. *Educause Review.* Accessed at https://er.educause.edu/articles/2015/10/on-becoming-a-leader-building-relationships-and-creating-communities on February 19, 2024.

School Mental Health Ontario. (2023, March 6). *Think in tiers and focus on the positive.* Accessed at https://smho-smso.ca/school-and-system-leaders/think-in-tiers-and-focus-on-the-positive/ on February 19, 2024.

Schuhl, S., Kanold, T. D., Barnes, B., Jain, D. M., Larson, M. R., & Mozingo, B. (2021). *Mathematics unit planning in a PLC at Work: High school.* Bloomington, IN: Solution Tree Press.

Scott, K. (2018). *Radical candor: How to get what you want by saying what you mean.* London: Pan Macmillan.

Sebastian, J., Allensworth, E., & Huang, H. (2016). The role of teacher leadership in how principals influence classroom instruction and student learning. *American Journal of Education, 123*(1), 69–108.

Serdyukov, P. (2017). Innovation in education: What works, what doesn't, and what to do about it? *Journal of Research in Innovative Teaching & Learning, 10*(1), 4–33.

Sethi, J., & Scales, P. C. (2020). Developmental relationships and educational success: How teachers, parents, and friends affect educational outcomes and what actions students say matter most. *Contemporary Educational Psychology, 63*, Article 101904. https://doi.org/10.1016/j.cedpsych.2020.101904

Sinek, S. (2009). *Start with why: How great leaders inspire everyone to take action.* New York: Portfolio.

Sinek, S. (2014). *Leaders eat last: Why some teams pull together and others don't.* New York: Portfolio.

Smith, J. (2022). *Why has nobody told me this before?* New York: HarperOne.

Smith, T. E., Reinke, W. M., Herman, K. C., & Sebastian, J. (2021). Exploring the link between principal leadership and family engagement across elementary and middle school. *Journal of School Psychology*, 84, 49–62.

Spira, D. (2010, November 3). *Advanced skill-will diagnostics: Distinguishing habits from values, incentives from attitudes.* Accessed at https://danspira.com/2010/11/03/advanced-skill -will-diagnostics-distinquishing-habits-from-values-incentives-from-attitudes on January 3, 2020.

Sridharan, M. (2022, July 9). *Situational Leadership Model: Adapting the leadership style to the follower.* Assessed at https://thinkinsights.net/leadership/hersey-blanchard-situational -leadership/#:~:text=The%20model%20consists%20of%20four,a%20single%20 approach%20to%20leadership on February 19, 2024.

Stronge, J. H. (2018). *Qualities of effective teachers* (3rd ed.). Alexandria, VA: ASCD.

Teotonio, I. (2023, March 20). Lockdowns, fights, weapons: Angst and fear in Toronto schools over rise in violence. *Toronto Star.* Accessed at https://www.thestar.com/news/gta /lockdowns-fights-weapons-angst-and-fear-in-toronto-schools-over-rise-in-violence /article_1474663f-374a-5334-abe0-897b9c3be163.html on February 19, 2024.

Thanem, T. (2013). More passion than the job requires? Monstrously transgressive leadership in the promotion of health at work. *Leadership, 9*(3), 396–415.

Theoharis, G., & Haddix, M. (2011). Undermining racism and a whiteness ideology: White principals living a commitment to equitable and excellent schools. *Urban Education, 46*(6), 1332–1351.

Tiddens, W., Braaksma, J., & Tinga, T. (2021). Decision framework for predictive maintenance method selection. *Applied Sciences, 13*(3). https://doi.org /10.3390/app13032021

Turkle, S. (2015). *Reclaiming conversation: The power of talk in a digital age.* New York: Penguin Press.

Tyler, D. E. (2016). Communication behaviors of principals at high performing Title I elementary schools in Virginia: School leaders, communication, and transformative efforts. *Creighton Journal of Interdisciplinary Leadership*, 2(2), 2–16.

U.S. Department of Education. (2024). Innovation and improvement: Fiscal year 2025 budget request. Accessed at: https://www2.ed.gov/about/overview/budget/budget25/justifications /g-ii.pdf on August 3, 2024.

U.S. Department of Health and Human Services. (n.d.). *Stop bullying on the spot.* Accessed at stopbullying.gov on February 19, 2024.

U.S. Government Accountability Office. (2022, July 14). K–12 Education: Student population has significantly diversified, but many schools remain divided along racial, ethnic, and economic lines. Accessed at www.gao.gov/products/gao-22-104737 on August 3, 2024.

Vallerand, R. J., Blanchard, C., Mageau, G. A., Koestner, R., Ratelle, C., Leonard, M., et al. (2003). Les passions de l'ame: On obsessive and harmonious passion. *Journal of Personality and Social Psychology*, 85(4), 756–767.

Visible Learning. (n.d.). *Collective Teacher Efficacy (CTE) according to John Hattie.* Accessed at https://visible-learning.org/2018/03/collective-teacher-efficacy-hattie/ on February 15, 2024.

Wahlstrom, K. L., Louis, K. S., Leithwood, K., & Anderson, S. E. (2010). *Investigating the links to improved student learning: Executive summary of research findings.* New York: The Wallace Foundation. Accessed at https://wallacefoundation.org/sites/default/files/2023 -09/Investigating-the-Links-to-Improved-Student-Learning-Executive-Summary.pdf on February 19, 2024.

Weber, C. (2020). *Doing what works: Ten common-sense leadership practices to improve student learning.* Bloomington, IN: Solution Tree Press.

Welch, J. (2005). *Winning.* New York: HarperBusiness.

Weldon, P., & Ingvarson, L. (2016, October). *School staff workload study: Final report to the Australian Education Union–Victorian Branch.* Camberwell, Victoria, Australia: The Australian Council for Educational Research. Accessed at https://research.acer.edu.au/cgi /viewcontent.cgi?article=1028&context=tll_misc on February 19, 2024.

Whitaker, T. (2020). *What great principals do differently: Twenty things that matter most* (3rd ed.). New York: Routledge.

Whitaker, T., Miller, S., & Donlan, R. (2018). *The secret solution: How one principal discovered the path to success.* San Diego, CA: Burgess.

Wolcott, G. (2019). *Significant 72: Unleashing the power of relationships in today's schools.* Winneconne, WI: FIRST Educational Resources.

World Health Organization. (2022, June 17). *Mental health.* Accessed at https://www.who.int /news-room/fact-sheets/detail/mental-health-strengthening-our-response on February 19, 2024.

Yan, R. (2020). The influence of working conditions on principal turnover in K–12 public schools. *Educational Administration Quarterly, 56*(1), 89–122.

Yumurtaci, O. (2017). A re-evaluation of mobile communication technology: A theoretical approach for technology evaluation in contemporary digital learning. *Turkish Online Journal of Distance Education, 18*(1), 213–223.

INDEX

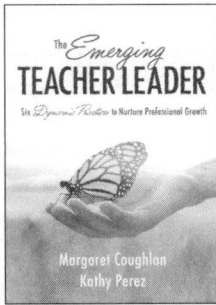

The Emerging Teacher Leader
Margaret Coughlan and Kathy Perez

Packed with insights from veteran teacher leaders, this book equips educators with six dynamic practices to empower their expertise and inspire their peers. Discover how to amplify success in the classroom and become an agent for change and school improvement.

BKG057

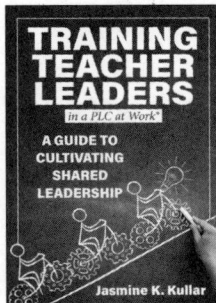

Training Teacher Leaders in a PLC at Work®
Jasmine K. Kullar

In this book, author Jasmine K. Kullar empowers teacher leadership teams with the knowledge to implement the PLC process successfully while developing ten essential leadership skills that will help influence their colleagues to advance student achievement.

BKG201

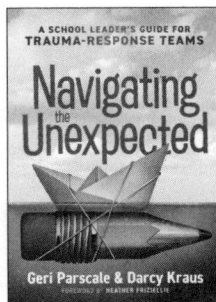

Navigating the Unexpected
Geri Parscale and Darcy Kraus

Nearly two-thirds of students show symptoms of traumatic stress. This book serves as a quick-reference guide for school and district leaders in designing their own Dynamic Problem-Solving Team (DPST). It also offers identified systems that allow the DPST to navigate traumatic situations with structured flexibility.

BKG150

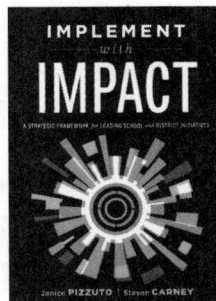

Implement With IMPACT
Jenice Pizzuto and Steven Carney

Learn how to build an implementation team that will bridge the implementation gap and prevent the adopt-and-abandon cycle that often comes with change. The IMPACT framework provides distinct stages and human- and learning-centered design elements to help you achieve quick, tangible wins and sustainable, scalable results.

BKG093

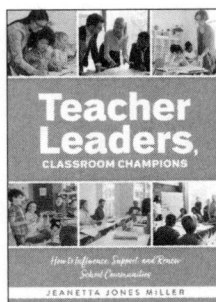

Teacher Leaders, Classroom Champions
Jeanetta Jones Miller

Gain a clear path to activate school improvement from within your classroom. This book shares a vision of teacher leadership not as teachers who lead other teachers but as those who take responsibility in supporting other teachers, students, and parents in a variety of ways.

BKG110

Solution Tree | Press
a division of
Solution Tree

Visit SolutionTree.com or call 800.733.6786 to order.

"Excellent engagement
in what truly matters
in **assessment**.

Great examples!"

—Carol Johnson, superintendent,
Central Dauphin School District, Pennsylvania

PD Services

Our experts draw from decades of research and their own experiences to bring you
practical strategies for designing and implementing quality assessments. You can choose
from a range of customizable services, from a one-day overview to a multiyear process.

Book your assessment PD today!
888.763.9045

Solution Tree